Thinking about
POVERTY

Thinking about POVERTY

Third Edition

Editor

Klaus Serr

THE FEDERATION PRESS
2006

Published in Sydney by

    The Federation Press
        PO Box 45, Annandale, NSW, 2038.
        71 John St, Leichhardt, NSW, 2040.
        Ph (02) 9552 2200. Fax (02) 9552 1681.
        E-mail: info@federationpress.com.au
        Website: http://www.federationpress.com.au

National Library of Australia cataloguing-in-publication

    Thinking about poverty.

    3rd ed.
    Bibliography.
    Includes index.
    ISBN 978 186287 626 2

    1. Poverty – Australia. 2. Poor – Australia. 3. Public welfare – Australia.
    4. Neo-liberalism – Australia. I. Serr, Klaus

362.50994

©   The Federation Press 2006

This publication is copyright. Other than for the purposes of and subject to the conditions prescribed under the Copyright Act, no part of it may in any form or by any means (electronic, mechanical, microcopying, photocopying, recording or otherwise) be reproduced, stored in a retrieval system or transmitted without prior written permission. Enquiries should be addressed to the publishers.

Typeset by The Federation Press, Leichhardt, NSW.
    Printed by Ligare Pty Ltd, Riverwood, NSW.

To Lyn Rose

With gratitude and appreciation

Table of Contents

List of Boxes, Figures and Tables	ix
Abbreviations	x
Preface and Acknowledgements	xi
Contributors	xiv

Chapter 1
Introduction:
Klaus Serr — 1

Chapter 2
Processes of globalisation: The generation of wealth and poverty
Frank Stilwell — 8

Chapter 3
Women and poverty: The application of feminism in overcoming women's poverty in the global context
Ruth Phillips — 24

Chapter 4
Understanding poverty
Eric Porter & Jennie Trezise — 35

Chapter 5
Concepts of poverty
Klaus Serr — 49

Chapter 6
Governing inequality: Poverty before the Australian welfare state
Karen Crinall — 66

Chapter 7
Poverty: The impact of government policy on vulnerable families and older people
Ruth Webber — 79

Chapter 8
Unemployment at 29-year low: Why unemployment still matters
Margot Rawsthorne — 92

Chapter 9
Poverty and crime
David Rose — 107

Chapter 10
The impoverishment of a people: The Aboriginal experience in Australia
Sue Green 118

Chapter 11
Poverty and mental illness
Robert Bland 131

Chapter 12
Poverty and people with a disability
David Sykes 142

Chapter 13
Government anti-poverty strategies in Australia
Benno Engels and Gavin Dufty 155

Chapter 14
The funding and provision of emergency relief in Australia
Benno Engels 170

Chapter 15
Moving forward: Alternative anti-poverty strategies
Klaus Serr 183

Chapter 16
Conclusion
Klaus Serr 197

References 200
Index 229

CONTENTS

List of Boxes

Box 5.1	Definition of Poverty Developed by Homeless Men	60
Box 5.2	Poverty Categories Identified by Poor Respondents	62

List of Figures

Figure 8.1	Estimated Poverty Rates for People Aged 15 and Over by Labour Force Status, 2001	96
Figure 12.1	International Classification of Functioning, Disability and Health	144
Figure 141	Types of Emergency Relief Distributed by Organisations in Metropolitan Melbourne, 2004	179

List of Tables

Table 2.1	Economic Performance and Human Development 2003: Selected Countries	13
Table 8.1	The Henderson Poverty Line Compared with Centrelink Income Support Australian Dollars per Week, Quarter Ending December 2004	97
Table 9.1	Imprisonment Rates & Prior Imprisonment, Australia 2005	111
Table 13.1	Main Income Support Payments and Allowances	158
Table 13.2	Commonwealth Concession Cards and Eligibility Requirements	159
Table 13.3	Other Commonwealth Funded Programs in Australia, 2005	160
Table 13.4	State and Territory Based Concessions, 2005	163
Table 13.5	Payment Differentials between the Aged Pension and a Sample of Benefits, September December 2005	167
Table 14.1	Commonwealth Government Emergency Relief Allocations to States and Territories, 1999-2000 to 2005/06, in AU$	172
Table 14.2	Type and Number of Emergency Relief Providers by State and Territory, Australia, 2005	174
Table 14.3	State and Territory Government Concessions for Low Income and Income Support Applicants, 2005	176
Table 14.4	Victorian Utility Relief Grant Scheme: Ratio of Processed and Approved Applications, 1999-2004	176
Table 14.5	Type of ER Provider Organisations Surveyed in Metropolitan Melbourne, 2004	178
Table 14.6	Sources of Funding to ER Providers, Metropolitan Melbourne, 2004	180
Table 14.7	Receivers of ER Assistance in Metropolitan Melbourne, 2003-04	181

Abbreviations

ABS	Australian Bureau of Statistics
ACOSS	Australian Council of Social Service
FaCS	Commonwealth Department of Family and Community Services
CIS	Commonwealth of Independent States
CIS	Centre for Independent Studies
COA	Commonwealth of Australia
COSS	Council of Social Service
CPI	Consumer Price Index
ER	Emergency Relief
EU	European Union
GAD	Gender and Development
GATT	General Agreement on Tariffs And Trade
GDI	Gender Development Index
GDP	Gross Domestic Product
HACC	Home and Community Care Program
HDI	Human Development Index
HPI	Human Poverty Index
ILO	International Labour Organisation
IMF	International Monetary Fund
IPA	Institute for Public Affairs
LETS	Local Area Trading Systems
NATSEM	The National Centre for Social and Economic Modelling
NGO	Non Government Organisation
OECD	Organisation for Economic Co-Operation and Development
PBS	Pharmaceutical Benefit Scheme
SAAP	Supported Accommodation Assistance Program
SAP	Structural Adjustment Program
SCARC	Senate Community Affairs References Committee
SPRC	Social Policy Research Centre
UNDP	United Nations Development Programme
UNICEF	United Nations Children's Fund
UNMDG	United Nations Millennium Development Goals
USBS	United States Bureau of Statistics
VCOSS	Victorian Council of Social Service
WB	World Bank
WCED	World Commission on Environment and Development
WEF	World Economic Forum
WHO	World Health Organisation
WTO	World Trade Organisation

Preface and Acknowledgements

In 1985, as a youth worker in Kensington, I had my first encounter with Australian youth homelessness and the problems of poverty in Melbourne. This experience sparked my ongoing interest in and commitment to social justice issues, especially in the midst of the dramatic changes during the 1990s in the Australian economy and society as whole. Some of these changes were certainly positive, but increasing inequalities and social problems also emerged, coupled with accelerating deregulation and privatisation. Since the 2000s, poverty also began to be felt more strongly by some sections of the community, as the effect of economic globalisation was much more apparent, and economic rationalism became the dominant policy and government approach.

In the late 1990s, after spending the past two decades working in both social work and academia in poverty-related fields, I developed the concept of *Thinking about Poverty* as a social justice project, with Social Work Services Pty Ltd (SWS). In many ways, this publication is part of my journey to advocate and work for positive social change and to make a difference in the lives of those who are disadvantaged and marginalised. The first edition of the book, published in 2001, was to encourage my social work students at La Trobe University to write on poverty issues, and to think critically about the great structural changes occurring in Australian society. As part of this social justice project, SWS donated 372 copies of the 2001 edition to all secondary schools in Victoria, and many copies were given to organisations and people around the State.

In 2004, SWS published the second revised edition with generous support provided by the Salvation Army Crisis Services (St Kilda). This allowed us to continue the contributions to the community and again to distribute widely the book free of charge, including to my Australian Catholic University (ACU) poverty students in 2005. By this stage *Thinking about Poverty* had created a commercial market for itself, and has been prescribed reading at Sydney University since 2002, the St Georges TAFE Sydney in 2004, and ACU in 2005.

This third and current edition, published by Federation Press, is much extended and totally revised. Based on the structure of the previous versions, however, the book maintains the three key areas of theory, policy and practice. *Thinking about Poverty* also keeps its social justice aim, and the current authors have stipulated that royalties from sales be donated to the Missionaries of Charity in Addis Ababa for poverty relief in Ethiopia.

Over the three editions of *Thinking about Poverty*, many people have contributed to the book's development and evolution. While it is not possible to name all of these people, their contributions are nevertheless appreciated. However, this book would not have been possible without the support of the authors, the SWS editorial committee and the following people and organisations: SWS, in particular Lyn Rose and David Rose, for its vision and financial support; staff and students of La Trobe University's School of Social Work & Social Policy, who encouraged and supported the first edition of this book, in particular Bill Healy, Cliff Picton, Helen Cleak and Jan Fook; the Salvation Army Crisis Services, especially Doug Parker and Sally Coutts who supported the project over many years; Ruth Phillips (Sydney University) and Kathryn Couttoupes (St Georges TAFE, Sydney) who, with their students, prescribed and used the book, thus ensuring the continuation of this publication.

This third edition of *Thinking about Poverty* was made possible through my secondment by the Australian Catholic University (ACU) to its Institute for the Advancement of Research (IAR). This secondment enabled me to concentrate on the writing and editing, for which I am most grateful.

As in any edited book, acknowledgement must go first and foremost go to the current contributing authors. They were a wonderful team to work with and I am very grateful for their personal and professional support to complete this third edition. Special thanks to Frank Stilwell who agreed to write the lead chapter and to Robert Bland and Sue Green who came on board late and therefore had extra pressures in completing their chapters. The contributions of the following people and organisations are especially appreciated:

- The Federation Press for agreeing to publish this edition. Special thanks to Chris Holt, Margaret Farmer, Trisha Valliappan, Clare Moss and the rest of the team for their continuing advice and support.

- Staff and students at ACU, in particular Peter Carpenter, John Coll, Jen Couch, Margot Hillel, Laurine Hurley, Michael McKay, Sue Rechter, Stewart Sharlow, Shurlee Swain, and Ruth Webber. My ACU students have continuously stimulated and encouraged my work.

- Staff and students at Addis Ababa University (AAU). Special thanks to Abeye Tasse and Melese Getu (Dean and Associate Dean) of the Graduate School of Social Work, Jim Rollin from the University of Chicago at Illinois, and to Meron, Zenebe and Mesret and all those students who cared enough about poverty to help me establish a new program to feed some of the poorest in Addis Ababa.

- Fathers Rogelio and Rizal of the Ethiopian Catholic University who invited me to stay with them in Addis Ababa so that I could work and live safely, and Annette Friala, a volunteer of the Missionaries of Charity, who let me come with her to hand out food to the poor and showed me what absolute poverty really means.

- Marie Lawson and Eric Porter who have read all chapters and made valuable editorial suggestions throughout various stages of the manuscript.

PREFACE AND ACKNOWLEDGEMENTS

- Last, but certainly not least, special thanks to Ling and Toby who put up with much during the process of the book and were supportive, patient and understanding.

Klaus Serr
Melbourne, November 2006

Contributors

Robert Bland is Professor of Social Work at the University of Tasmania. He has worked in mental health services in hospital and community settings and has a life-long interest in the welfare of people with long-term mental illness. He has been an advocate for families of people with mental illness and is a life member of the Association of Relatives and Friends of the Mentally Ill. His other research interests include professional practice, and spirituality and mental health. Robert is the Convenor of the National Social Work and Mental Health Network, represents Social Work on the Mental Health Council of Australia, is a Board member of Anglicare Tasmania, and is President of the Australian Council of Heads of Schools of Social Work.

Karen Crinall lectures in Social and Community Welfare and Human Services Management at Monash University. She has over 25 years experience working, researching and teaching in social welfare in the areas of family violence and homelessness. As a researcher Karen has conducted practice-based and academic projects utilising feminist, visual and participatory action research methods. Karen has presented conference papers and published on the topics of women and homelessness, rural and regional responses to social change, working with young women, and the visual representation of homeless women and young people. She has conducted consultancies for the Department of Human Services on homelessness and family violence service responses. Karen's qualifications span the visual arts, education and social sciences. She is currently researching integrated responses to family violence and the photographic representation of women as being disadvantaged.

Gavin Dufty is the Manager of Policy and Research at St Vincent de Paul Society Victoria, and has also worked in policy and research with the Victorian Council of Social Service and the Energy Action Group. Gavin has published widely in the area of income inequality and poverty over the past 15 years, and has worked on numerous advisory bodies, including ministerial appointments. In 2001 he received a Centennial Medal for services to the community.

Benno Engels – BA (Hons), Diploma of Teaching, Ph.D (Sydney) currently lectures in politics and public policy in the School of Global Studies, Social Science and Planning, City Campus, RMIT University. Benno is presently engaged in research on emergency relief, urban poverty, the locational distribution of services for the elderly, and the

CONTRIBUTORS

reporting of social policy issues within the mainstream Australian media. He is a member of the editorial board of Just Policy.

Sue Green is an Associate Professor of Indigenous Education at the University of New South Wales, the Director of Nura Gili (Indigenous Programs at the University of New South Wales), and the 2005 recipient of the Neville Bonner Award for excellence in university teaching. Sue is a Wiradjuri woman from western New South Wales and was born on Eora land. As an Indigenous woman Sue is extremely interested in both history and welfare. Thus much of her teaching and research are focused on these two areas and often the focus is on welfare history. Sue teaches Aboriginal studies within a variety of areas including social work at the University of New South Wales.

Ruth Phillips is a lecturer in the undergraduate and postgraduate programs in Social Work and Policy Studies in the Faculty of Education and Social Work at the University of Sydney. She is an active researcher in the areas of global social policy, feminism and social policy, third sector studies, and social work education.

Eric Porter completed his PhD at La Trobe University in 1992 and has worked as a tutor, lecturer, researcher, editor and writer at a number of Melbourne universities. Since 1999, he has held the position of Lecturer in Politics and History at RMIT University.

Margot Rawsthorne is a lecturer in Community Development at the University of Sydney, with over 15 years of leadership in community development practice and community-based research. Margot has actively participated in many community sector debates and has published extensively on government/non-government relations. She is particularly interested in policy relevant action research, the transformation of the welfare state and the experiences of disadvantaged people.

David Rose is a social worker with over 15 years experience in alcohol and drug treatment, mental health and offender support services. He has worked in direct practice, management, program design and policy development roles in both prison-based and post-release support services for offenders. He has been responsible for developing pilot transitional support programs for mentally ill offenders and their families, and for high need offenders with serious drug use problems. His Master's degree research involved an evaluation of a transitional support service for mentally ill offenders. He is currently the Manager of Special Projects at Uniting Care Moreland Hall (a drug treatment service) and also undertakes a range of consultation, research and evaluation projects within the human services field.

Klaus Serr teaches at Australian Catholic University (Melbourne) in sociology and youth studies. Over the past 15 years, he has also taught on poverty and globalisation issues at RMIT University, La Trobe University and Addis Ababa University. Klaus has written a PhD on community-based anti-poverty strategies and developed the concept of *Thinking about poverty*, which he edited in 2001 and 2004. He has actively been engaged in research on homelessness and poverty since the 1990s. His recent study *Shattered Dreams* (Catholic Social Services Victoria) is the basis for a comparative international study between Addis Ababa (Ethiopia) and Munich (Germany). Klaus is also a founding director of Social Work Services P/L and has worked in the human services sector for more than 20 years in Australia, England and Hong Kong.

Frank Stilwell is Professor of Political Economy at the University of Sydney. He is well known as a critic of orthodox economics and as an advocate of economic policies that prioritise social justice and ecological sustainability. He is the author and editor of 13 books, including *Political Economy: the Contest of Economic Ideas* (Oxford University Press, 2002) and *Changing Track: a New Political Economic Direction for Australia* (Pluto Press, 2000). He is also the coordinating editor of the *Journal of Australian Political Economy*. Currently he is the economic policy spokesperson for the NSW Greens.

David Sykes is the Manager of Policy and Education at the Office of the Public Advocate (OPA) Victoria, and also worked as an advocate at OPA for six years. David has been the co-ordinator of a Citizen Advocacy program and has experience in volunteer management and workcare rehabilitation. He has a long-standing commitment to the rights of people with disabilities and a particular interest in seeking ways to effectively promote their rights, while at the same time ensuring adequate safeguard of their needs.

Jennie Trezise is a social work trained outreach support worker with Homeground Services, working with the homelessness and people with multiple needs in the City of Yarra. Over the past 18 years Jennie has also worked in aged care, the psychiatric disability rehabilitation support sector, and on a mental health pilot project funded by the Victorian Homelessness Strategy.

Ruth Webber is an Associate Professor in sociology at Australian Catholic University, and the Director of Quality of Life and Social Justice Flagship, a research centre. She has published extensively on youth and families both nationally and internationally.

Chapter 1

Introduction

Klaus Serr

> [T]here is growing concern about the direction globalisation is currently taking. Its advantages are too distant for too many, while its risks are all too real. Its volatility threatens both rich and poor. Immense riches are being generated. But fundamental problems of poverty, exclusion and inequality persist. Corruption is widespread. Open societies are threatened by global terrorism, and the future of open markets is increasingly in question. Global governance is in crisis. We are at a critical juncture, and we need to urgently rethink our current policies and institutions. (World Commission on the Social Dimension of Globalisation 2004, p 3)

In 1944, leaders of 44 countries met to discuss 'the re-construction of the world economy' at Bretton Woods, New Hampshire (Hill & Scannell 1983, p 14). One of the reasons for this meeting was that the post-war industrial nations were trying to prevent the re-occurrence of the post-war chaos of the 1920s. Some policy makers, including Keynes, recognised that unregulated capitalism periodically fails as an economic system, and therefore creates conditions of war as a way out of the economic dilemma. Keynes also recognised that among the key factors playing a part in the Great Depression in the 1930s, were speculative economic behaviour, unemployment, and the enormous concentration of wealth, which was controlled by a very small number of individuals and companies forming huge monopolies. During that time the greater the inequalities of income and wealth became, and the higher the number of the unemployed, the more an over-supply of goods created the conditions for economic depression. While the wealthy had so much money that they did not need to spend it, the unemployed could buy very little to put back into the economy (Serr 2000). However, providing an adequate income for the greater part the population seems necessary to create demand for the economy. A fair distribution of income, therefore, makes good economic sense and 'is highly functional' in economic terms (Galbraith 1995, p 82). In this context, Keynes clearly understood that in order to sustain the global economic system, regulatory bodies must be built into the structure. Keynes also wanted to ensure 'that the pursuit of national interests would never again subvert the entire international economic monetary order' (Corbridge 1986, p 193).

THINKING ABOUT POVERTY

At the Bretton Woods meeting there were two main options for consideration. The Keynesian or British model advocated monetary regulations which would achieve a more equal partnership between national economies. To that end, Keynes was in favour of all countries joining a world bank that 'would issue its own money – called Bancor' (Barratt Brown 1984, p 63). Bancor would be outside the control of any country and be used to settle international accounts. The American model advocated a world currency linked to the value of gold. That currency was to be the US dollar. The negotiations at Bretton Woods therefore had far-reaching implications for the development of the global economy. As the American model was accepted, the global economy became dominated by the US dollar, through which most international transactions were exchanged. This decision also secured US domination over the ensuing trade institutions: the World Bank, the International Monetary Fund and the General Agreement of Trade and Tariffs (now the World Trade Organisation (WTO)), controlling international trade and finance (Held et al 1999). The other major outcome of Bretton Woods was that the world embarked on a large-scale implementation of so-called 'free trade policies'. Based on neo-classical economic principles, these policies promote economic growth, privatisation, rationalisation and deregulation, and advocate competitive social behaviour and self interest (Korten 1995). In effect, this approach resembled the earlier system that had failed and led to the Great Depression.

The leaders at Bretton Woods had hoped to create a better world without want, but it was soon apparent that their development model was not working as planned. In the 1950s poverty was recurring in many parts of the world, and disparities were increasing between the wealthy and the poor both in and between developed and developing countries.

> Despite great increases in wealth and productivity in some sectors of the developed economies, even the richest and most industrialised nations have not been immune from poverty, and relative poverty is increasingly touching millions of people in these nations. As Sachs points out (1992, p 159), this poverty has occurred 'precisely in the shadow of wealth', and paradoxically includes those nations that had pursued neo-liberal policies most vigorously. An estimated 60 million people are living below the poverty threshold in Europe (see the European Communities 2002), with poverty rates varying from 6.8 per cent in Sweden (incidentally the slowest to adopt neo-liberal economic policies at home), to 15 per cent in the UK which, with the US, has been at the forefront of implementing 'free trade' policies (UNDP 2002, p 21).

The US, the richest nation on earth, has a poverty rate of 16 per cent, the highest amongst developed nations (Mishel et al 2003). Already in the 1950s, Harrington (1962) found a 20-25 per cent poverty rate and in a follow-up study in the 1980s, concluded that poverty in the US had not changed during the previous 30 years (Harrington 1984). This finding was accepted in official government estimates at the time, accepting that 'there were almost as many poor people in 1987 (32.5 million) as there had been in

INTRODUCTION

1963' (Schiller 1989, p 26). By the early 1990s, the plight of children in the US was particularly reprehensible, with up to 12 million children estimated to be living in poverty (United Nations Children's Fund (UNICEF) 1992.). While US child poverty has declined somewhat in the 2000s, it still stands at 23 per cent (UNDP 2005).

The US also has one of the most unequal distributions of wealth among industrialised nations, and some large corporations have a higher annual turnover than many poor countries and are said 'to rule the world' (see Korten 1995). The growth in the fortunes of the super rich has been equally pronounced. For example, in 2000 there were 306 billionaires commanding US$1.27 trillion of personal wealth (Forbes Magazine 2000); by 2004 there were 587 billionaires worth US $1.9 trillion (Forbes Magazine 2004); by 2006, 793 billionaires owned a staggering US $2.6 trillion (Forbes Magazine 2006). Thus the world's wealthiest 500 people have a combined wealth of more than 420 million people (UNDP 2005, p 4).

In Australia poverty rates are in dispute, but the general rate is estimated at about 13 per cent (see Harding 2001; UNDP 2002; Peter Saunders* 2005), and child poverty at 14.7 per cent (UNICEF 2005). Poverty in Australia has been of active concern since the 1970s. a large Melbourne poverty survey (Henderson et al) 1970 was followed in 1972 by the Commonwealth Commission of Inquiry into Poverty (Henderson 1975) which also led to the Henderson Poverty Line, discussed further in Chapter 5. In 1982 the Senate Standing Committee on Social Welfare (1982) found evidence of high unemployment and significant social dislocation resulting in family break down and youth homelessness. Poverty was again confirmed by the Department of Housing and Construction in 1985 (Coopers & Lybrand, 1985), and in 1989 The Human Rights and Equal Opportunity Commission (Burdekin 1989) reported about 25,000 homeless youths and children in Australia. During the 1990s many studies by academics and welfare agencies such as the Brotherhood of St Lawrence and the Salvation Army continued to raise concerns about disturbing trends of poverty and homelessness (Hirst 1989; Neal & Fopp 1992; Peter Saunders 1994; Fincher & Nieuwenhuysen 1998; Serr 2003). While disputed by some commentators, the 2004 Senate's Inquiry into Poverty (Senate Community Affairs Reference Committee 2004) found that in the early 2000s poverty was increasingly being entrenched in Australian society. The Senate's report raises many concerns about the loss of Australia's egalitarian aspirations, noting that economic growth has not been able to alleviate poverty and that there are increasing inequalities in Australian society. As in other Western countries, wealth

---

* There are two researchers called Peter Saunders. One works at the Centre for Independent Studies, the other at the University of New South Wales. Throughout this book, The former will be referred to as 'P Saunders' and the latter as 'Peter Saunders'.

and income inequality (see UNDP 2005) have become more prominent since the early 2000s, and 'one-tenth of Australian families has 45 per cent of the wealth and the top half has 93 per cent of the wealth. The bottom half of families have only seven per cent' (Kelly 2001, p 15). The latest *Business Review Weekly* (BRW) Rich List reports 'an embarrassment of riches' for the 200 wealthiest Australians in 2006; the combined wealth for these 200 people increased from AU$63.2 billion in 2003, to AU$71.5 billion in 2004, to AU$ 83.37 in 2005, and to a staggering AU$105.5 billion in 2006 (BRW 2006). This wealth creation has occurred while poverty becomes more concerning and the recently introduced industrial relation laws might extend poverty further by reducing wages and conditions for poorer workers.

Thus it is clear that although the Bretton Woods policies were enormously profitable for industrialised nations and especially for Western banks, within these nations a large cohort continues to exist in poverty, and disparities between rich and poor continue to increase. However, the Bretton Woods system had much more dramatic effects on the so-called 'third world' nations. In the 1980s a financial crisis developed in poor nations, which by then had accumulated a US$854 billion debt (George 1992). Despite paying back the enormous sum of US$1345 billion (George 1992), between 1982 and 1990 these countries found themselves even worse off. According to the United Nations Development Programme (UNDP), by the mid-1990s their debt reached a massive US$ 2.2 trillion (UNDP 1999), crippling the economies of poor nations around the world and impoverishing the lives of millions of people. For example, in the developing nations, more than 2.5 billion live on less than US$2 per day, one billion people lack safe drinking water, and about 2.6 billion lack even basic sanitation (UNDP 2005, p 24).

Disparities are also problematic between nations. While 'the global economy has grown sevenfold since 1950 ... the disparity in per capita gross domestic product between the 20 richest and 20 poorest nations more than doubled between 1960 and 1995' (Renner & Starke 2003, pp 88-89). As the world spends more than US$ 1,000 billion on weapons each year (about 7.8 million per minute), the UNDP estimated that at the beginning of 2000, the universal provision of basic services in developing countries would cost about $80 billion a year (UNDP 2000). In other words, the annual weaponry expenditure could provide basic services to the world's poor 12.5 times over.

This disparity not only exists, but is increasing. According to the UNDP: '40 per cent of the world's population account for 5 per cent of global income. The richest 10 per cent, almost all of whom live in high-income countries, account for 54 per cent' (UNDP 2005, p 4). This 40 per cent of the global population forms an underclass 'faced daily with the reality or the threat of extreme poverty', while 'more than 10 million children die each year before their fifth birthday' from mainly preventable diseases (UNDP 2005, p 24).

INTRODUCTION

Instead of solving poverty, the continuation of neo-liberal polices has meant vast profits for a few corporations and people, and the increasing tendency to see profits ends in themselves rather than as the way to serve the needs of all humanity. As a result large parts of the global population are threatened with insecurity, lack of well-being, and an increasingly shameful poverty amid vast and alienated wealth. In developing nations this situation means extreme deprivation, where not even the most basic services can be taken for granted. In developed countries it increasingly means relative poverty, unemployment, and a continual reduction of public services (Serr 2004d).

Over the past two decades there have been some attempts to address this situation. By the 1980s, it was increasingly obvious that the chosen neo-liberal economic principles had generated extreme poverty and wealth, and that the associated environmental costs were unsustainable. Consequently, over two decades, a number of United Nations inquiries investigated these enormous challenges; inquiries included The Brandt Commissions (1980 & 1983), The World Commission on Environment and Development (1987), and the UN Millennium Summit (see UNDP 2003), the World Commission on the Social Dimension of Globalisation (2004). The earlier commissions in particular recognised the seriousness of the crisis faced by humanity, and recommended changes to economic practices. They also acknowledged in many ways that a continuation of the development orthodoxy could lead to the extinction of the human race. However, while all commissions generated thoughtful and well-meaning reports, their work did not translate into concerted efforts by governments, corporations or international institutions, such as the IMF, World Bank, and the World Trade Organisation (Serr 2004d).

What was really needed was structural change in global and national institutional arrangements to regulate and balance the global economy against the well-being of other important areas such as environmental and community needs around the world. Poverty was therefore again a focus when various heads of states and governments met at the UN Millennium Summit in September 2000. The subsequent Millennium Declaration committed 189 countries to collective action to alleviate the poverty of the 1.2 billion people who continue to live in severe deprivation and survive on less than US$1 per day (UNDP 2003). The Millennium Declaration aims to halve the proportion of people in extreme poverty by 2015, declaring that:

> We will spare no effort to free our fellow men, women and children from the abject and dehumanising conditions of extreme poverty, to which more than a billion of them are currently subjected. We are committed to making the right to development a reality for everyone and to freeing the entire human race from want (United Nations Millennium Declaration, The General Assembly, see UNDP 2003, p 5).

The aim of this book is therefore to delineate current global poverty and inequality, and then to explore aspects of Australian poverty in the context of the persistent application of neo-liberal economic policies by Australian policy makers. Setting the scene, Frank Stilwell outlines the global aspects of poverty and the interdependence of global and local problems, identifies the underlying non-egalitarian tendencies in capitalist economies, and shows how neo-liberal policies have progressively undermined egalitarianism and notions of social justice. However, Stilwell argues that neo-liberalism is not inevitable and can be challenged by social movements and by commitment to values of human dignity, liberation and social cohesion.

Chapter 3 continues the global context. Here Ruth Phillips shows that women are the main victims of poverty in every region in the world, and that a feminist analysis is required to understand the causes of this situation. Phillips locates the issue of poverty within the paradigm of citizenship status, and argues that countries with strong notions of human welfare and equality have a stronger level of citizenship than in those with a weak welfare state.

Since social policy is underpinned by theory, Chapter 4 explores individual and structural explanations of poverty. Porter & Tresize demonstrate that current government policies spring from predominately individualistic models and do not address the structural causes of poverty. As Serr points out in the next chapter, individualistic notions of poverty also relate to neo-liberal ideas of how the economy should run, and are form the background for an increasingly hostile debate about the definition and extent of poverty in Australian society. At the heart of this debate is the ideological divide between neo-liberal perspectives and notions of egalitarianism, redistribution and social justice. In turn this discussion affects the way poverty is conceptualised and measured. Chapter 5 thus reviews existing poverty definitions in a historical context, explores the relationship between conceptualisation and economic thinking, and argues for an alternative definition of poverty which does not rely on purely economic measurements but takes qualitative aspects into account, including the voices of the poor themselves.

Chapter 6 demonstrates how poverty and inequality were already implicated in governmental practices in Australia's early years. As Karen Crinall argues, some of the policies from the time of settlement can be traced back to mid-sixteenth century Europe. In Chapter 10, Sue Green points out that past and current policies have contributed to the highly disadvantaged situation of Aboriginal people. Ruth Webber (Chapter 7) and Margot Rawsthorne (Chapter 8) both locate current government polices within economic rationalism, and demonstrate such policies' negative impact on vulnerable groups in Australia, including families and the unemployed. David Rose (Chapter 9) examines the association of poverty and crime and the extent to which crime is a product of either individual characteristics or social, economic and cultural factors. Exploring issues of mental health and poverty, in Chapter 11, Robert Bland looks at the policy and demands of mutual obligation, alerting the

INTRODUCTION

reader to the potential negative effects such a policy can have on people with mental health problems. In Chapter 12 David Sykes considers the welfare of people with disability and the kind of approaches taken by policy makers.

Gavin Dufty & Benno Engels (Chapter 13) take a practical approach in assessing potential anti-poverty strategies based on welfare provision at the three levels of government. This is followed by a discussion by Engels (Chapter 14) about the capacity and status of the provision of emergency relief in Australia. In Chapter 15, Klaus Serr looks at alternative economic thinking and how this has influenced community-based anti-poverty approaches.

Chapter 2

Processes of globalisation: The generation of wealth and poverty

Frank Stilwell

To address any problem systematically requires an analysis of its character and causes. Thus understanding the problem of poverty, and its relationship to the processes of wealth creation, needs an analysis of the economy and the processes that reproduce economic inequality. These political economic features are increasingly global in character. The analysis of contemporary 'globalisation' and its implications for inequality and poverty presents a big challenge for political economists. Some see the globalisation process as an extension of the increased role of the market in economic and social life, a process that has been ongoing for centuries and has generated prodigious increases in wealth. Others emphasise the distinctive features of the past three decades, such as the impact of neo-liberal policies in breaking down the relative autonomy of national economies, thereby making more people directly vulnerable to the interests of corporate capital.

So an analysis of the nature of poverty can usefully begin with a broad consideration of these political economic forces and increasingly global processes. For this purpose it is useful to trace the drivers of globalisation, their impacts on the distribution of income and wealth, and the alternative policy responses. Such an analysis is particularly pertinent for those who wish to ameliorate the problem of poverty and/or to tackle its underlying causes. What can be done within an individual nation, such as Australia? What can be done on a global scale? What politics are implied? This chapter provides an exploration of these big issues, considering the international situation and making particular reference to the Australian experience.

Drivers of wealth and poverty

Poverty persists amid growing material affluence. In a generally wealthy nation like Australia, for example, particular social groups, such as single-parent families, recent migrants from non-English-speaking countries, and the long-term unemployed, commonly experience unacceptable levels of poverty. Many Aboriginal communities have living standards more typical of poor people in 'third world nations'. Meanwhile, on a global scale, there are enormous disparities in living standards. Some nations, like China and India, have seen a rapid growth during recent years in the number of people with 'middle class' living standards, although hundreds of millions still lead lives of material deprivation. Other nations, particularly in Africa, have slipped backwards, and their people as a whole are now poorer than they were a decade ago (UNDP 1999; 2005). According to the most recent United Nations (UN) estimates, 2.5 billion people (over 40 per cent of the world's population) are in, or at risk of, extreme poverty, surviving on less than US $2 per day (UNDP 2005, p 4).

The eradication of these problems of poverty has often been claimed as a reason for seeking faster economic growth, both nationally and globally. The expectation of orthodox economists has been that producing and consuming more goods and services will rescue people from lives of drudgery and destitution. Even if they are not the main producers or consumers, the poor are presumed to benefit from the 'trickle down' effects of an economy generating more incomes and wealth. From this perspective, the ongoing globalisation of capital, the growth of transnational corporations, and the further expansion of international trade are regarded as benign processes of capitalist expansion (Irwin 2002; Shipman 2002).

However, critics of such economic orthodoxy (for example Korten 2000; Tabb 2004) have argued that processes of economic growth in capitalist economies are inherently inequitable. Certainly, capitalism is a dynamic system of economic organisation. It is based on the relentless pursuit of profit, and both nature and society are continuously transformed by that systemic imperative. One should always be wary of the use of metaphors in social science, but it is tempting to liken the capitalist economy to a bicycle – likely to be stable and to function effectively only when moving forward. But for whom does the economy function?

The fruits of economic growth under capitalism have always been unevenly distributed, because those who own most of the capital have the capacity to use it for whatever productive and speculative activities that may expand their personal wealth. However, those without capital depend on the sale of their labour, which places them in a subordinate economic position, except in the relatively rare situation of labour shortage. Where there is an excess of labour relative to the number of jobs available, workers may be condemned to striving for mere subsistence. In the extreme instance, they may be unable to generate sufficient income even to maintain their personal health which, in turn, renders them less capable of productive labour, let alone upward social and economic mobility. In effect, 'capital makes capital' and 'poverty breeds poverty'.

Globalisation reproduces these trends on a world scale. Driven by technological change, corporate interests, and neo-liberal policies, the forces generating economic inequality within individual nations now operate transnationally. Concurrently, the institutions that historically kept these processes in check at the national scale now have less traction. The most important of these institutions are governments and trade unions. National governments pursuing policies of progressive redistribution through taxation and expenditure had some modest effect in ameliorating economic inequalities in the decades before neo-liberalism gained dominance over the policy-making institutions (Stilwell 2000). Concurrently, trade unions' capacity to resist the persistent downward push on wages by firms seeking to minimise production costs has been eroded, as union membership in the workforce in the OECD nations has declined (now down to 23 per cent in Australia, for example). Neo-liberal governments have also promoted more 'flexibility' in labour markets (King & Stilwell 2005).

Many observers (see, for example, Bryan & Rafferty 1998; Buckman 2004; Davis 2004) cite evidence of a 'beggar-thy-neighbour' competition between nations as they strive to attract investment by multinational corporations. To attract this investment, countries may lower wages, company taxes, and environmental standards. This process causes a 'race to the bottom', undermining the living standards of the bulk of the people. However, countries can compete in other ways too. For example, they may offer highly-skilled labour or technological know-how that is crucial in particular industries, rather than cheap unskilled or semi-skilled labour. But the dominant drive towards 'international competitiveness' exerts a general downward pressure on workers' incomes. Meanwhile, managerial incomes experience a quite different 'race to the top' as companies compete to attract executives by offering prodigious remuneration packages. The growth in these executive incomes has been spectacular in recent years (Shields 2005). Evidently, class power and sectional interests are only thinly shrouded by the so-called imperative of 'globalisation'. Transnational corporations are the principal institutional vehicle through which these power relations and economic inequalities operate.

Other institutions are also involved in globalisation. International political and economic institutions such the International Monetary Fund (IMF), the World Bank (WB) and the World Trade Organisation (WTO) advocate the pursuit of faster economic growth as the means towards social progress on a global scale. They have embraced neo-liberal ideologies and policy practices, particularly the expansion of trade and investment in the private sector, and containment of the public sector. There are ongoing debates about their policies and their effects, with critics strongly arguing that their activities have compounded global inequalities (Peet 2003; Buckman 2004). In practice, all three of these global political economic institutions have been vehicles for policies supportive of the interests of international capital, notwithstanding the rhetoric about their concerns with social aspects of economic development.

The question then arises as to the politics of coping with, and challenging, the prevailing processes and institutions that create the poles of wealth and poverty. Is a progressive internationalism the appropriate emphasis? Or would a more defensive nationalism be appropriate? The two are not mutually exclusive. Progressive internationalism, aimed at redressing economic and social inequalities, requires international cooperation. Whether such co-operation is best focused on the expansion of trade, on policies to steer foreign investment, on increasing the volume of direct foreign aid, or on a combination of all three is a continuing debate (Stutz & Warf 2005).

If one considers that foreign aid is important, it is clear that much can be done to improve the current situation. In practice, the current foreign aid commitment is tiny. The UN target is for donor countries to commit 0.7 per cent of their gross national income to direct foreign aid to poorer countries. In 2003, the average for the OECD nations was 0.25 per cent, ranging from 0.92 per cent of gross national income in Norway to only 0.15 per cent in the United States. In Australia, this figure fell from 0.34 per cent in 1990 to 0.25 per cent in 2003 (UNDP 2005, p.278). Increasing aid contributions may seem an obvious target for 'citizens of the world' wishing to contribute to poverty alleviation. However, there is also concern that foreign aid, especially when 'tied' to requirements that the recipients use services and businesses in the donor nations, has quite marginal – or even negative – contributions to fostering economic development in the poorer nations. Anderson (2006) argues that aid has increasingly become 'corporate welfare' since it mainly focuses on payments made by governments to businesses based in the donor countries.

Meanwhile, poverty also persists in richer nations. In Australia, for example, its incidence has been estimated at between about 8 and 17 per cent of households, depending on how poverty is defined. If, for example, the poverty line is set at half of the median income for different types of household, about 11 per cent of households fall below it (Lloyd et al 2004). Much can be done to address the problem of particular social groups who are over-represented in this economically marginalised stratum of the population. Tackling the entrenched disadvantages that perpetuate poverty among Aboriginal peoples is an obvious priority. So too, more generally, are improvements in the provision of social security, public employment and public housing that could reduce the vulnerability to poverty, unemployment and homelessness.

However, policies to ameliorate poverty, whether nationally or internationally, are operating only at the margins of a more deeply-seated political economic problem – the tendency for the capitalist economy to generate economic inequality. Poverty is one manifestation of this more general problem of economic inequality. Indeed, if poverty is considered in relative terms (that is, relative to the social norms associated with the prevailing standard of living), it is clearly insoluble without a challenge to the forces reproducing and intensifying economic inequalities. Therein lies the even larger challenge than alleviating poverty: to promote egalitarian principles and to implement practical policies that can bring them to fruition. Together with the challenge of ecological sustainability, this is the most important issue for progressive political economic reform in the 21st century. The possibility of reforms which get to the root of the problems of poverty and economic inequality needs to be considered in relation to the current effects of globalisation and neo-liberalism.

Globalisation and income distribution

How has globalisation affected poverty and inequality on a world scale? The question is deceptively simple but difficult to answer.

Some writers have claimed that the expansion of international trade and investment in recent decades has produced a decrease in poverty. For example, Burbach & Robinson (1999) state that the globalisation of capital has meant a breakdown in divisions between the 'First' and 'Third' worlds. Journalist Martin Wolf (2002, p 13) states, more boldly, that 'evidence suggests that the 1980s and 1990s were decades of declining global inequality and reductions in the proportion of the world's population in extreme poverty'. Economist Richard Cooper asserts that the poverty alleviation record of the late 20th century is 'unambiguously positive' (quoted in Hoagland 1999, p 8).

However, such claims have been challenged. For example, political economist Robert Wade points out that, while the evidence on global poverty alleviation is ambiguous, the evidence on economic inequality indicates generally wider disparities, particularly when considered in terms of absolute differences between living standards in rich and poor countries (Wade 2002). The link between trade liberalisation and poverty reduction is yet more problematic. World Bank economists cited by Wade posit a positive connection between countries' economic performance and the extent to which they have opened their economies to international trade. However, this statistical relationship depends on how one interprets the economic progress made by China and India, the two most populous developing nations, and that of other growing economies like South Korea and Taiwan. Wade's conclusion is:

> [T]hat countries do not have to adopt liberal trade policies in order to reap benefits from trade and in order to grow fast. It shows only that as countries become richer they tend to liberalise trade, which is not the same thing (2002, p 53).

To get a basic understanding of the extent of inequality and poverty in different countries, some United Nations figures for 2003 are reproduced in Table 2.1. The variations are enormous. The per capita Gross Domestic Product (GDP) ranges from over $37,700 in Ireland, to a miserable $711 in

Table 2.1. Economic performance and human development 2003

Selected countries	GDP per capita (PPP US$)*	Human Development Index
Rich countries:		
Norway	37,670	0.963
Australia	29,632	0.955
Canada	30,677	0.949
Sweden	26,750	0.949
Switzerland	30,552	0.947
Ireland	37,738	0.946
Belgium	28,335	0.945
United States	37,562	0.944
Japan	27,967	0.943
Netherlands	29,371	0.943
Finland	27,619	0.941
Denmark	31,465	0.941
United Kingdom	27,147	0.939
France	27,677	0.938
Austria	30,094	0.936
Italy	27,119	0.934
New Zealand	22,582	0.933
Germany	27,756	0.930
Some poorer countries:		
Brazil	7,790	0.792
China	5,003	0.755
Indonesia	3,361	0.697
South Africa	10,346	0.658
India	2,892	0.602
Pakistan	2,097	0.527
Papua New Guinea	2,619	0.523
Nigeria	1,050	0.453
Burundi	648	0.378
Ethiopia	711	0.367
Burkina Faso	1,174	0.317

* PPP (purchasing power parity) accounts for price differences across countries, allowing international comparisons of real output and incomes. It takes account of the exchange rate between the currencies and differences in cost of living. So it provides a better indication of real material living standards in different countries than simply GDP per capita.

Source: UNDP (2005 p 219)

Ethiopia and $648 in Burundi. The 'human development index', a composite index that takes account of a wider array of social as well as economic variables, ranges from 0.963 in Norway and 0.955 in Australia, to 0.317 in Burkino Faso. Of course, using other indicators, such as infant mortality rates or the proportion of people living on less than two dollars per day, would produce different patterns, more or less striking in character (see O'Boyle 2004; Thompson 2004). The yet more contentious statistical issue is how to aggregate this sort of information to get a picture of global economic inequality and how it has been changing over time.

According to Australian Reserve Bank economists Gruen and O'Brien:

> [T]here appears to be widespread agreement that global inequality widened for much of the past two to three centuries, and the absolute number of people living in extreme poverty rose (even though the proportion in extreme poverty fell over this time). From around 1980, however, there is some evidence that these trends have not continued, and may in fact have reversed (2002, p 2).

Between 1980 and 1997 the population-weighted annual growth rate in GDP per capita was 4 per cent for the poorest one-fifth of countries, compared with 1.7 per cent for the richest one-fifth of countries (Gruen & O'Brien 2002). So, setting aside all questions about inequality within these countries, it seems that there is some evidence of a narrowing in the overall economic relativities during the last two decades of the twentieth century. However, the above figures are worldwide aggregates, and hide the effects of specific nations. Again, the data is dominated by China and India, both of which have experienced considerable economic growth during the last two decades. The effect is that, on a per capita basis, there appears to have been a diminution in the total number of people living in abject poverty. However, given that economic inequality has risen sharply within both of those countries, the net outcome may be greater economic inequality on a global scale (see Table 2.1, p 13).

Another specific situation not reflected in the global data is the position of sub-Saharan Africa. By any standards its economic conditions have deteriorated. According to the Reserve Bank analysis, Africa as a whole accounted for only about one-tenth of the world's extremely poor in the 1970s, but this proportion had risen to about two-thirds by 1998 (Gruen & O'Brien 2002). The ravages wrought in recent years by AIDS, periodic famines, wars and despotic regimes have further accentuated the fundamental economic problems in many of the nations. The continent, particularly the countries south of the Sahara, seems locked into an intractably difficult economic situation, other than in places such as the Republic of South Africa where a combination of natural resource wealth and some degree of industrialisation has produced affluence for a substantial minority. The economic growth impulses of modern capitalism have effectively by-passed much of the continent.

The problem of underdevelopment of Africa is quite different from that of Latin America, for example. Historically, all the nations in South and Central America have been victims of imperialism, and most have continued to be vulnerable to exploitation by international capital and a local comprador class. That subordination has been challenged by Cuban socialism, of course, and recently by anti-imperialist parties gaining political power in other nations, most notably Venezuela. The problems of imperialism have also constrained the development of Africa since its annexation by colonial powers in the 19th century, but the more modern problem – over and above the persistent ravages noted above – is one of marginalisation from the global economy. The continent does not even participate much in the processes elsewhere generating 'trickle down' economic development (Kitching 2001). The statistics for poor African nations, shown in Table 2.1, illustrate the outcome of extreme poverty, both absolutely and relatively.

However, broad-brush economic statistics alone tell only part of the poverty story. It is necessary to consider the diversity of experience of poverty in different nations. This is addressed in an important book by Michael Chussodovsky (1997) which, country by country, presents a depressing parade of the abuse of power by transnational institutions, often working in tandem with corrupt and authoritarian governments. Case studies from sub-Saharan Africa, South and South-East Asia, Latin America and the former Communist bloc are considered in detail. The 'structural adjustment programs' (SAPs) of the IMF are a particular target: SAP basically means forced privatisation and eliminating barriers to foreign investment and trade as conditions for getting financial assistance. As Chossudovsky puts it:

> While adopted in the name of democracy and so-called good governance, the structural adjustment programme requires the strengthening of the internal security apparatus: political repression – with the collusion of the Third World elites – supports a parallel process of economic repression. (1997, p 36)

The resulting situation 'is one of social desperation and the hopelessness of a population impoverished by the interplay of market forces' (Chossudovsky 1997, p 36). Australia's situation may appear relatively unproblematic by those standards. But even in Australia poverty is pervasive and persistent and the gulf between rich and poor is tending to widen (Stilwell 2003). These features have become more starkly pronounced in the last two decades as the unequalising forces of the globalisation of capital have been accompanied by the embrace of neo-liberal policies.

The influence of neo-liberalism

Neo-liberalism has been the dominant political economic ideology in the industrialised capitalist nations during the past two decades. It puts economic concerns above broader social concerns and asserts that economic progress is better sought through market processes than through 'interventionist' government policies. These two aspects of neo-liberalism are incompatible with other social and economic beliefs about the need to create institutions for the purposes of nation-building, planning and other collective political purposes, including the creation of a more egalitarian society. They are based on narrow conceptions of efficiency and individualism that supplant concerns about redistributive social justice. In this way neo-liberal ideology displaces the influence of Keynesian economic management and the commitment to a welfare state, as well as social democratic and socialist ideas.

However, in practice, neo-liberalism operates somewhat differently from its ideology. As some of its critics have pointed out, the policies of governments promoting neo-liberal ideology are often less about 'slimming the state' than about redistribution of social resources – from labour to capital and from poor to rich (Stilwell 2000; Beder & Cahill 2005). In Australia, for example, despite the neo-liberal philosophy of 'small government', the size of the public sector (measured in terms of federal government revenues and expenditures as a percentage of gross national product) has not fallen since the Howard Government came to office. This is disguised by the fact that revenue from the Goods and Services Tax (GST) is reported as a State tax rather than a federal tax. Yet neo-liberal policies have certainly had a major impact through other channels, such as the privatisation of public enterprises, contracting-out of service provision to private enterprises and growth of private-public partnerships for the provision of infrastructure.

In relationship to poverty and inequality, two interdependent aspects of neo-liberalism may be distinguished – its legitimation of disparities in living standards. and its practical policies which accentuate those disparities. Each aspect will be considered in turn. 'Incentivation' is the key concept in the neo-liberal legitimation of economic inequality. The term itself, though grammatically awkward and recently declining in common use, reveals what is at issue. The posited driver of economic activity is material incentives. So what is necessary to transform otherwise inert human beings into economically active ones is a wide gulf between the top and bottom of the income distribution. Political economist JK Galbraith once commented that this belief assumes rather different behavioural responses by the rich and the poor – the former will work harder when their incomes are raised while the latter will work harder when theirs are lowered (Davidson 1987). The narrow emphasis on individual monetary incentives also ignores personal, social and institutional factors that shape people's capacity for productive economic activity. Yet the 'incentivation' argument retains a widespread and simple appeal. Even relatively poor people sometimes subscribe to a belief that the system can, like a lottery, sometimes confers big wins, or that the economic system is a meritocracy in which everyone gets their just reward.

Neo-liberalism also operates in the realm of specific policies, both at the national and supranational levels. As previously noted, it is manifest typically at the national level in policies of privatisation of public enterprises, deregulation of private sector businesses and reductions in public sector expenditure on social services. Reductions in the higher rates of income tax are also a recurrent theme. These policy commitments have been accompanied by unwillingness to run fiscal deficits, as advocated by Keynesians, where they could operate as a counter-cyclical policy to reduce unemployment and finance public infrastructure and services. At the supranational level, neo-liberal policy is manifest through the practices of the IMF, WB and WTO. As noted earlier, these institutions, ostensibly charged with goals of ensuring financial stability and promoting economic development, have tended towards policies supportive of the interests of transnational capital. The 'structural adjustment programs' enforced by the IMF and WB on poor debtor nations have been particularly notorious for their financial stringency and damaging impacts on living standards and development prospects. Even some of their own leaders, such as the former chief economist at the WB, have come out openly as critics of those global institutions (Stiglitz 2003).

The pursuit of this neo-liberal agenda in the context of corporate globalisation produces major problems. The three-part 'race to the bottom' (in wage rates, tax rates, and environmental standards) reverberates with particularly deep tensions. Living standards for workers and the capacity of governments to finance necessary infrastructure and social services are common casualties. Lowered company taxes and less progressive income tax scales shift the tax burden to indirect taxes that impact more heavily on low and middle-income earners. The growing inequalities in living standards also vitiate our collective ability to achieve more ecologically sustainable development, because the cooperation necessary for commitment to the necessary changes in production and consumption patterns is less forthcoming in those circumstances. How to deal with these real dangers is the analytical and political challenge. Evidently there is a need to differentiate between the potentially progressive aspects of globalisation and its damaging effects. This differentiation requires exploration of alternatives that offer better prospects for economic and ecological security, social harmony and the reduction of poverty, nationally and internationally.

Progressive alternatives

Progressive internationalism, defensive nationalism and alternative localism are three strikingly different strategic options (Goodman 2002; Buckman 2004). After outlining each of these strategies, an argument will be made that a synthesis of the three can provide the basis for a constructive way forward. Progressive internationalism emphasises the potential for 'citizens of the world' to cooperate in the pursuit of human rights, labour rights, rights of indigenous people, and improved environmental standards on a global scale. Thus progressive internationalism involves building a progressive transnational consciousness. This means bringing indigenous peoples, environmental groups, and other progressive activists in different nations into closer contact (either face-to-face or via Email and Internet) to share experiences and ideas about alternatives to neo-liberal globalism. As such, progressive internationalism is not opposed to all aspects of global integration, but does stand in opposition to the globalisation of capital, seeking to combat corporate globalisation with a more progressive 'grass-roots' globalisation.

This position is supported by intellectuals such as Waldon Bello (2002), who has written about the prospects of 'deglobalisation' as a process whereby nations, and the communities that comprise them, can regain more control over their political economic futures. The globalisation of the interests of capital is thereby countered by a global peoples' movement with a more radical agenda. Its most public face has been its 'anti-globalisation' protests in recent years. Thousands of demonstrators have taken to the streets in cities such as Seattle, Prague, Melbourne, Gothenburg, Genoa and Hong Kong, where meetings have been held by the World Trade Organisation, the World Economic Forum, the G8 (the political leaders of the eight most powerful nations) and Forbes (the pro-business magazine that organises meetings for CEOs of transnational corporations). The concerns of progressive internationalism also find regular expression at the World Social Forum, a huge annual gathering first held at Porto Allegre in Brazil and now partially decentred to other localities. The protestors and participants in these events have focused their protests on the concentration of power in the hands of transnational corporations, the massive economic inequality on a global scale, the ultimate futility of consumerism, the problems of environmental decay, and the undermining of indigenous people's rights, workers' rights, and human rights.

Progressive internationalism had significant success in helping to thwart the introduction of the Multi-lateral Agreement on Investment in the late 1990s, an agreement that would have further restricted the capacity of governments to regulate the activities of transnationals operating in their nations (Goodman & Ranald 1999). More recently, the WTO's push for more trade liberalisation has been partly stalled by concerns coming from the poorer Third-World nations about how those aspects of the neo-liberal agenda disproportionately advantage the wealthier nations. Advocates of defensive nationalism adopt a different strategic stance. They stress that it is within the nation-state that our principal democratic institutions, however imperfect, exist. So it is at that level that the possibility is most viable for tempering, even taming, the unequalising effects of the capitalist market economy through reformist policy interventions. Anti-poverty programs targeted at the groups who are most socially disadvantaged and vulnerable to inadequate incomes are obvious examples. Policies emphasising the provision of affordable housing, education and health care for all also have an important role. A more radically redistributive tax system, and policies for more balanced industry and regional development can also be pursued at that level as part of a reinvigorated social democratic agenda. There is no fundamental incompatibility between progressive internationalism and the alternative strategy of defensive nationalism. Pursuing the globalisation of human rights and environmental consciousness is consistent with working within nation states for policies that can produce more egalitarian and sustainable outcomes.

The challenge to neo-liberal globalism can also be waged simultaneously on a third front – through the politics of localism. Indeed some political economists have argued that 'a return to the local' is an essential element in the struggle against neo-liberal globalism (Goldsmith & Mander 2001). Locally organised cooperatives for producing and distributing food and necessary social services can be fostered for this purpose. The experiments with cooperative businesses and with local area trading systems (LETS) in some Australian communities also reflect an ambition for partial disengagement from the institutions of global capitalism. A similar aim drives the development of community banks, although one must be wary of the ways in which the interests of finance capital can subvert the progressive potential of such institutions.

The well-known Green adage 'think global, act local' makes obvious sense in this context. Indeed, the current political economic context is one in which Green politics have particular resonance, linking a global analysis of the economic, social and environmental challenges that we face with practical actions to 'make a difference' at the local level. That sort of Green politics is evidently appealing to an increasing number of people who might otherwise have limited their political horizons to a focus on particular welfare or labour issues.

Towards more egalitarian outcomes

Proponents of a more egalitarian society, locally and globally, face enormous analytical and political challenges. 'Pessimism of the intellect, optimism of the will' – the much-quoted aphorism of Antonio Gramsci (Stilwell 2000, p 13) – seems even more relevant. Analytically, the challenge is to understand the factors shaping poverty and inequality. These factors are: (i) systemic, deriving from the intrinsic nature of the capitalist economy, (ii) temporally and spatially variable, dependent on country-specific features and on changing political economic circumstances, and (iii) malleable through public policy, either at the level of the locality, the nation or through supranational institutions. If we can develop a coherent analysis of these factors causing poverty and inequality then we are in a better position to see what different directions of economic and social development could contribute to their resolution.

Politically, it is also necessary to establish the case for prioritising egalitarian policies and to mobilise support for that sort of change of direction. We have to challenge the neo-liberal notion that substantial inequality is necessary for creating the economic growth that will eliminate poverty. Expressed like that, there is an evident internal contradiction in the neo-liberal position – reducing poverty requires more inequality! But the challenge is not purely one of logical consistency. A growing body of evidence shows that the neo-liberal model is simply not working in practice. Economic growth is being achieved – albeit unevenly over time and space, as has always been the case in the capitalist economy. However, the problem is that poverty and economic inequality persist – indeed, are reproduced in yet more intractable forms. The correlation between economic growth and improvements in wellbeing, particularly the wellbeing of people vulnerable to poverty, is quite weak. After reviewing the evidence on this issue, the Executive Director of The Australia Institute concluded that economic growth 'not only fails to make people contented [but] destroys many of the things that do' (Hamilton 2003a, p x).

Economists have usually justified their emphasis on economic growth as the primary goal of public policy on the grounds that the rising material living standard thereby generated will eradicate poverty and enhance happiness. It is not an altogether unreasonable expectation. Indeed, there is significant evidence that increases in the income of poor people correlate positively with increases in their happiness (Layard 2003). Liberation from grinding poverty, not surprisingly, generally makes people feel better about their lives. But, beyond that poverty threshold there is very little correlation between further increases in income and increases in happiness. This is revealed by within-country studies of the subjective wellbeing reported by people in different income groups (Peter Saunders 2002b; Hamilton 2003a), and by cross-country comparisons (Frank 1999). In both cases it is evident that major economic inequalities vitiate any positive association between material economic conditions and people's own perceived well-being. In brief, economic growth does not live up to the neo-liberal claims that it is the key to improved personal satisfaction, either for individuals or whole nations.

Meanwhile, the persistence and intensification of economic inequality has socially damaging effects. It consigns substantial sections of society to relative poverty, which depresses their well-being. Even those in the middle of the income distribution in a generally affluent nation like Australia commonly complain of their economic hardships (Hamilton 2003b). The relevant goal becomes, in effect, 'the life styles of the rich and famous' and ever-larger personal debt is embraced as the means of pursuing that aspiration. Unequal societies are also more prone to social conflict and crime, and to more ill-health among their citizens (Wilkinson 2001). As these uncomfortable facts come to be more widely recognised, the politics of egalitarianism should come to be viewed more favourably.

Indeed, in Australia today, opinion polls indicate strong public support for the view that the gulf between rich and poor is too wide, albeit with weaker support for any actively redistributive policies by government to redress it (Wilson et al 2005).

Equality of opportunity is an uncontested political goal: even neo-liberals assert it, although their policies ensure that it is more honoured in the breach than the observance. Greater equality of outcome is a taller order. Yet countries do vary enormously in terms of distributional inequality. Capitalism does not come as 'one size fits all'. In the Scandinavian nations, the ratio of the top ten per cent of household incomes to the bottom ten per cent of household incomes is typically around 5:1. In Brazil and South Africa the corresponding figures are over 50:1. Britain and Australia come in at around 13:1, somewhat more egalitarian than the USA at 17:1 (Stilwell 2002, p.30). These variations reflect long-standing historical, institutional and cultural differences between these societies. Australia cannot instantly become Sweden, but public policy could steer the nation in that direction rather than in the other direction towards the US 'model'.

There is no shortage of policy instruments that can be used to reduce inequality and poverty within a nation, if there is the political will to use them. Three clusters warrant particular attention – policies that redistribute income, create jobs, and provide affordable homes. A more egalitarian distribution of net incomes can be achieved directly through the implementation of appropriate structures of taxes and transfer payments. Current arrangements could be made much more effective for this purpose. For example, the existing progressive income-tax system in Australia is undermined by pervasive tax avoidance and evasion, such as the use of 'family trusts' by wealthy people to reduce their tax payments, and the misrepresentation of personal income as company income which attracts a lower rate of tax (Stilwell 2000). The greater emphasis on indirect taxes since the introduction of the GST has been another factor reducing the progressivity of the overall tax system. Significantly, income from capital is taxed more lightly than income from labour (because the rate of capital gains tax is well below the top marginal income tax rate), and income from inheritance is not taxed at all. The inadequacies of the current land tax system also produce a situation where land price inflation, experienced in all Australian cities over the last decade, produces a more unequal distribution of wealth. Large-scale property investors have reaped huge capital gains as land prices have risen, particularly in the major State capitals, while those seeking first homes are increasingly excluded from the market because of the cost of acquiring land and housing. A more broadly based land-tax could reduce the attractiveness of land as a speculative investment, and thereby help to stabilise land and housing prices. It could also generate more tax revenue which could be used to finance a larger stock of public housing, which would help those on low incomes (Stilwell & Jordan 2005). Major reforms in all these areas could produce radically redistributive effects.

On the expenditure side, many benefits designed to assist low-income earners are often claimed by upper-income groups. Tax relief for work-related expenses, such as the purchasing of overalls, are now used by business people to claim their international travel and luxury hotel accommodation costs for attending conferences and seminars. And social security beneficiaries commonly face high effective marginal tax rates because their benefits taper off sharply when they earn additional wage income, thereby catching them in notorious 'poverty traps'. These problems reflect the tension between two principles: 'universality,' in which social security is considered a right, and the goal of 'targeting expenditures at the needy', which requires means-testing. One means of reconciling these principles would be to introduce a 'guaranteed minimum income' system, so that all citizens automatically avoid poverty. There are real concerns about the level at which any such income level should be set, of course. And, despite some support that has come from figures on the political right, such as Milton Friedman (1962, Ch.12), there is an evident lack of political momentum for the introduction of such a scheme at present.

Measures to deal with poverty through the provision of public employment and public housing seem to be similarly out of favour. State provision of employment and housing runs counter to the neo-liberal preference for market provision. But these two policies are fundamental to tackling poverty in a nation like Australia. Unemployment has a strong correlation with poverty, so one can be confident that government policies emphasising job-creation will make a direct contribution to poverty-alleviation. Of course, there can be disagreement over whether job creation is better done through stimulus to the private sector via business subsidies, through general expansion of public employment, or through more targeted schemes like 'work-for-the dole'. However, at a bare minimum, the general principle of government as 'employer of the last resort' is essential. John Maynard Keynes emphasised that capitalism cannot reliably produce full employment unless government plays this role (Stilwell 2002). Otherwise the uncertainties created by the labour market inevitably result in the continued reproduction of a 'reserve army' of unemployed persons.

Concurrently, intervention in the housing market is essential to combat the tendency, evident in recent Australian conditions, for housing costs to push people on modest incomes into poverty. Again, the most appropriate policy instruments are debatable. Increased provision of public housing and government housing subsidies (for example for first home-buyers or, more generally, for means-tested applicants) are the most direct mechanisms. More indirectly, raising property taxes can have the effect of reducing the price of land by driving out the speculative element in housing demand. A combination of policies could be particularly potent – for example, a nationally uniform system of land-tax that generates the revenue for dramatically increasing the public housing stock. Such a policy would reverse the current trend towards running down the stock of public housing and redistributing the nation's wealth towards land-owners at the expense of those seeking affordable rental housing.

Conclusion

Poverty and inequality are features of a capitalist system that tends to polarise the distribution of income and wealth both within and between nations. But this chapter has argued that there is nothing 'natural' or inevitable about these outcomes. Historically, the extent of poverty and inequality has varied according to how effectively the democratic institutions of government and trade unions have ameliorated, even reversed, the underlying inegalitarian tendencies in capitalist economies. The rise of neo-liberalism during the past three decades has tended to roll back those interventions and undermine their perceived legitimacy. However, it is not all one-way traffic. Neo-liberalism can be, and recurrently is, challenged by social movements, including the 'green', 'anti-globalisation', and labour movements, which seek to prioritise issues of social justice and sustainability. Progressive politics in the current era necessarily involves linking those concerns with egalitarian and welfare policy initiatives within the nation-state. It also requires, more locally, a focus within particular communities on practical down-to-earth measures that directly address the needs of the poor and redistribute economic and social opportunities more equitably.

There need be no major tension between policies that tackle inequality and poverty 'at home' and those that tackle inequality and poverty on a global scale. It is not just a matter of a nation or a region showing that it 'can get its own house in order first', although that is always important in establishing credibility as a progressive player in the international arena. It is also a matter of recognising the interdependence of local and global problems of economic and social justice. An attack on 'third world' living conditions, whether focused on remote Aboriginal communities in Australia or on aid to the poor in Africa, is essentially similar. There are issues of priority to be established, as in any matter of public policy, of course. But the unifying element in the struggle against poverty and for a more egalitarian society, both locally and globally, is the commitment to the values of human dignity, liberation and social justice.

Chapter 3

Women and poverty: The application of feminism in overcoming women's poverty in the global context

Ruth Phillips

> Women are the majority of the world's 1.3 billion people living in extreme poverty, often surviving on less than one dollar a day. As globalisation continues to influence economic opportunities worldwide, the number of women living in poverty has increased compared to men. With little education, basic work skills or access to credit, many women are not able to start businesses or other income-generating projects to participate in the global economy (Women's Edge Coalition 2005).

The claims about women's poverty in the above quote are made repeatedly by women's organisations throughout the world. Such claims, along with evidence discussed below, paint a consistent picture of women's inequality and disadvantage, as they endure economic, political and social exclusion, and gender-based discrimination. Therefore this chapter aims at increasing understanding of the issue of women's deprivation in a globalised world, and highlights the importance of feminism in addressing women's poverty. It is argued that achieving equal citizenship for women is important for overcoming poverty, which in this chapter is based on two broad concepts of poverty. The first is absolute poverty, generally understood as a lack of 'the most basic of life's requirements and is measured by estimating the numbers of individuals or families who cannot provide for the necessities of life such as housing, food or clothing' (Senate Community Affairs Reference Committee (SCARC) 2004, p 5). A global measure of absolute poverty is based on the number of people living on less than one US dollar per day (World Bank 2000a). The second concept is relative poverty, usually measured within countries rather than globally. Relative poverty 'refers to individuals and families that have low incomes or other resources relative to other individuals or families' within the society in which they live (SCARC 2004, p 6). Thus to be relatively poor is to be excluded from the choices and opportunities to participate in the lifestyle enjoyed by the majority in a given society. The terms absolute or relative poverty are both relevant to a discussion of women's poverty, and are both related to ideas of inequality.

Why focus on women? Why do women experience poverty differently to men? There are two basic answers to these questions: one, gender inequality is a direct cause of poverty; two, research at national and international levels shows that women experience poverty more than men.

Women and poverty

There are two widely accepted facts about poverty in the global context. First, despite significant economic growth throughout the world and apparent reductions in 'world poverty', absolute poverty is still increasing (World Bank 2005, p 1). Second, women are over-represented among the poorest of the poor (Beall 1998; Dewan 1999; Anderson 2000; Nussbaum 2000; Pressman 2003; Gupta 2005). The most recent research available from the United Nations Development Program (UNDP) reported that in 1995 women comprised 70 per cent of the world's poor, and accordingly women's poverty is now a focus of global social policy responses to poverty. These policies, highlighted in the United Nations Millennium Development Goals (UNMDG) (UN 2005), are central to the poverty strategies of many governmental and non-governmental organisations.

Since the advent of the second wave women's movement in the late 1960s, feminists have striven to highlight the nature and extent of women's poverty (Glendinning & Millar 1987; Mies 1998; Friedman 1995; Nussbaum, 2000; Feminist Majority Foundation 2005). A broad feminist perspective of women's poverty argues that more women than men experience poverty because of entrenched gender inequalities in most societies (Mies 1998, Nussbaum 2000). Although it cannot be argued that globalisation has ameliorated world poverty, George and Wilding (2002) claim that in many ways women have benefited from globalisation, because a globalised women's movement has challenged many entrenched gender inequalities and freed women from traditions of second-class citizenship. Nevertheless many women continue to experience inequality, and this chapter explores some of these inequalities as they are central to an understanding women's ongoing poverty.

It is further argued here that the most effective means of addressing the impact of gender inequality on women's poverty is to improve women's citizenship status. Having unequal access to political, social and economic resources and political power, women clearly face more barriers than men in any attempt to move out of poverty. Definitions of and arguments for the importance of citizenship are presented later in the chapter.

Feminism and women's poverty

Feminist theory and action have transformed over time and place, and the feminist theories that have been most applied to poverty and development are socialist or Marxist feminism, liberal feminism, radical feminism, post-modern feminism, post-colonial feminism, and third-world feminism (Narayan 1997). Although the divergences between these approaches have preoccupied many feminist theorists and activists in the West for the past two decades, such preoccupations are not necessarily of value to women engaged in women's equality activism and development programs across the world.

For this chapter, the most relevant aspect of theoretical and political transformations in feminism is the rethinking in approaches to how women's experiences are perceived and addressed. For example, the second wave movement of the late 1980s to the early 1990s was predominantly liberal or radical (structuralist) feminism, and regarded women as a homogeneous group suffering the dominance of men. In turn this approach gave way to types of feminism that challenged the hegemony of Western feminism. This rise of post-modern feminism was seen to fracture the Western women's movement, as it shifted the politics of feminism away from the universal experience of being a woman in a world dominated by men, to the differences between women and their experiences of oppression (Thompson 2001; Bryson 2002). Thus post-modern feminism emphasises the diverse ways in which women experience gender relations, opening opportunities for women of diverse cultural and religious backgrounds to speak about their specific experiences. The complexity of these shifts in approach is highlighted in the following observation:

> The challenge of feminist scholarship to replace the analysis of women's lives based solely on the commonality of sex with a more inclusive methodology that recognises the intersection of differences compelled feminist scholarship to widen its horizon, explore its possibilities, and gain a new lease on life ... In assessing the feminist challenge and the challenges of feminism, I, an African women from Igboland, think of 'when and where I enter', both in the larger feminist movement and the women-of-colour variant (Nnaemeka 2005, p 54).

Third-world feminism, influenced by post-modern feminism, draws heavily on the frameworks of post-colonial feminism, which sees the impact of globalisation as crucial. Post-colonial feminism is not a grand narrative for feminism, but focuses on the legacies of colonialism, seeking 'to extend the analysis of sexism and multicultural identity formation to include the effects of Western colonialism that still exist today' (Mack-Canty 2004, p 164). Third-world feminists are described by Narayan as 'feminists who acquired feminist views and engaged in feminist politics in third-world countries and who continue to do so' (1997, p 4). This position is founded on identity and is linked to the specificity of the lived experience of women in different cultures and nations.

Women from developing countries initially rejected feminism in the1970s, believing that it would divert political efforts from poverty and development, the most pressing questions for their countries. However, women's movements in developing countries have been growing since the 1980s (Mies 1998), and key social policy issues have been placed on state and international public agendas. Issues such as violence against women, sexual assault, sexual exploitation and gender equality have become central to women's struggles for equality throughout the developing world.

Feminism thus engages in women's struggles, where states ignore or even perpetuate women's inequality and suffering. As Dewan points out, 'the absence of gender incorporation and analysis in economic policies leads to both the misallocation of resources and a virtual denial of the existence of households and 'vulnerable' sections of the community' (1999, p 426).

It is useful and appropriate to view women's poverty through a feminist lens because social, cultural, religious and gender conditions affect women's experience of poverty (Leonard 2003). Therefore a key strategy is to strive for women's equal citizenship, as daily life is often determined by how women are treated and regarded in their own communities.

Citizenship

Citizenship exists in an individual's relationship with the state and wider society (Lister 2003). Lister also pointed out that citizenship is a 'slippery concept', perhaps best explained by Marshall's 1950 definition:

> [Citizenship is] a status bestowed on those who are full members of a community. All who possess the status are equal with respect to the rights and duties with which the status is endowed (cited in Lister 2003, p, 14).

Drawing on the definition of citizenship above, the idea of 'global citizenship' has emerged:

> The idea of global citizenship leads us to focus on the responsibilities of rich countries towards countries which are impoverished enough not to be able to translate international principles of human rights into citizenship rights. It also leads to a focus on the action of global civil society to ensure equal rights for citizens world-wide (Sweetman 2004, p 6).

Because women are often not granted the rights of first-class citizens by their own communities, it can be argued that a structural cause of women's disproportionate poverty is their second-rate citizenship status. In response to this situation, women have organised their own global networks, mostly emerging from international conferences that effectively legitimised feminist agendas for equality on a global scale and provided important resources for women from developing countries in particular (Keck & Sikkink 1998). The legitimacy of women's networks was strengthened by the use of the UN as a key forum. The key objective of this networked activity is to influence states' policies and to bring about legislative changes that address women's inequality, security and protection as citizens of their country (Keck & Sikkink 1998).

A part of global feminist activity has been the growing trend for women from developing countries to make connections between women's rights or gender equality and the much broader mandate of human rights. This connection originated as a platform at the 1955 UN Conference on Women's Issues, when 'violence against women' was launched as a global social policy issue. This issue then became a common advocacy cause in both the women's movement and the human rights movement (Bunch 1995; Townsend 1996; Keck & Sikkink 1998; Bahar 2000). Bunch describes this shift as a means of moving women from the margins to the centre of policy concerns for the state and international institutions, 'by questioning the most fundamental concepts of our social order so that they take better account of women's lives' (Bunch 1995, p 11).

However, some feminists have argued that in a world dominated by male power, the blending of women's specific needs into a human rights agenda may lead to ignorance of the fact that women are generally worse off than men, and that the human rights agenda itself has been established by a measure of what might happen to men in denial of their rights (Flew et al 1999). Ezeilo also questions the human rights framework as appropriate for women's rights struggles:

> [W]omen's freedom, dignity and equality have been grossly eroded by law and, in fact, inequality developing from cultural patterns deprives women their opportunity of full and equal participation as citizens within their own societies and within international society (2005, p 231).

This type of argument reflects the lively feminist debates that continue among women activists and theorists, and highlights the importance of questioning changes that may threaten the core agenda for improving the status of women.

The need to improve women's citizenship

Sinha, in a discussion about Indian women in a modern state but a premodern society, observes:

> A current challenge for development workers is to decide whether and how their interventions should address cultural beliefs and practices which challenge the idea of women as equal to men, and hence undermine the idea that women are full citizens of the states in which they live (2004, p 19).

As stated above, cultural and structural barriers often limit women's citizenship. Social relations that influence the experience of citizenship are bound by gender, class, race and religion, and are often played out in the legal and political status of citizens, particularly women (Sinha 2004). For example, where laws do not recognise rape in marriage, women are excluded from the responsibility of the state to protect its citizens from such assault. In many societies, a few of which are India, Uganda, and Algeria, women are legally designated second-class citizens (Sweetman 2004). For example, the 1984 'Family Code' laws in Algeria make it a legal duty of women to obey their husbands (Sahli 2004). All of these states have high levels of poverty and poor economic outcomes for women: population poverty rates for Uganda, India, and Algeria are 55, 35, and 23 per cent respectively. Of these, Algeria has the world's lowest earnings ratio for women compared to men, based on the Human Development Index measures (UNDP 2005). Thus it is clear that poverty and citizenship are related, and where women are denied full citizenship, they are more likely to experience poverty.

In a call for a focus on citizenship in India, John (2002) argues that feminism in India must move beyond its engagement with women as 'the poor', to study the processes that relegate women to a secondary place in Indian society. Such a focus would involve examining the non-poor, understanding gender inequalities across economic and social classes, raising issues of the disproportionate number of males over females, and understanding transitions into and out of poverty (John 2002). Another problem is the entrenched preference for male children in a number of countries, such as China, Korea, and Japan. Where birth rates are legally controlled, families have chosen to keep boy children over girls, reflecting both traditional and current gender inequalities in those countries.

Income and employment security are also determinants of citizenship, and in 'a private and market setting ... income and employment security cannot be as far-reaching as is the security inherent in citizenship status' (Rieger & Leibfried 2003, p 77). Rieger and Leibfried point out that the social benefits provided by a strong welfare state act to secure a living standard for all, as a guard against poverty, and 'a kind of indemnity against economic risks' (2003, p 78). They also point out that as an economy becomes more 'open' or globalised, there is a much greater volatility of employment and this 'takes on a different significance in welfare states than it does in societies lacking economic protection schemes' (Rieger & Leibfried 2003, p 78). Social protection ensures a security for individuals while keeping labour markets intact, so that waves of economic growth can be sustained (Rieger & Leibfried 2003).

In both developing and developed countries women's status as citizens is a key feature of their comparative economic position. Recent research commissioned by the World Economic Forum (WEF) examined the status of women across the world and rated 58 countries on five criteria: economic participation, economic opportunity, political empowerment, educational attainment and health, and wellbeing (Lopez-Claros & Zahidi 2005). These criteria are not dissimilar to qualitative measures of relative poverty and, from a feminist perspective, reflect key areas of exclusion or second-class citizenship for women across the world. The results of the WEF research are startling. The Nordic states of Sweden, Norway, Iceland, Denmark and Finland rate the highest in gender equity (in that order); it is no coincidence that these countries have the world's strongest welfare states, highest levels of taxation, and the lowest levels of poverty. Australia ranks tenth and the United States seventeenth, reflecting a diminution of equity as the breadth of social citizenship (essentially provided by the welfare state) becomes weaker. Countries with no welfare infrastructure or social citizenship rank at the bottom, with Egypt the lowest and Turkey, Pakistan and Jordan just above it (Lopez-Claros & Zahidi 2005). The set of countries studied does not include the poorest in the world, as they could not rate at all on indices of health outcomes or wellbeing. However, countries such as India have a high level of poverty, a relatively good political empowerment rank, but a very poor educational attainment rank, reflecting the importance of state infrastructure in addressing gender equity (Lopez-Claros & Zahidi 2005).

Due to the integral relationship between social citizenship and the welfare state, in countries with strong welfare systems, women generally have a stronger level of citizenship. Where there is no welfare state, notions of gender equality tend to be absent, and women lack social and economic status. This position is supported by the WEF research described above, where the top rating states have very strong gender equity principles in their social welfare and legal systems. Key causes of women's poverty in developing countries relate to failures of those states to provide fundamental welfare that support women's citizenship. Education, health services, housing, rights to control their own fertility, access to resources, access to work and income, freedom from violence and appropriate nutrition are primary steps in alleviating women's poverty. Without equal and legitimate access to these essential elements for a fair or good standard of living as equal citizens, women (and those they care for) suffer social and political exclusion.

Research on women's poverty

Women's poverty in the developed world is growing, partly due to women's increasing longevity and consequent over-representation among the aged. Globally, in 2000-05 women had a life expectancy of 68 years, compared to 63 years for men; however, women's advantage is larger in developed countries (seven years) than in less developed countries (three years) (UN 2004). The gender gap in life expectancy is narrowest in the least developed countries (two years), where the impact of HIV/AIDS on mortality is estimated to be more detrimental for women (UN 2004).

Older women's poverty in developed countries is likely to be compounded by a number of factors. One such factor is their work histories, which have left them with few savings. Another factor is their experiences of domestic violence which excluded them from support from partners. Poverty is also due to women's traditional roles as caregivers where their unrecognised labour has excluded them from independent economic citizenship. In Australia this is reflected in a range of ways. For example, the 2001 Census revealed an increase in the number of homeless women and older women living alone, compared to men (SCARC 2004).

Older people living alone are prone to poverty, as despite the material asset of housing, they may not be able to utilise services, maintain appropriate nutrition, manage their financial affairs, or maintain their own health care.

According to Cagatay (1998), much of the international poverty research literature claims that women are poorer than men for three main reasons: one, women experience a higher incidence of poverty therefore are at greater risk of poverty; two, women's poverty is more severe; and three, the incidence of women's poverty is increasing over time. Cagatay critiques these claims as limited and dated means of understanding the gendered nature of poverty, and refers to more complex measures such as the Gender Development Index (GDI) used by the UNDP (1998). As Cagatay observes, 'norms about child marriage of girls, gender biases against girl's education, women's limited mobility, and gender gaps in wages all contribute to difficulties of escaping poverty' (1998, p 11).

The UNDP makes strong links between its measures of GDIs and Human Poverty Index (HPI). For example, the four lowest ranking countries on their GDI (Sierra Leone, Niger, Burkina Faso and Mali), are also ranked the lowest on HPI (UNPD 1997). Catagay (1998) suggests that this type of research demonstrates that gender inequality, although important in itself, is also a poverty issue. Even without such historically- and culturally-entrenched gender inequalities, in one of the wealthiest nations in the world, the United States, women are poorer than men. According to the US Bureau of Statistics (USBS), in 1997 there were more women than men (135,865,000 females and 130,353,000 males), and more poor women than poor men. Of the almost 14 per cent of Americans considered poor, 57 per cent were women (USBS 1997). Much research on women's poverty has focused on sole parent female-headed households as they stand out as the most vulnerable to poverty in most societies (Nicholas-Casebolt & Krysik 1993). In some societies, whether women are abandoned, widowed or divorced, they experience social and economic exclusion (Cagatay 1998), and in many cases must balance care of children and work.

Women who are sole parent heads of households are a group in great need of social protection (SCARC 2004). In countries such as Australia and USA, where welfare state provisions are available, 'single mothers' are highly stigmatized politically as 'dependent' on the state, and have become a target for welfare reform policies such as those undertaken by the current Australian government (ACOSS 2005a, 2005b). As outlined in the Australian Senate Report on Poverty, sole female-headed households are poorer than their male equivalents (SCARC 2004), with 104,000 female-headed families measured as poor, compared to 34,000 male-headed families in Australia in 2000 (Harding et al 2001, pp 15-23).

As stated above, women in developed countries have consistently been over-represented among the poor. However, in Australia in 2000, after two decades of protective and targeted welfare state policies, and concerted women's equality policies, there appeared to be a reduction in women's poverty. Broad national research covering people over 15 years of age indicated that women and men were equally represented among the poor (Harding et al 2001). Hill counters this finding by stating that more in-depth research suggested gender differences regarding living standards within households in Australia, as 'many studies have found that when resources are limited it is most likely that the female adults, particularly mothers, will go without' and 'no studies have found that, on average, men experience greater deprivation overall than their female partners' (2004, p 4). Hill also argues that in Australia, conventional research probably both underestimates the extent of women's poverty and overestimates the extent of men's poverty (Hill 2004). The underestimation of women's poverty is due to a failure to identify groups of poor women hidden within household statistics because of assumptions of equal sharing of income (Hill 2004).

Hill's research demonstrates the value of a feminist framework, for example, in methodology that separates out the experience of poverty for women within households, thus highlighting the inequalities of power relations between women and men. In this way feminism contributes to a specific understanding of women's poverty that under broader research frameworks is lost.

Gender inequality as a cause of poverty

From a broad liberal feminist perspective, one that focuses on equality for women in a society that has been traditionally dominated by men, the unequal ownership of power and resources by men has resulted in a greater risk of poverty for women. This power imbalance has meant that women suffer social disadvantage, exclusion and inter-personal violence because they are women. Kaplan (1992) describes liberal feminism as organised, hierarchical, negotiative and working toward coalition building. That leads to liberal feminism seeking to influence and change public opinion through formal networks such as the United Nations, and the progressive reform of laws within states, in pursuit of greater equality for women (Kaplan 1992). One way of understanding the scope of women's inequality at a global level is to examine the set of problems addressed by some advocacy-oriented women's developmental organisations. For example, the Australia-based International Women's Development Agency (IWDA) responds thus to the question 'Why focus on women?':

- Women have a right to a sustainable livelihood. More than a billion people live on less than US$1 a day; 70 per cent of these are women. Worldwide, over 60 per cent of people working in family enterprises without pay are women.

- Every minute, a woman somewhere in the world dies in pregnancy or childbirth; almost half of births in developing countries take place without the help of a skilled attendant.
- Around the world, one in three women has been beaten, coerced into sex, or abused in some other way; one woman in four has been abused during pregnancy.
- Women hold only 16 per cent of seats in parliament worldwide; currently there is not a single female parliamentarian in the Solomon Islands.
- More than a billion people lack access to clean drinking water; in developing countries, women can spend several hours a day collecting water (IWDA 2005).

These issues highlight the gendered nature of poverty, reproductive health, sexual and domestic violence, lack of political representation and the unequal division of labour. These issues are also core areas of action for feminists working toward addressing women's poverty in developing and developed countries. A further indicator of women's inequality is education. This contention is supported by data that shows a gap between the education of girls and boys in primary and secondary schools, reflecting the maintenance of male privilege at a young age, and is a primary driver for one of the UNMDG (beginning in 2000 to be reached by 2015) to promote gender equity and empowerment of women (UN 2005). The UN also argues that:

> [G]ender equity is at the core of whether the Goals will be achieved – from improving health and fighting disease, to reducing poverty and mitigating hunger, to expanding education and lowering child mortality, to increasing access to safe water, to ensuring environmental sustainability (2005, p 50).

The UNMDG is currently the most prominent global initiative against world poverty, and is supported by the world's most powerful leaders. The fact that women's education and gender equity are key objectives of the UNMDG is recognition of the importance of gender equality and the need to address women's poverty in the global context. In its development and aid policy, the Australian government also acknowledges that issues of gender are critical to addressing poverty. An AusAid policy statement explains the Gender and Development (GAD) approach to overseas aid and development:

> Gender equity refers to equal opportunities and outcomes for men and women. This involves the removal of discrimination and structural inequalities in access to resources, opportunities and services, and the promotion of equal rights (AusAid 2005, p 2).

The Australian government argues that over the past decade changes in the way development agencies and NGOs seek to advance women's status through development programming are reflected in the GAD approach (AusAid 2005). This policy position recognises that women are a key target in addressing poverty and economic development, the core purposes of official overseas aid. The GAD approach also acknowledges that some barriers to overcoming poverty are embedded in discrimination and structural inequalities. Women continue to experience sex discrimination and structural exclusion in societies that still see women as subordinate or unequal to men. Gender equality is important both for women living in developing countries and experiencing absolute poverty, and for women in developed countries, where a disproportionate number of women endure relative poverty.

Conclusion

The central purpose of this chapter has been to prompt thinking about women's poverty in the global context. It has also set out to explain, briefly, feminist frameworks in strategies to address women's poverty, and argues that a core strategy for gender equality is action to bring about equal citizenship for women.

Gender equality has been presented as a central feminist social policy principle for addressing women's poverty at both national and global levels. Although not discussed in depth in this chapter, the global context is now an important broad arena for addressing women's poverty. Women's networks are linked by both formal, institutional processes such as conferences conducted through the United Nations and, perhaps more effectively, thousands of women's advocacy and development organisations. Women's activism against poverty also supports localised activities for countering the negative effects of globalisation on women's economic participation through social movement and NGO engagement (John 2002; McCann & McClosky 2003; Mukhopadhyay 2003).

As economic development is increasingly viewed as the cure for global poverty, both in its capacity as a global free market and via its imposition as a model for development placed on countries seeking to establish their place in the globalised economy, it will continue to be an important arena for action against poverty. However, resistance to the negative effects of increasing marketisation and globalisation must continue within nation states, and the original purpose of the welfare state and its links to citizenship must continue to be a focus of challenges to gender inequalities. Social protection afforded by income security policies, free school education, universal health care, accessible child-care and state assured access to basic resources such as clean water and food are of particular importance for women. Addressing such fundamental needs will often be women's only means of gaining equal citizenship. As Yuval-Davis observed of struggles for equal citizenship, 'without 'enabling' social conditions, political rights are vacuous' (1997, p 92).

Chapter 4

Understanding poverty

Eric Porter & Jennie Trezise

Recent years have witnessed intense debate on the nature and extent of poverty in Australia. In generating significant and challenging research, this debate has helped refigure understandings of poverty at a fundamental level. By uncovering the social, cultural and inter-generational complexities of poverty, the research data has now discredited any notion that poverty is merely a lack of financial resources. But data alone will not settle this debate. Data must be interpreted, and all interpretation rests implicitly on existing values, anxieties and motives – that is, on ideology. The poverty debate is thus essentially and unavoidably political. As Peter Saunders (2005b) notes, analysis of poverty in Australia has developed largely through efforts to reform welfare, rendering the current poverty debate unintelligible and hence unresolvable in isolation from the parallel debate on welfare. This chapter demonstrates, however, that while continued research has steadily improved and refined our understanding of poverty, welfare reform follows a separate trajectory guided purely by a political agenda.

Despite over a decade of economic growth, recent studies suggest that poverty in Australia is increasing (Melbourne Institute 2003). The tax burden underpinning the welfare system is growing even more rapidly, despite the well-publicised 'crackdown' on 'welfare cheats' by the Coalition Government, and other policies designed to shift the unemployed and pensioners into the workforce (P Saunders 2004b). Indeed, the broader debate on poverty has been fuelled by changes to welfare, instigated by the government since 1996. Whether government policy is directly motivated by the poverty debate is a moot point, but the government clearly shares the general ideals and objectives favoured by one side of the debate. It is this shared ideology rather than any research that shapes Coalition policy.

The poverty debate resolves into a contest between two main theoretical approaches. One emphasises individual choice and responsibility, drawing attention to the roles of moral character and motivation in determining an individual's socio-economic status. This 'right-wing' approach draws support from prominent conservative think tanks including the Centre for Independent Studies (CIS), the HR Nicholls Society (HRNS) and the Institute for Public Affairs (IPA). The second theoretical approach, generally characterised as 'left-wing', highlights broader social and economic structures. This structural approach explores the class and economic processes that limit and anticipate the opportunities open to individuals and the choices they can make. Advocates include the Melbourne Institute of Applied Economic and Social Research at Melbourne University and the Social Policy Research Centre at the University of NSW.

This chapter argues that current government policies designed to target poverty are based predominantly on individual explanations. It also argues that these policies have proved largely ineffective. While choice plays an important role in determining any individuals' economic fate, such choices are not made in a vacuum. Unless government addresses the cultural and socio-economic contexts within which these choices are made, such policies will miss by a wide margin (Pusey 2003). Starting with a discussion of these two major explanations of poverty, this chapter locates choice within these contexts, exploring the broader structures that both facilitate and restrict the actions of individuals and governments alike.

Individual explanations of poverty

Individual explanations have a long history, typified by the laissez-faire social and economic ideas of the mid-19th century. Influential English sociologist Herbert Spencer (1820-1903), for instance, saw life as an inherent struggle. Success or failure depended upon an individual's physical, intellectual and moral resources. Inevitably some would fail 'to fulfil all the requirements of life' (Spencer 1969, p 106). Those who could not compete were of a weaker type, 'good-for-nothings, vagrants and sots, criminals... men who shared the gains of prostitutes' (Spencer 1969, p 106). Efforts, financial or otherwise, to assist the 'idle', 'weak', 'inferior' and 'improvident' meant only that they would 'thrive and multiply as much as, or more than' those who had proved themselves in life's struggle (Spencer 1969, p 137). Most importantly, charitable intervention was seen as counter-productive, allowing the 'inferior' to thrive, and thus causing social decline (Spencer 1969, p 137).

Spencer articulated attitudes popular across 19th century British social and political ideas. At heart, these aimed to separate the 'deserving' from the 'undeserving' poor, moralising poverty by making it indicative of personal virtues (Carney & Hanks 1994). By this definition, physically fit individuals in poverty were immoral.

Spencer wrote at a time of enormous socio-economic change. Today, in another period of instability and social dislocation, similar views have resurfaced (Phillips 1990), in a form adapted to the current context. Though both classic and contemporary neo-liberal policies exhibit moralising tendencies, there are important differences. For example, the poor are still treated as 'incapables', but are also seen as victims of the welfare state, corrupted by 'welfare dependency' (Cox 2001; Murray 2001; P. Saunders 2004c). Spencer by contrast saw the poor not as victims but as a threat to society, furnished by charity with a chance to out-breed those of superior virtue. Today, society still 'suffers' from welfare dependency through the tax burden (see below), but it is the plight of individual beneficiary that attracts moral censure (Cox 2001; P Saunders 2005b).

Neo-liberals such as the CIS cast welfare as a 'trick' that feigns help as it undermines poor people's initiative and chance of independence (Cox 2001; P Saunders 2005b). The loss of healthy 'self-reliance' is thus seen as the core of poverty – any other deprivation is contingent on that. Inspired by Charles Murray's critique of the 1960s' 'war on poverty' in the United States (Murray 1984; 2001), CIS commentators view the poor as dependent on welfare, much as drug users are dependent on drugs (P Saunders & Tsumori 2002). Here financial dependence is recast as psychological dependence, a failure of the individual rather than of economic process or government policy. Only 'tough love' strategies that force 'self-reliance' on the poor, making them take responsibility for their own condition and use their own moral resources, will really help (Cox 2001; P Saunders 2004a).

In this sense, individual explanations of poverty contribute to a broader attack, developed since the 1970s, on the traditional rights-based agenda of the left (McKnight 2005). Speaking generally, this attack has shifted the focus of government policy from rights to obligations. In a liberal democracy, rights are common to all citizens, justifying entitlement to welfare for all, regardless of personal characteristics. McKnight argues that, by contrast, obligations can be tied more directly to a person's particular circumstances. Thus welfare can be made conditional on specified obligations. For this reason, neo-liberals can accept rights as abstract and universal, while using obligations to articulate what seems a simple and symmetrical relationship between individuals and society. This approach makes harsher government policy easier to sell. Only the 'deserving' poor receive assistance, and they in turn reciprocate through defined obligations and responsibilities.

For this reason, individual explanations are associated closely with conservative 'mutual obligation' policies. As such, they are often accused (Knight 2005) of disadvantaging the poor and unemployed, the finer points of theory dismissed as mere rhetoric to justify welfare cutbacks (see below). Under mutual obligation, the poor must exhibit responsible attitudes to justify receipt of welfare. It is tempting to regard this emphasis on morality as both a sign of, and fig leaf for, conservative power. But it is a mistake to dismiss these ideas simply as right-wing populist parsimony. McKnight (2005) documents how using rights to displace rather than complement obligations discourages a sense of responsibility among recipients of welfare. Noel Pearson's critique of 'handouts' for Aborigines targets this very issue: in his view, Aborigines see 'handouts' as a right, and reject any responsibility for their own plight. Notably, Pearson is not blaming the victim. Instead his aim is to activate Aborigines, to make them realise that increased assistance is useless unless they, the victims, take a more proactive role (Pearson 2001a; 2001b).

Similarly, explaining poverty from the perspective of individual responsibility is not helpfully dismissed as simply 'right-wing': after all, individuals do make choices that can determine their socio-economic status. Rather, the central issue is how a focus on individual responsibility typically treats individuals as autonomous agents, masters of their own destiny, and capable of entirely rational and independent choices. Challenging those assumptions and focusing instead on the fields of action in which individuals must work and live, leads to a structural understanding of poverty.

Structural explanations of poverty

During the 19th century, while Spencer was promoting his views, others were laying the foundations for structural explanations for poverty. Most notably, Karl Marx and Friedrich Engels emphasised that the socio-economic mechanisms central to capitalism have generated an increasingly unequal distribution of wealth (Desai 2004). In their view, wealth and poverty are structurally linked: the very processes that facilitate burgeoning wealth in one sector leave others destitute. Competition is central to this imbalance: though it encourages excellence and innovation, it also creates more losers than winners, forcing worsening poverty upon workers as businesses downsize to make themselves more competitive.

While Marxism has generated many variants and other structural explanations of poverty have pursued alternative lines of inquiry, all such approaches share an interest in the structures, processes and mechanisms that shape individual behaviour. Choice is one thing – opportunity another. Individuals choose from the opportunities available; but what influences those choices and what determines the options themselves? Where neo-liberalism sees individuals as autonomous agents mastering their destiny through rational choice, structural explanations situate people in complex webs of socio-economic relations, forces and processes. To a considerable extent, these structures anticipate choice and opportunity, creating both wealth and poverty independently of the choices individuals make. From this perspective, policies that target individuals but ignore broader structural determinants, treat the symptoms rather than the causes of poverty. Research from the Melbourne Institute supports this observation (Melbourne Institute 2003). The data reveal a marked degree of income mobility in Organization for Economic Cooperation and Development (OECD) countries. Over a single year, only a minority of both rich and poor remained at the extremes, while

13-14 per cent shifted from one extreme to the other. Several individual countries showed even higher mobility, particularly for the poor. But while choice clearly influenced income status, and individuals climbed in and out of poverty, actual poverty levels and wealth ratios across society remained unchanged. Roughly one in eight of the lowest income decile climbed into the highest decile within a year, without altering income ratios overall.

Data like these help shift the focus from individual choice to the broader structures that generate and maintain poverty, structures that limit and often determine both choice and opportunity. Such data also confirm Marx's observation that poverty is generated essentially by the same structures that generate wealth (Desai 2004): both poverty and wealth are symptoms of the inequalities that characterise modern capitalism. Individual explanations of poverty take capitalism as a given and define poverty in its terms. Thus competition is seen as a Darwinian-like mechanism for identifying individuals of worth, and freedom is preferred to equality which militates against competition. Talk of a 'level playing field' sounds like equality, but in the individual approach it means only freedom to compete in the marketplace – equality of opportunity, not equality of access.

Conversely, structural explanations use equality of both access and opportunity, to measure the worth of capitalism itself. In this view, freedom without equality is little more than licence for the strong and well-resourced to exploit the weak and the poor. In this sense, structural explanations of poverty highlight socio-economic processes that favour and are maintained by social elites (Spicker 1993). This is an analysis of power – and not just of top-down power where one group exploits another, but of structures and practices that run through the very fabric of society. At a macro-level, these structures are represented most prominently in the distribution of property and control of production. As demonstrated below, however, they are reproduced in the daily minutiae of cultural and social practices that reinforce overall patterns of domination on a micro-level.

Structural inequalities

Widening definitions of poverty in recent years suggest that effective solutions will only come from an in-depth understanding of the diverse and often hidden problems the poor face (Peter Saunders 2005b). To achieve this requires, first, a wider understanding of the groups affected. The Australian Council of Social Services (ACOSS 1998) has identified several groups as particularly vulnerable to structural inequalities in society:

- Indigenous Australians;
- single unemployed people;

- sole-parent families;
- unemployed and low income couples with children;
- people with disabilities or chronic illness.

The diversity of these groups supports the idea that poverty involves problems and inequalities that are not purely economic: various forms of discrimination are involved. Structural inequalities, however, present all such groups with a common risk: poverty. Thus poverty threatens all who do not 'succeed' – that is, those who do not measure up to dominant social, cultural, economic and sexual values (Jamrozik & Nocella 1998; Peter Saunders 2002a). In this sense, poverty means more than a low income (Townsend 1979; Peter Saunders 2005d): the poor are also marginalised, excluded from experiences that promote 'belonging', and alienated from group identities that help mediate an individual's place in society.

Among groups most at risk are young single parents, a majority of whom are women. Because women traditionally take responsibility for the children when families break up, and their wages are lower, they are afflicted by poverty in greater numbers than are men (Spicker 1993; ILO 2004). Such inequalities are caused mainly by structures – in this instance, cultural traditions and values that determine behaviour across society – and not simply by individual choices. While women are legally entitled to equal pay for equal work, their central child-rearing role disadvantages them in the work place, relegating them in disproportionately high numbers to more lowly paid jobs (Peter Saunders 2002a).

For this reason, the spread of user-pays systems has also been particularly disadvantageous to women (Pusey 2003). At base, user-pays systems mean that resources and services are available to those with money, rather than to those in need. The introduction of user-pays for childcare and playgroups hit women, particularly poor women, very hard. The spiralling cost of childcare has forced many out of the workforce; this in turn frequently generates feelings of social isolation, a major problem for those in poverty (Jamrozik & Nocella 1998). Isolation generates a snowball effect, creating stress and depression, depriving the poor of hope, and making them vulnerable to physical and mental illness, hence reducing their ability and desire to work.

As contributors to the 'poverty cycle', these cultural and psychological difficulties indicate deep problems that require remedy at a structural level. For instance, the health problems of the poor are not solved simply by more health services (though these are, of course, needed), because such increases treat symptoms not causes. Frequently such health problems spring from generational lifestyles and the stress of social discrimination. To address these multiple layers, health services must be integrated with broader strategies that address structural change (Pusey 2003; Peter Saunders 2005b).

For instance, early intervention policies aimed at preventing lifelong poverty and exclusion are the most effective use of government resources (Taylor & Fraser 2003). Direct support for children and families, particularly the vulnerable and disadvantaged, does much to reduce the social and personal costs of mental and physical illness. Lack of skills and opportunities for social participation can perpetuate disadvantage and increase the chances of contact with child protection and juvenile justice (Taylor & Fraser 2003). Strategies addressing these deficiencies pre-empt other problems and reduce social stigma. For example, the Home Instruction Program for Parents of Preschool Youngsters (HIPPY), run in Australia and internationally, is conducted by the Brotherhood of St Laurence in Melbourne in two inner areas where there is much disadvantage and where people from diverse nationalities are trying to establish families with preschool children (Brotherhood of St Laurence 2003a). For a minimal cost over two years parents and children work with a tutor at home to develop teaching and learning skills, using regular practice and activity packs (Gilley 2003). Research has found that outcomes for the children include improvements in family relationships, an increase in eagerness to learn new concepts, and increased self-confidence. Parent meetings decrease isolation, and improve parents' confidence to participate in their child's education and interact with their child (Gilley 2003).

Another micro-level example of structural problems is the tax system which provides a ready-made mechanism for redistributing wealth to those areas of the community most in need, but which increasingly serves instead as an impediment to poverty reduction and to the achievement of social equality (Hudson 1998). In this regard, tax minimisation is a major problem. Successive governments promise to crack down on 'tax cheats' but repeatedly fail to supply the legal armoury to achieve anything substantial. Tax minimisation in contrast to tax avoidance is, after all, perfectly legal – witness the Australian Taxation Office's seven year investigation of Kerry Packer that netted only $25,000 of an estimated $300 million allegedly owed in tax (White 1998). When the rich use the law to minimise their tax, they are also using their associations, wealth and knowledge to improve their own financial situation. This system deprives the community of public revenue for services needed by the poor and unemployed (Wiseman 1998).

ACOSS (1998) identifies similar problems with the Goods and Services Tax (GST). Assessed on a sliding scale proportionate to earnings, income tax helps redistribute wealth more equitably. In contrast, the GST taxes expenditure at a flat 10 per cent regardless of income. Thus those whose expenditure represents a larger proportion of their income—the poor—are especially hard hit by a GST. The same principles that underpin individual explanations of poverty are used to justify this tax mix: the funds raised through GST enable lower income and business taxes which then enable rewards for hard workers, entrepreneurs and investors. With more money in the pocket, these same 'deserving rich' also receive increased freedom of choice (P Saunders 2005a).

Structural inequities discussed so far relate directly to opportunity; these are mostly socio-economic structures that restrict opportunities available to the disadvantaged. Behavioural and cultural structures relate strongly to inequities of choice, and influence choice in two ways. First, structural inequalities restrict what the disadvantaged see as credible possibilities. Second, such inequalities encourage the poor to make choices that lead to bad results; that is, the disadvantaged often suffer for choices that can have a positive outcome when made by more affluent individuals.

Consumer behaviour is a prime example. The general prosperity and consumer spending that developed from the early 1990s has created hidden poverty traps (Frankel 2001). Most concerning is the explosion of credit that has fuelled this prosperity. Individual interpretations of poverty treat this credit revolution as extending individual choice and facilitating the spread of the 'goodies' of capitalism and technology to broader sectors of the community. Structural interpretations, however, assess consumer choices against the external forces that encourage certain types of behaviour; such forces include advertising, social conformity, and pressure buying (Consumer Credit Legal Centre 2004). Structural explanations associate the debts of sections of the community with the manner in which finance operates and with cultural pressure concerning what constitute necessities (Ife 2002), as outlined in more detail below.

The current private debt explosion can be traced back to the deregulation of banking and finance that started in the mid-1980s (Frankel 2001). Financial institutions jumped at the opportunity. Encouraging cultural rather than rational definitions of 'need', these institutions promoted their own profitability by pushing instant gratification through credit. When problems emerged, the Economic Planning Advisory Council (1989) suggested greater control over institutional practices to minimise exploitation. Legislation introduced in the 1990s did reintroduce some debt controls, but private debt continued to balloon and the poor remained the major victims.

People using credit to make purchases are committing future income before it is received (Consumer Credit Legal Centre 2004), thus risking over-commitment and attracting condemnation from those who believe consumption should be deferred until it can be afforded. Holders of this latter view believe that people are capable of accurately estimating outcomes based on information available, a view that assumes individuals employ reason to calculate their expenditure, have access to all necessary information, and can do without the items they purchase on credit. There is no evidence that this is so.

With relative poverty, almost anything can be a 'need' depending on one's circumstances: age, status, education, gender, values, resources etc; 'reason' typically plays a minor role. In this respect, the poor are no different from anyone else. Thus a television may be considered essential, particularly if the people are unemployed. Many other forms of entertainment are expensive, children may need to be 'distracted', or the boredom and limitations of poverty that create social isolation may be overwhelming. Similarly, where there are young children, a properly functioning washing machine is essential in today's society. Further, a large family may see a new machine as easier or more economical despite the financial risk, particularly if they are unable to secure one through other avenues or because available facilities are shared or badly maintained.

Again such inequalities result from culturally-structured social behaviour and not simply individual choice. Urged on by felt 'needs', by advertising and by easily available credit, people readily burden themselves with debt. With few checks, credit is provided on request to virtually anybody (Consumer Credit Legal Centre 2004). Criticism has been levelled at lenders for not providing adequate information about the financial commitment being made, and insufficient assessment of debtors' and guarantors' ability to honour the debt is a major part of the wider problem (Economic Planning Advisory Council 1989).

For people of low socio-economic status, these problems are accentuated. With generally lower education and fewer options, the poor are vulnerable to high interest loan-sharks (Consumer Credit Legal Centre 2004). Knowing less about how the system works and having fewer sources of money open to them, the disadvantaged have less power when negotiating contracts with creditors. Pawnbrokers are also used for immediate cash for goods. Retrieving goods usually requires repayment/s with interest. The poor thus frequently pay higher interest rates than those with the security of additional monies or assets and knowledge of the law and their rights (Consumer Credit Legal Centre 2004). At the same time, with tighter finances and lower incomes, the debts of the poor are more likely to become unmanageable.

Poverty and welfare

In 1985 Francis Castles famously described Australia as a 'wage-earner welfare state', meaning that jobs provided an adequate income without direct government support. Government did, however, provide three central guarantees: the minimum wage, a commitment to full-employment, and wage justice calibrated to need rather than to productivity. Welfare itself was 'needs-based', but available to all save the well-off in a non-discretionary way (Castles 1985, 2001; Jamrozik & Nocella 1998).

Since 1990, all this has changed. Now productivity rather than need sets wages, and welfare is subject to harsh eligibility tests to weed out the 'undeserving' – a reversion to the 19th century model (Castles 2001). In addition, there is increasing focus on seeing 'welfare dependency' as a threat to moral wellbeing of recipients and, by extension, to society at large (see below). At the same time, recent Industrial Relations reforms have withdrawn the three guarantees that once underpinned the system. Now the Fair Pay Commission is charged with ensuring the minimum wage does not 'obstruct' employment opportunities, keeping interest rates low takes precedence over full employment, and productivity rather than need increasingly determines wage levels. The welfare state is stripped back, leaving only a safety-net of benefits designed principally to catch those who 'fail'.

Delivered in this manner, welfare perpetuates the poverty cycle (Spicker 1993). First, welfare eligibility tests have become deliberately harsh and benefit levels inadequate. Second, safety-net welfare has been decoupled from employment and economic policies, leaving the systemic causes of poverty undisturbed (Peter Saunders 2002b). Moreover, because such welfare is targeted at individual problems and works to dissuade those in need from seeking assistance, it invalidates structurally-focussed analyses and conceals structural inequalities.

The hierarchy of benefits – aged pensions at the top and unemployment benefits at the bottom – indicates the underlying philosophy. Aged pensioners have earned their right to assistance; the unemployed still have to prove themselves. Thus, under the present government, aged pensions have been indexed to male total average weekly earnings, whereas unemployment benefits are indexed to the Consumer Price Index (CPI). As the former grows faster than the latter, so pensions steadily outgrow unemployment benefits (Gittins 2005). The disabled, whose pensions are indexed in the same fashion as aged pensions, also attract scrutiny for being on a more 'lucrative' benefit. The government thus saves money through policies that force disability pensioners into the workforce, even if the only result is to shift beneficiaries onto the dole. Attempts to lift the retirement age point in the same direction.

Moreover, unemployment benefits are already set so low that beneficiaries find it difficult to change their circumstances, even where this would improve their chances of obtaining work (Peter Saunders 1994; 2005b). The government rationale for not increasing payments or providing more equitable income support is that working-age individuals on benefits lack the skills to manage their resources effectively. This is an assumption about the moral character of those in need, an assumption that the poor are, in many ways, to blame for their own plight (Fook 1993). Moreover, there is a perception that increasing welfare would look as if the government was rewarding the unemployed for being 'bludgers', thus discouraging them from seeking work. This perception reflects a double standard on 'incentive': the poor and unemployed are thought to require punishment to motivate them, whereas the rich and successful are rewarded with tax breaks and higher salaries (Mendes 2003).

Recent changes in the character and delivery of welfare benefits extend these inequities. First, welfare for the disadvantaged has become increasingly selective and punitive. Witness the policies introduced under the rubric of 'mutual obligation': designed to punish the 'undeserving' and break 'dependency', they in fact widen the poverty gap and impede the transition to independence. International and local studies (Borland & Tseng 2005) suggest that the negative results of 'work for the dole' programs stem largely from the resultant reduction in and adverse affects upon the type of job search activities undertaken by participants. Other contributing factors include stigma effects where participation acts as a negative signal to potential employers, and the fact that work for the dole programs are a relatively minimalist intervention. Thus, though sold to the public as both assistance for the unemployed and a duty for those in receipt of benefits, these programs actually hamper their efforts to find work (Borland & Tseng 2005; Schubert 2005). Now disability and aged pensioners face the same crackdown as do 'welfare cheats', and are subject to the broader surveillance apparatus instituted by the government to weed out unworthy recipients (Gittins 2005).

Secondly, and simultaneously, so-called 'middle-class' welfare is extended to subsidise 'choice'. Though the high unemployment of the 1991 recession fell through the following decade, the national welfare bill increased (P Saunders 2004a). During this period, the proportion of working aged people receiving income support rose from 10.6 per cent (1965) to 27.4 per cent (1998). Though the Government warns of the welfare costs of an aging population, the proportion of pension-aged people receiving income support has actually returned to the levels of the late-1960s (65 per cent) after peaking at over 80 per cent around 1980. Increases in income support rates combine with major changes in the types of benefits available, and hence with the profile of recipients. Barns documents how the Coalition used welfare to attract disaffected voters – 'Howard's battlers' – in the wake of the Pauline Hanson debacle of the late-1990s (Barns 2003). Mendes concedes that middle-class welfare does help shore up general community support for welfare (2003). But such welfare involves a reorientation of welfare around individualist interpretations of poverty and unemployment, and supports conservative ideals of family and hard work.

Those who favour a structuralist approach are highly critical of these policies, treating them as a diversion from the true causes of poverty. As Fifer argues:

> The current approach of narrowly targeted welfare spending highlights a fundamental misunderstanding of the structural issues that cause and perpetuate the cycle of poverty (1998, p 16).

We examined a range of those structural issues in the previous section. Narrow targeting suggests 'accountability' understood in terms of both 'value for money' and the 'worthiness' of recipients. Mutual obligation policies achieve both objectives. Recipients prove their worth through tests of eligibility; those who fall short save the government money. Delivered in this manner, welfare alleviates the individual's experience of poverty while the underlying, structural causes of poverty remain undisturbed. Exactly why governments prefer this style of welfare 'safety-net' rather than systemic reforms that address the underlying causes of poverty, is a political question.

The politics of poverty

By couching debate in terms of 'welfare wars' and 'poverty wars' (Mendes 2003; Peter Saunders 2005b), recent books indicate that the issues at stake are not just academic. When critics attack government policy, they challenge social elites who favour those policies. Since the 1970s, critics such as Townsend (1979) have argued that poverty persists because it benefits elite social groups. In this sense, current welfare policies do not eradicate poverty but serve rather as safety valves, maintaining poverty at levels that are 'beneficial' to the elites. Positions like those advanced by the CIS (P Saunders & Tsumori 2002; P Saunders 2004a) which recast poverty in Australia as personal failure of poor people, are merely extreme varieties of this defence of the status quo.

A number of commentators (Squires 1990) have suggested in more detail how poverty serves the elite:

1. Poverty ensures that dirty, dangerous, menial and undignified work gets done. High unemployment provides, in Marxist parlance, a 'reserve army' of labour willing to do anything because these people lack choice.

2. Poverty nurtures marginal occupations (for example. drug peddlers, prostitutes) that, though illegal, serve a wider public function. At the same time, by exacerbating poverty and threatening law and order, those occupations themselves create demand for social and welfare workers, and police and security.

3. Poverty secures the status of the non-poor. Poverty, perceived as deviant behaviour and other failings, creates a contrast for superiority of higher classes.

Welfare also functions as a safety valve to keep poverty at manageable levels. For this reason, neo-liberals tolerate welfare, as long as it meets their expectations about individual, moral responsibility. But even this is changing. Neo-liberal critics now link their criticism of welfare to a call for lower taxes, part of a campaign to promote individual freedom of choice. In Australia, the CIS leads this attack. Rather than supporting high taxes that fund welfare services whether needed or not, the CIS argues that low taxes will put money in consumers' pockets and allow them to finance the services they choose from private suppliers (P Saunders & Tsumori 2002). In this neo-liberal scenario, private suppliers are considered able to provide services more efficiently than government (P Saunders 2005a). The CIS thus treats the welfare state as an unnecessary burden on today's affluent society. Consumer 'choice', already available to a large extent in health cover and education, should be extended to privatised welfare, with assistance costs to be repaid once the recipient rejoins the ranks of the affluent.

Public welfare is also attacked for degrading recipients' character and virtues. In this view, the mere receipt of welfare renders beneficiaries 'dependent', depriving them of the invigorating moral benefits of 'self-reliance' (P Saunders 2004c; 2005b). This is not simply a call for a reduction in welfare and the restructure of what remains. It is also a defence of the prevailing free market system. Welfare should be delivered in a way that promotes individual self-reliance but does not challenge principles like competition that encourage individual excellence and innovation.

Paradoxically, the neo-liberal emphasis on the market thus justifies government intervention in the lives of the poor. Determined to rescue the poor from 'dependency' and promote 'self-reliance' through their re-entry to the labour market, the government has instituted a regime of 'mutual obligation'. To both reduce direct government action and highlight the perceived individual, moral dimensions of poverty, welfare is increasingly farmed out to private suppliers, most notably church-based charities and non-government organisations (NGOs) (Maddox 2005). These NGOs include that icon of new right conservatism, the Hillsong Church in Sydney, with its prosperity doctrine. Having privatised welfare as neo-liberals want, the funding arrangements 'discourage' these NGOs from criticising government neo-liberal policies (Maddox 2005). Here the politics of poverty are made explicit: when these organisations lobby for actual 'political change' instead of simply addressing the needs of individuals in poverty, they cross the line (Milne 2005). When they cross the line, they jeopardise the funding they need to assist the poor. Again, casting poverty as an individual moral failing is used to divert attention from the broader structural causes of poverty and relieve the government from fundamental systems change.

Conclusion

Poverty is too readily dismissed as the result of individual choice and personal moral failure. As the example of Herbert Spencer demonstrates, such views have been popular for at least two centuries, and are symptomatic of our affluent society's reluctance to acknowledge and understand inequality and the problems of the disadvantaged. Individual effort is eulogised to justify inequitable distribution of wealth and to explain poverty, while excusing those in power from remedial action that might threaten the status quo.

The very structures and mechanisms that generate affluence also maintain poverty. Because these structures appear distant and abstract, they often attract little interest. For the poor, however, such structures have a very immediate reality, imposing themselves in the daily difficulties and frustrations of life, and reproducing broader social inequalities on the micro-scale. Poverty is thus more than simply a shortage of financial resources; it affects every facet of life, intruding on areas only remotely linked to financial issues. To be effective, anti-poverty policies must tackle these entrenched structural issues. Tinkering around the edges may give temporary relief for individuals but, left undisturbed, deeper structural inequalities will continue to reproduce the problem.

Unfortunately, though poverty remains unacceptably widespread in Australia and other Western countries, its causes continue to be individualised and moralised by government. Ignorant of the daily lives of the poor, governments neglect the deeper structural causes of the problems the poor face. Indeed, rather than challenge the ingrained structural causes of poverty with policies that will actually make a difference, the current Australian Coalition Government prefers to set responsibility for poverty on the shoulders of poor individuals. Neo-liberal think tanks and ideas that advocate and defend this approach gain favour because they excuse the government from risky and possibly unpopular policies. As long as this approach prevails, the structures that maintain poverty will remain and poverty will persist.

Chapter 5

Concepts of poverty

Klaus Serr

The question of what constitutes poverty has always been central to social and political debate. However, the answer remains contentious as concepts of poverty are embedded in social and economic conditions and concepts, and are therefore open to a range of interpretations. Current debates about globalisation and free market policies are thus closely linked with the ways in which we understand and define poverty. For example, the 2000 research findings by the Smith Family (Harding et al 2001) about the extent of poverty in Australia prompted an ongoing dispute of words between the Centre of Independent Studies (CIS) and the key researcher on the Smith Family project about how to measure and understand poverty. Further, a 2004 inquiry into poverty by the Senate Community Affairs Reference Committee (SCARC) found increasing levels of deprivation, but acknowledged difficulties in forming a consensus about what constitutes poverty. The ensuing public debate was thus underpinned by an ideological divide between neo-liberal perspectives and notions of egalitarianism, redistribution and social justice.

This chapter explores different concepts of poverty in an historical context, showing how they reflect fundamental assumptions about human need, poverty measurements, and societal arrangements. It argues that while quantitative measures have contributed to the understanding of poverty, a deeper understanding requires a more qualitative perspective, one that acknowledges the non-monetary aspects of deprivation. The central argument of this chapter is that poverty should not be defined solely by the 'experts', but that the people experiencing poverty and deprivation should be included in the development of the definition.

Concepts of poverty, economic thinking, and society

Although poverty has always been part of European social discourse, the massive social dislocation and poverty brought by the Industrial Revolution necessitated a correspondingly massive change in thinking. Thus with industrialisation came a range of new interpretations of what it means to be poor, and new questions about the causes of poverty and its explanations (Lutz 1999). In the 18th and 19th centuries, these radical social and economic changes led political economists such as Adam Smith, David Ricardo and Karl Marx to view poverty in one of two main ways: 'either as the necessary price of social progress or as evidence of the inefficiency of the system' (Geremek 1997, p 1). Thus began two basic approaches to understanding poverty: poverty as a product of an inadequate system, and poverty as an unavoidable by-product of growth. This chapter shows how these themes underlie mainstream concepts of poverty and its remediation, then goes on to suggest a third, alternative conception.

In Britain, the poverty studies of the late 1800s and early 1900s by Booth (1969) and Rowntree (1901) set the trend for a narrow poverty definition related to classical and neo-classical ideas of the economy as based on 'income, subsistence or the maintenance of physical efficiency, and consumption' (Taylor 1992, p 101). Subsequently this subsistence model of poverty has diversified to include concepts such as absolute poverty, basic needs, and relative poverty, all of which measure human needs in mainly material terms, and correlate 'with a strict market logic, with competitive ethics, and with the acceptance of ... inequalities' (Townsend 1993, p 41).

The neo-classical orthodoxy has tended to produce economically-oriented poverty solutions based on economic growth. As shown earlier in this book, the dominant poverty debates today are still intrinsically linked to the idea that economic progress and growth will eventually alleviate poverty (see also Fincher & Nieuwenhuysen 1998; Serr 2001; Stilwell 2002; Social Watch 2005). This focus on economic progress also implies that the best way to define poverty is in monetary terms, with numerical data measuring consumption, expenditure and income poverty lines. However, these purely quantitative concepts of poverty are inadequate in dealing with the complexities of poverty at either the practical or conceptual levels because they neglect the qualitative experiences of what it is to be poor (Narayan, Patel et al, 2000; Peel 2003; Peter Saunders 2005b; Serr 2006). The anticipated consequences of social change also influence thinking about poverty and economics. For example, the Industrial Revolution precipitated deep anxieties about social dislocation creating too great a potential for large-scale social unrest and increasing crime, neither of which were in the best interest of capitalist industrialisation. Thus, the 'nineteenth century brought with it the realisation that there was a 'social question', and that the poor were a threat to the rich' (Beilharz et al 1992, p 15). Fear of violence and crime was therefore at the heart of the creation of welfare provision (Geremek 1997).

As many governments in the 21st century fundamentally adhere to the same economic market mechanisms and economic development as institutions in the 1900s, the minimalist conceptualisation of human need continues as an underlying influence on social policy. This influence is especially evident in Anglo-Saxon countries such as Australia, Britain and the US (see Pusey 2003), where the influence of neo-classical economics has been particularly pronounced. For example, Australian researchers from the currently influential Centre for Independent Studies (CIS) are critical of the provision of welfare services, and are a persistent voice for the reduction of the welfare state, deregulation, privatisation of public utilities, and increasing inequality in society (see Marston & Watts 2004; Serr 2004a; Peter Saunders 2006).

The CIS has been successful, particularly in recent times, in shifting the poverty debate away from important discussions on the incidence and extent of poverty, to a renewed focus on 'the failings of the poor' (Peter Saunders 2005b). Any suggestion that poverty is a broader societal problem receives a harsh response. For example, when the Senate Poverty Enquiry found unacceptable levels of poverty in Australian society, its report was roundly condemned as 'one-eyed, misleading, inaccurate and deeply ideological' (P Saunders 2005a, p 14). Similarly when a recent paper by the St Vincent de Paul Society (see Wicks 2005) warned of significant social dislocation and an increasing shift towards great inequalities in Australia, the CIS suggested that:

> The St Vincent de Paul report reflects an unthinking, egalitarian political agenda which is never questioned, explained or justified. It fails to understand that inequality is not always unfair and that equalisation of incomes can be very unjust. The report also reflects the anti-market, anti-capitalist ideology which has characterised much of the output produced by the St Vincent de Paul Society's research arm since 2002 (P Saunders 2005a, p 1).

The influence of this approach on the Australian government is clear, and the government called the findings of the Senate Poverty report 'a shallow, naïve and purely political attempt to condemn the government of the day' (Australian Government 2006, p 1).

Peter Saunders (2005) calls this current debate 'our war on poverty', but suggests that it is not 'driven' by a great vision for a better and more egalitarian Australian society. Instead, history seems to repeat itself. Neo-liberal forces of today are, in Peter Saunders's words, trying to:

> [D]iscredit the poverty statistics and the credibility of those who produce them, in order to deny the existence of poverty and absolve government of responsibility for addressing it (Saunders 2005b, pp 2-3).

After presenting a historical overview of absolute poverty, the following section argues that this agenda underpins current policies on poverty. A more productive policy approach involves perspectives on poverty that distinguish between how poverty is experienced and how it is measured. How poverty is talked about and understood is relative to national and local economic and social contexts definitions and measurements of poverty that are applicable to different contexts are crucial to engaging in relevant and appropriate solutions for people living in poverty. In order to understand these distinctions it is important to examine the broad concepts of absolute and relative poverty and more contemporary ways of understanding poverty.

Absolute/subsistence poverty

Historically, the absolute poverty model is based on the notion of 'subsistence' and assumes universal 'standards' of existence. Because a person is said to be in absolute poverty when he/she lacks the minimum requirements for sustaining life, such as food, shelter and clothing (Townsend 1970), the absolute poverty concept is based on monetary/ material deprivation and:

> [I]s generally measured by pricing the basic necessities of life, drawing a poverty line in terms of this price, and defining as poor those whose income falls below that figure (Haralambos & Holborn 1991, p 192).

One of the first studies applying a subsistence approach was carried out in the late 1880s by Charles Booth, a conservative 'merchant, ship owner, financier and later social surveyor' (Taylor 1992, p 25) and Beatrice Webb, a founder of Fabianism. In an attempt to prove that contemporary claims of about 25 per cent poverty in London's working class districts were exaggerated (Beilharz 1992), Booth selected London's East End, one of the most destitute areas in England, and found a 35 per cent poverty rate, amounting to 'one-eighth of the metropolitan population' (Taylor 1992, p 37).

Booth's subsequent 1887 study is significant in that it conceptualised a poverty line, estimated to be 21 shillings per week of earnings (Taylor 1992, p 39). Of the six working-class groups identified by Booth, four were below the poverty line (Novak 1988); in all, 31 per cent of the survey population lived in poverty (Taylor 1992). For two groups Booth had little sympathy, referring to them as 'beggars', 'incapables', and 'unfit' (Novak 1988), but conceded that the other two poor classes were poor because of their precarious and unstable employment situation. Despite his finding that the lack of stable employment was a key factor in causing poverty, Booth's recommendations 'proved to be little else than a doctrinaire defence of the capitalist system. ... [for which] Booth could see no safe policy but laissez-faire' (Taylor 1992, pp 41-43).

In 1899, building on Booth's work, Seebohm Rowntree (see Townsend 1993; Peter Saunders 2003) studied York's wage-earning families, and calculated total family incomes deemed as the absolute minimum for an adequate existence (Taylor 1992, p 92). Despite the austerity of his measure, Rowntree found a 33 per cent poverty rate in York, a typical English town. Like Booth, Rowntree did not attempt a thorough analysis of the structural issues of poverty and inequality, and although insecure casual labour was found by both to contribute largely to the extent of poverty, little was made of these findings (Taylor 1992).

Although others had already argued that insecure employment was not accidental but integral to capitalism (Marx 1954; Novak 1988; Geremek 1997; Lutz 1999), this link was not recognised by most influential people in England at this time. For example in the 1860s Marx had described the poor as a 'surplus-population' necessary to capitalism, a population which could be drawn upon as an 'industrial reserve army', so that pauperism was a 'condition of capitalist production and of the capitalist development of wealth' (Marx 1954, p 603). In Marx's words, capitalism:

> [E]stablishes an accumulation of misery, corresponding with accumulation of capital. Accumulation of wealth at one pole is, therefore, at the same time accumulation of misery, agony of toil slavery, ignorance, brutality, mental degradation, at the opposite pole, ie, on the side of the class that produces its own product in the form of capital (Marx 1954, p 604).

In contravention of Marx's view, Rowntree's belief that laissez-faire economics would deliver prosperity for more people in the end, seemed vindicated in his studies in 1930s and 1950s. Rowntree found that the poverty rate had dropped from 33 per cent in 1899 to 18 per cent in 1936, and finally to 1.5 per cent by 1950 (Haralambos & Holborn 1991). However, later analysis has attributed this reduction of unemployment-related poverty to the introduction of welfare programs (see Townsend 1993; Geremek 1997) and to the re-building efforts after two world wars (see Galbraith 1995). Therefore since the 1970s unemployment-related poverty has re-appeared in many developed countries (WCSDG 2004; UNICEF 2005), and the dramatic increase of casual and part-time employment, especially in Australia, was identified as a great concern during the 2004 Senate Poverty Enquiry (SCARC 2004).

The concept of subsistence has been widely criticised for its minimalist approach to poverty because it measures only the absolute survival threshold (Peter Saunders 2003). Policies applying this concept condemn the poor to live not only on the margins of existence but also on the margins of society. Although notions of absolute poverty take no account of social, cultural, emotional/ psychological and other forms of human needs, this approach has guided a number of governments around the world, including the United States, which still 'relies on an "absolute" measure of poverty defined in the early 1960s ... and held constant in real terms since that time' (Smeeding 2005, p 4). This history makes it clear that the absolute/subsistence concept arose in the political and economic climate of the 19th century, and has shaped much of today's thinking about the economy, the nature of poverty, and its possible solutions.

Like Booth's contemporaries in the 1900s, current neo-liberals support market mechanisms as the best way to organise both the economy and society as a whole. They do not support welfare, arguing that the market should be complemented (if at all) by a very basic social safety net. Despite evidence to the contrary (see Stilwell 2002; Stiglitz 2003; Wicks 2005; UNDP 2005), neo-liberals play down the existence of poverty and suggestions about its structural causes. The Australian government's response to the Senate Poverty Inquiry predictably supports this view, arguing that: 'Social welfare is generated by a strong and growing economy' (Australian Government 2006, p 2).

Basic needs and the internationalisation of the poverty definition

The growth of the global economy also meant that poverty concepts became international. As globalisation grows, many related concepts have to change in parallel, so definitions of terms such as wealth, poverty, and productivity have changed to become internationally applicable. Making poverty concepts international was achieved through the idea of 'development', a term closely related to the laissez-faire market model where 'the degree of civilisation in a country could be measured by the level of its production' (Sachs 1992, pp 157-158). Constructed by the United States after World War II, productivity and economic growth are intrinsic to 'development'.

Within this framework the concept of basic needs, largely adopted by international organisations in the 1980s, was based on a subsistence notion of poverty. Basic needs, defined by Western countries and employed in developing nations, came to be seen as the maintenance of physical necessities such as food, shelter and clothing, plus minimal provisions such as basic health care and other social services, basic sanitary standards, and minimum education (Townsend 1984). In economic terms these needs were said to apply to all societies. They can be measured, quantified, limited, and universalised and, moreover, '[a] major redistribution of existing wealth and income can be avoided or at least postponed' (Townsend 1993, p 37). This version thus fits well with the development model's prescribed economic growth approach, where 'experts' can decide what people need and how 'basic' is defined (Sachs 1992, p 169). In this way the basic needs concept of poverty is related to absolute poverty as it:

> [R]epresents only a slightly extended version, and one which is rather less coherent. It goes beyond the recognition of physical need and some allowance is made for an environmental infrastructure of physical services for local communities (Townsend 1984, p 57).

While the post-war achievements of capitalist development were very impressive (Renner & Starke 2003; WCSDG 2004; UNDP 2005), by the late 1970s and early 1980s it was clear that mainstream economic development was failing to eliminate poverty, especially in many developing nations (Hettne 1995; UNDP 1998). Many argued that economic development was bringing the world closer to a major crisis, not only of economic failure, but also of environmental disaster, and a dangerous arms race. Accompanying this argument was a debate, initiated in developing countries, about whether the definition of basic needs should have more qualitative and normative aspects (Ekins 1992; Hettne 1995).

A number of United Nations inquiries investigated these enormous challenges: the Brandt Commissions 1980, 1983; and the World Commission on Environment and Development 1987. These inquiries were followed by the World Summit for Social Development in 1995 and the UN Millennium Summit in 2000 (see UNDP 2003). The earlier commissions in particular 'recognised the serious nature of the total crisis faced by humanity, recommending changes to the traditional practices of development. They also acknowledged in many ways that a continuation of the development orthodoxy could lead to the very extinction of the entire human race' (Serr 2004d, p 2). Although these UN reports demonstrated awareness of the failings of the mainstream model, the UN commissions continued to advocate for economic growth. The Brundtland report by the WCED (1987) in particular recommended a renewed phase of economic growth. Many of the criticisms of mainstream economic processes were not addressed and the report's concept of sustainable development (further economic growth) allowed multilateral organisations like the World Bank to continue on the mainstream development path (see World Bank 2000b; WCSDG 2004).

These developments also meant that normative values were not accepted into the basic needs concept. The purpose of omitting normative values was to safeguard the continuation of neo-classical practices and the idea of development based on economic growth (Sachs 1992). However, continued criticisms of purely economic indicators of human needs led to the Human Development Report by the UNDP in 1990. The UNDP devised the Human Development Index (HDI) to better measure the human dimension of development. The HDI focused less on Gross Domestic Product (GDP) data, and re-introduced normative aspects of human needs such as a country's literacy rate, longevity, and school enrolment (UNDP 1990). Despite initial criticism, especially by economists, the index is now a welcome addition to the international literature on development and poverty. Subsequently the UNDP introduced its Human Poverty Indexes (HPI-1 & HPI-2). The HPI-1 measures deprivation in developing countries through three dimensions: longevity, knowledge, and a decent standard of living. The HPI-2, designed for selected developed nations, uses the same three dimensions plus social exclusion (UNDP 2005).

Relative poverty

The concept of relative poverty is now widely used in Australia and other developed nations (Saunders 2005b). It can be seen as an extension of the basic needs approach, as there are similarities between basic needs as defined by the International Labour Organisation (ILO 1976) and relative poverty as conceived by Henderson et al (1970) and Henderson (1975).

For example, the ILO's subsistence concept, like the Henderson definition, included:

> Firstly ... adequate food, shelter and clothing, as well as certain household furniture and equipment. Second, they should include essential services

provided by and for the community at large, such as safe drinking water, sanitation, public transport and health education and cultural facilities (ILO 1976, pp 24-25).

Both also agreed on the relativity of poverty, suggesting that poverty was to be defined in relationship to living standards typical within a community (Henderson et al 1970).

The poverty line and its problems/limitations

Poverty lines are based on disposable income, and measure the level of income poverty within a community. The poverty line is therefore drawn by 'poverty experts', so that 'someone whose income is one dollar below the poverty line is defined as poor, whereas someone whose income is one dollar above the line is not' (Peter Saunders 2003, p 5). While few countries have an officially accepted poverty line, conventionally most researchers set it at 50 per cent of 'median (or middle) income of all people' (Harding et al 2001, p 2). However, problems remain with setting the poverty line against a measure of central tendency. One problem lies in the decision about where to set the line; for example, the 50 per cent line defines proportionally fewer people in poverty than does the 60 per cent line used in the European Union (EU) (Smeeding 2005). Another problem concerns whether the mean or the median best defines the middle income, as one of these measures can be higher than the other, depending on the distribution of incomes. Both measures have their weaknesses: means are susceptible to being skewed by a few extreme incomes, while medians take no account of skew in the distribution of income. Thus by selecting specific measures, researchers and policy makers can define a wide variety of poverty lines within the same population. The most fundamental problem, however, is that, whatever the measure of central tendency used, and whatever the numerical 'cut-off' point selected, the resulting poverty line is a statistical artefact that is unlikely to relate to the experiences and needs of the poor.

Disagreements are therefore understandable between those who support neo-liberal market forces and greater inequalities in society, and those who believe in more egalitarian and just societal structures (see P Saunders & Tsumori 2002 versus Harding et al 2001; Peter Saunders 2006). While the relative poverty conception is useful in providing some indications of society's material poverty, it has become increasingly clear that quantitative poverty lines omit many of the qualitative factors of poverty, and how poverty is actually experienced. The shortcomings of research relying too heavily on income-based poverty measurement were already identified in the 1960s by Henderson et al (1970, p 34), who stated that the income unit was 'an artificial concept'.

Seen in a historical context, the current poverty dispute makes it obvious that the field of poverty research, and its debates, have long been dominated by economists, with their narrow conceptions of consumption-based needs, economic growth, and efficiency. Although neo-liberals continue to assert that the application of economic principles and anti-egalitarian policies is the best way forward (see Marston & Watts 2004; P Saunders 2005b), questioning the reliance on economic indicators to understand societal processes is long overdue. Indeed, mounting evidence suggests that free market forces do not eliminate poverty, and that increased levels of consumption do not increase people's happiness (WCSDG 2004; Hamilton & Dennis 2005).

Alternative poverty concepts

A number of alternative frameworks bring useful perspectives to the poverty debate: relative deprivation, the concepts of capability and social exclusion, and self-identification approaches are examples. All conceptualise needs in a much wider context. They go beyond monetary values and income poverty to bring out the multifaceted nature of poverty. There is also a new trend in acknowledging the need to consult with the poor themselves and include their voices in the conceptualisation of poverty (Narayan, Patel et al, 2000; Serr 2000, 2004b, 2006; Peel 2003; Peter Saunders 2005b). Here it is argued that the poor could play a significant role in re-formulating existing definitions and could work with other stakeholders on anti-poverty measures.

Relative deprivation

Townsend (1979) embarked on an ambitious study of poverty in Britain and, with nine researchers, he collected data on over 2000 households and 6000 individuals. The concept of relative deprivation thus developed by Townsend, and later revised by Mack and Lansley (1985), aimed to incorporate other aspects of deprivation, defining the poor as 'those who are excluded from social intercourse: the isolated, the invisible, the hidden and the overlooked' (Townsend 1984, p 57). For this study Townsend developed the relative deprivation index (RDI) comprised of 12 survey questions. The RDI can be criticised for not allowing for the fact that some people may choose not to have certain items in their daily lives. They may, for example, decide not to eat meat, never to have friends, or go the cinema, even though they can afford it. Similarly, a person may have all of the above but not have the resources to engage adequately in society. Nevertheless Townsend's contribution was very important for the development of other recent research that stresses the need for 'an explanation or understanding of poverty as the outcome of the irresponsible exercise of overly concentrated social, economic and political power' (Dennett, et al 1982, p 159).

Extending the concept of relative deprivation, many European projects have investigated patterns of consumption, lack of participation and decision-making in society, patterns of employment, and the lack of opportunities, choices and social justice for the poor. These conceptual developments have been important for our broader understanding of poverty, as they point towards essential non-monetary aspects of the human condition, so vital for well being. The concept of relative deprivation seems to have influenced the 1999 Poverty and Social Exclusion Survey of Britain (PSE), which aimed to measure the complexities of poverty and to operationalise 'social exclusion' in Britain. An extensive survey index then tried to measure, among other items, income, available support services, social and educational participation (Gordon et al 2000). This significant development fits well with the European adoption of the concept of social exclusion discussed in the next section.

A small number of researchers in Australia have also started to look at alternative conceptions of poverty, to form a broader view of the problem (see Travers & Richardson 1993; Serr 2000; SCARC 2004; Peter Saunders 2005b). However, none of these approaches attract the attention of policy makers within government, where they could inform and enhance policy debates on poverty. Indeed, Australia is falling behind these new developments in Europe.

Capability and social exclusion

The notions of capability and social exclusion make a useful contribution to widening the poverty debate away from the narrow focus on income poverty. While Amartya Sen was seen by some as one of the main proponents of absolute poverty in the early 1980s, he later developed the notion of 'capability'. Here poverty is associated with the lack of basic 'capabilities', where the necessary resources to 'function' in a given society must be 'relative'. While income is still seen as important, Sen, like Townsend, conceptualises poverty more broadly:

> [T]here is a strong case for judging individual advantage in terms of the capabilities that a person has, that is, the substantive freedoms he or she enjoys to lead the kind of life he or she has reason to value. In this perspective, poverty must be seen as the deprivation of basic capabilities rather than merely as lowness of incomes (Sen 1999, p 87).

What is essential then is the fulfilment both of basic needs such as food, shelter, clothing, and of 'more complex social achievements such as taking part in the life of the community' (Sen 1992, p 23). Thus 'capability deprivation' refers to the lack of choice or freedom to be able to function in society, where a poor person is unable to fulfil basic/ absolute needs such as housing.

The notion of capability is useful in that it goes beyond income, and has informed the Human Development Report of the UNDP, especially in its 1996 version (UNDP 1996). However, Townsend (1993, p 136) questions the concept's ability to shed light on structural issues, claiming that the approach is 'a sophisticated adaptation of the individualism that is rooted in neo-classical economics ... and will never ....

provide a coherent explanation of the social construction of need'. There are many problems in how to develop and operationalise the indicators of capability (Townsend 1993; Peter Saunders 2005b), and questions remain about how the capabilities are to be selected and in what way they are considered 'absolute'.

'Social exclusion' (SE) was coined in France in the 1970s, and has become increasingly popular in Europe and particularly in the United Kingdom (UK), which set up a Social Exclusion Unit (SEU) in 1997. Since the early 2000s, the concept has been adopted by many European Union (EU) members, as a strategy to reduce poverty-related problems (Estivill 2003), with the rationale that SE 'is a broader concept than poverty, and that direct measures of deprivation and exclusion are required in addition to income data income' (UNICEF 2005, p 22). Poverty and SE are not identical but are complimentary, so that income poverty is one indicator of SE, along with other issues of deprivation such as: 'unemployment, poor skills, low incomes, unfair discrimination, poor housing, high crime, bad health and family breakdown' (SEU 2004, p 4).

Because SE means exclusion in the social, economic and political dimensions, it has been criticised for being too encompassing and open-ended, as everybody in the community could be seen as excluded. As SE embraces a variety of needs, there are many methodological problems in trying to select, operationalise and quantify these needs (Estivill 2003). In Europe, for example, 'there are as yet very few widely deployed indicators designed to monitor trends in poverty and social exclusion' (UNICEF 2005, p 22).

Despite methodological problems, SE makes a useful contribution to our understanding of social processes related to poverty. As Estivill (2003, p 13) points out: 'exclusion is related to the dissatisfaction or unease felt by individuals who are faced with situations in which they cannot achieve their objectives for themselves or their loved ones'. This is echoed by an ILO study (International Institute for Labour Studies 1996) arguing that individual disadvantage is multi-dimensional, where people lack social ties to the family, local community, voluntary and other organisations, or even the whole country. In this context SE sheds some light on the experiences of the poor, and their interconnectedness with other people and communities.

Despite advances, the key weakness of the poverty conceptions discussed so far remains the fact that poverty is defined by 'poverty experts' who have failed to consult the very people most affected by poverty – the poor themselves. The next section therefore looks at how poor people define their problems; it then compares that with the views of the so-called experts (see Serr 2006).

Box 5.1. Definition of poverty developed by homeless men

Category 1
Lack of: good health; belonging; care; money; food, shelter and clothing; hygiene; housing; love; self-esteem; trust in other people; confidence; motivation and energy.

Category 2
Having to: live from day to day; live in overcrowded places; face problems with the police/ courts; roam the streets; experience violence on the streets; tolerate vandalism in public places.

Category 3
Being: physically drained; bored; insecure; lethargic and despondent; divorced; segregated from friends, community, family and churches; dependent on alcohol, drugs and gambling; weak within yourself; unemployed.

Category 4
Feeling: outside society; trapped; depressed/ anxious; feeling and looking like a bum.

Category 5
Unable to: live in a family; change the future; manage money; live in a permanent home; sleep: stop worrying about life; know what's going to happen; plan ahead

Category 6
Not having enough: alcohol; smokes; drugs; money to gamble.

Source: Serr 2004c, p 144

Self-definitions of the poor

A number of studies show that the poor themselves can offer great insights into the poverty condition, and that their knowledge and experiences should be taken seriously by researchers and policy makers (Peter Saunders 2005b). The importance of this has been confirmed by research conducted by the World Bank, which consulted with poor people in 23 countries (see Narayan, Chambers et al, 1999; Narayan, Patel et al, 2000). This global *Consultations with the Poor* was the first large-scale participatory study eliciting from the poor the nature and causes of poverty. Indeed, Narayan, Chambers et al (2000, p 2) argue that 'there are 2.8 billion poverty experts, the poor themselves'. Their report revealed that problems for the poor are increasing and that some of the needs identified by the poor were universal: 'poor people care about many of the same things all of us care about: happiness, family, children, livelihood, peace, security, safety, dignity, and respect' (2000, p 2).

There is growing interest in the application of this method in Australia (see Gilley and Taylor 1995; Johnson 2000; Serr 2000; Cameron & Duncan 2001; Peel 2003; Serr 2006). All these studies echo the World Bank findings, and show that poverty is much broader than income poverty, including many multi-dimensional factors. For example, a small study conducted at a Salvation Army hostel shows how a group of homeless men define their deprivation (Serr 2000, 2004b, 2004c). As shown in Box 5.1, the men's definition brings out the multi-dimensional nature of the poverty experience; further, because experiences often overlap, the dimensions themselves are complex and multifaceted. The men identify six categories of what poverty means to them, making it difficult to grasp what factors influence which event in peoples' lives.

Indeed, much of what is presented here shows a poverty cycle that is hard to break, especially when seen in its totality. For instance, lack of family and community contribute to feelings of social isolation; this isolation in turn can be exacerbated by lack of a job, money, unaffordable housing – all of which can be linked to ill-health, substance abuse and crime.

The multifaceted poverty dimensions were also found in the CSSV *Shattered Dreams* project (Serr 2006) that interviewed a number of poor men and women in inner-urban Melbourne.

As Box 5.2 shows, the poor in the *Shattered Dream* study identified seven main categories, including multi-dimensional aspects, lack of money and housing etc. Unpacking what the seven categories actually refer to, Serr reports that the associated issues of the participants ranged from:

> [B]ad and insufficient diet to the lack of access to health care, from substandard living arrangements to unsatisfactory social relationships. All of these factors result in a growing sense of insecurity and loss of self-esteem. As many of the disadvantaged have experienced family conflict/breakdown

Box 5.2. Poverty categories identified by poor respondents

1. Multi-dimensional aspects
2. Lack of adequate income
3. Substandard accommodation
4. Family conflict/breakdown
5. Lack of social/community networks
6. Personal problems
7. Negative outlook on life

Source: Serr 2006, p 7

they often also lack supportive social or community networks. Without these necessary support structures they find it even more difficult to escape the endless spiral of unemployment, personal problems, ill health, physical hardship and social isolation. Many of these difficulties faced by the poor therefore lead to a deep level of deprivation, explaining the negative outlook and personal degradation felt by this group (Serr 2006, p 31)

How the multi-dimensional aspects are described by poor people is demonstrated by two women in the study, fictitiously called Jemma and Jody. For Jemma poverty was:

> [A] total castration of the soul, depressing, claustrophobic, with some good days, bad days, where the pressure is constantly on, and you always carry a weight, juggling funds and resources. It is like robbing Peter to pay Paul – a downward spiral, slipping further and further away and ever getting harder to get out of the mess (Serr 2006, p 8).

Jody described her life as:

> [H]aving low resources and living on the streets – being homeless. Having to stay in refuges with criminals [and] drug addicts and fighting for a meal every day. Lack of belonging, being depressed, angry and afraid that it gets worse. Being unhealthy from having a cold and if you haven't got the money it can get worse and life-threatening (Serr 2006, p 8)

Shattered Dreams argues that the poor themselves are the leading poverty experts, since it is they who experience the deprivation, and the interviews confirm that:

- most participants were highly aware of poverty issues and their answers reflected serious hardships stemming from unmet needs and poor living conditions;
- their deprivation included social and psychological factors, which cannot be described simply as 'lack of money', thus underscoring the multifaceted nature of poverty;

- participants demonstrated their ability to conceptualise and understand many of the issues of poverty, and their responses reflect people's living conditions and experiences of deprivation in a way that allows them to formulate relevant poverty solutions in both policy and practical terms (Serr 2006, xii).

To compare the data generated by the disadvantaged with those of poverty professionals, this study also interviewed policy makers and service providers. When the data of the three groups are compared, some interesting points arise. For example, while service providers were aware of many of the needs of the poor, it was apparent that they were one step removed from the actual poverty experience. Being less familiar with some of the details of a deprived life, this group defines poverty categories as 'multi-dimensional issues, structural issues, lack of income and resources, and emotional/psychological issues'. A typical response from a service provider was: 'Poverty is more than finances: it is poor quality of health, education, food, housing' (Serr 2006, p xiii). Interviews with the policy makers demonstrated that they were even further removed from the poverty experience. The disagreement about what poverty means was also strongest among this group. While these policy makers acknowledged that poor people should be part of the poverty debate, some of their comments about the lives of the poor were disconnected from a felt reality.

The definition devised by policy makers had four broad categories: philosophical aspects, multi-dimensional aspects, lack of adequate income, and the inability to participate. While knowledgeable, this group classified poverty in a way that did not reflect well how the poor themselves perceived their lives. A typical policy-maker comment reflects this distance, saying that poverty is: 'the relativity of not having, going without, standard and availability of accommodation, food, having the wherewithal to manage' (Serr 2006, p 107).

A case for a combined poverty definition

The material presented so far gives only part of the picture. While service providers and policy makers were not as familiar with the actual poverty experience as were the poor, both groups understood structures and societal processes better than the disadvantaged. The service providers' knowledge of available and necessary welfare provisions was greater than those of the poor, and providers had a good 'understanding of some of the economic and political impediments to a more just and equal society' (Serr 2006, p 31).

Knowledge of structural issues was very pronounced in the group of the policy makers. Like no other group in the study, they understood structural issues of globalisation and some of their negative impact on

Australia. There also was awareness of current Australian government policy and its fixation on neo-liberal economic principles, where:

- current public policy is based on an economic rationalist ideology which the government formulates to 'the detriment of the poor. This results in continuous structural change, including the restructuring of the labour market, and increasing privatisation of public and other services;
- poverty cannot be solved without fundamental changes at governmental and societal levels (Serr 2006, p xiii).

Many of the policy makers believed that the current policies put Australia's national interest unnecessarily at risk, resulting in:

> 1) structural issues such as unemployment, accelerating living costs and inadequate income, lack of access to education and opportunities; 2) Social dislocation, lack of belonging; 3) Inadequate support provisions for the aged, disabled, the ill, social security payments and public housing (Serr 2006, p 32).

This then:

> [D]ivides and perpetuates the haves and have nots, [and] has implemented the rather judgmental approach of the 'undeserving poor', who 'don't appreciate what they get'. This is why government puts much effort into punishing and vilifying the unemployed, with no benefit to anyone (Serr 2006, p 32).

Although this was a small and exploratory study, the data from the *Shattered Dreams* project and similar research appear to support the value of involving the poor in the study of poverty. However, while this chapter is critical of poverty definitions developed exclusively by professional 'poverty experts', it is not argued that 'professional' definitions should simply be replaced by those given by the poor. As *Shattered Dreams* demonstrates, all relevant stakeholders need to be consulted in order to develop a more coherent approach to poverty conceptualisations, measurements, and solutions. Nevertheless, the voices of the poor can help to inform and re-interpret alternative notions of poverty which are open to a more normative approach and the analysis of economic, social and political structures.

Conclusion

This chapter looked at different poverty concepts in a historical context and demonstrated how economic principles have influenced definitions and poverty policies. In many ways current thinking is still being influenced by past poverty definitions which rely on income measures and monetary values. The chapter makes a case for alternative conceptualisations of poverty that not only take non-monetary values into consideration but argues for a place for the voices of poor people to be part of poverty research and policy-making. The discussion demonstrated that poor people themselves have an enriching and appropriate role to play in the poverty debate, and that poor people can and should assist in the development and re-interpretation of existing approaches to poverty. This is not to suggest that 'poverty professionals' should be replaced by poor people: rather it is an argument for more coherent and relevant definitions of poverty. To achieve this, all stakeholders, including governments, need to be included in the process.

Leading politicians in Australia have been all too readily influenced by neo-liberal conceptions of the free market economy rather than by arguments for a fair and egalitarian society. By refusing to acknowledge the existence of poverty the government has lost its focus on its responsibility to look after the welfare of all its citizens. As solutions presuppose the willingness to act, short-term thinking on economic growth and efficiencies that exclude certain groups in society are ineffective in dealing with social problems such as poverty. In years of record budget surpluses, the choices being made by governments indicate a neo-liberal approach that promotes the interests of the individual consumer over the broad needs of a 'better' society. As Peter Saunders points out:

> Rich countries like Australia can afford to abolish poverty. The financial cost of doing so represents only a small fraction of our national income. We can thus pay to remove all Australians from poverty if we want to: the fact that we don't do so is a matter of choice, not affordability (Peter Saunders 2003, p 1).

Chapter 6

Governing inequality: Poverty before the Australian welfare state

Karen Crinall

On the 18 August 1786 Lord Sydney announced to the British Treasury that Botany Bay, on the coast of New South Wales, was to be the new destination for British prisoners sentenced to transportation (Clark 1957). Seventeen months later 11 ships and 1000 British subjects, including 586 male and 192 female convicts, arrived at Port Jackson (Pownall 1983), bringing 'a culture attuned to producing and controlling poverty' (Garton 1990, p 15). After they disembarked, the land was seized, sanctioned as a colony and prison, and the lore and laws of the indigenous people were overridden (Jones 1996; Cadigal Wangal 2005). Along with fatal infections and plagues, poverty was introduced to the Aborigines by 'colonisers who sought to destroy (rather than learn from) a society in which welfare as an activity distinct from the daily processes of sharing and caring for others and the land was unthinkable' (O'Conner et al 2003, pp 24-25).

Previous chapters describe how conceptualisations of poverty vary across time, place and context. The history of dominant beliefs regarding poverty's causes trace a convoluted path, oscillating between explanations that include moral, spiritual and physical deficiencies, bad luck, economic exploitation, and structural inequality. Neglect by governments, whether deliberate or unintentional, is often cited as a barrier, if not a cause. This chapter explores responses to poverty in Australia before social security legislation was introduced in the early 1900s. In the context of this chapter, a related concern is the extent to which pre-welfare state attitudes towards poverty endure in contemporary social policy and practice. The principle focus in this chapter, however, is to advance understanding about how poverty and inequality were implicated in strategies of governmental practice in Australia's early years.

The settlement by the British of Australia in 1788 cannot be considered separately from Europe's cultural, political, social and economic history. Therefore the chapter begins with a discussion about the system for governing land and people that emerged in Europe during the mid-16th century know as governmentality. The development of the British Poor Laws is then described before turning to consider how poverty was addressed in the Australian colonies prior to Federation in 1901.

Governmentality, the state and dividing practices

During the 16th century a change in the exercise of sovereign rule, referred to in treatises of the time as the 'action' or 'art' of government, erupted throughout Western Europe and Britain. Foucault named this new approach 'governmentality' and observed that it sought to regulate almost every aspect of life including households, armies, parishes, souls, the poor, the criminal, and the conduct of families and individuals (Rabinow 1991, pp 4-15). Governmentality involved instituting systems of efficiency and order for achieving the most effective and economical management of territories and subjects. The state as a new form of political and administrative structure emerged with this shift in governance. The modern state, which began to take shape in the 18th century, exercised a form of power and knowledge that individualised the subject (Foucault 1983, p 214). At a macro level, governmentality circumscribed a domain comprising land, administrative systems and people, in which constituents could only operate with reference to the state. At the micro level, governmentality sought to regulate and intervene in the way people behaved, and in their development of self and identity, thereby constituting them as discrete objects of knowledge and power. Foucault regarded the modern state as a complicated structure, concerned at a fundamental level with the individual subject and individuality, the construction of which 'would be shaped in a new form and submitted to a set of specific patterns' (Foucault 1983, p 214).

Foucault described the process for subjecting people 'to a set of specific patterns' as 'dividing practices' (Rabinow 1991, p 8; Chambon 1999, p 67). By this he meant techniques of objectification for producing subjects more suitable for fulfilling the requirements of the state, such as the normalising definitions and standards established by the rise of medicine, psychiatry and criminology (Danaher et al 2000). These human sciences measure groups and individuals against normalising criteria and accordingly label and divide them into a series of oppositional hierarchies such as sane/insane, criminal/citizen, and poor/wealthy. These classifications then divide into types. For example, people classified as belonging to the insane pole of sane/insane are subdivided into and labelled as schizophrenics, psychopaths and hysterics; the criminal pole is elaborated into murderer, thief and rapist; 'the poor' become typified as deserving and undeserving. In further degrees of differentiation:

> [T]hese divisions expand into elaborate classification systems with internal graduations. They locate individuals within a series and assign them a relational rank. They partition age groups and break the difficulty of tasks into subtasks. They define degrees of development and hierarchies of deviance.

> They establish the multiple processes of affirmation and reward, surveillance and exclusion (Chambon 1999, p 67).

In these deliberate and diffuse ways, dividing practices separate the abnormal and deviant from the normal and compliant, structuring difference and inequality into almost every context and exchange. Actions to correct the deficient and their deficiencies are administered by qualified agents such as doctors, police, teachers and social workers who operate within state-authorised institutional contexts (Foucault 1991; Danaher et al 2000). Another quality of governmentality is that it does not have a singular source of administration that is 'the government'. Individuals govern themselves and one another as they are subject to the technologies of governmentality from wider political, social and economic institutions and interests.

While the path from 16th to 20th century offers historical signposts and linked events, there is no essential progression in governmental strategy. Circumstances caused by war, climate, famine, disease, economic failure and success, human error and changes within regimes of knowledge and power impelled states to adopt, discard and reformulate tactics for maximising administrative efficiency and economic productivity. The Enlightenment, industrialisation, population changes in rural and urban areas, revolutions in France and America, scientific invention, the human sciences and the rise of capitalism and liberalism were amongst many factors that informed governmental action.

Mitchell Dean observes a shift in the way poverty was constituted and addressed at the end of the 18th century, proposing that changes in the British Poor Laws reflect the institution of a liberal form of governance that promoted self and familial responsibility while bureaucratising the administration of poor relief. According to Dean (1991, pp 211-212), this 'responsibilisation of the poor' established the wage-labourer, the male breadwinner, the dependency of women and children, and 'the limits of state responsibility for relief and subsistence'. Dean's analysis is significant to this discussion because convict transportation to Australia, and subsequently the social, economic and political formation of the colonies, began during this transition in governance. Australia's establishment as a penal colony occurred amid the transformation from feudal, agrarian, traditional societies to industrial, capitalist, modern social states, and was in many respects a socio-economic experiment driven by liberal enterprise and desperation. The first governor, Arthur Phillip, was expected to fulfil Britain's need to establish new trade routes, markets and destinations for transportees in harsh and adverse conditions.

Uncharitable actions

As suggested above, tracing the history of the British Poor Laws highlights values, traditions and prejudices that informed early Australian responses to poverty. It also exposes the dominance of economic interests and the age of some contemporary social policy debates (Carney & Hanks 1994). While historical continuities emphasise enduring attitudes and practices, the identification of discontinuities can also reveal strategies of governmentality.

The main form of poor relief from about the 500s-1500s in Britain and Western Europe was Church-based charity (Garton 1990). Churches gathered tithes from parishioners and redistributed a proportion as poor relief. Responsibility resided with every Christian, although offering alms was more often about personal salvation than altruism (Webb 1963). Christian charity at this time was not overly concerned with the character of the recipient, the way alms were used, or the overall effect on pauperism. Assistance was based on need, relief was given when requested. Christian teachings reinforced belief that poverty was a spiritual virtue (Geremek 1997) and the judgment of God was believed to be directed at the alms-giver (Webb 1963). Unlike the Christian obligation to lessen suffering, the Monarchy feared the disorder and crime associated with vagrancy, and imposed severe punishments on mendicants (Webb 1963).

Charity and punishment began to converge in the mid-1300s as the feudal system dismantled and the plague and famine created widespread labour shortages. Freed from Lord and manor, labourers took advantage of these circumstances by pursuing higher wages in neighbouring parishes. In response, the Statute of Labourers was introduced in 1350 to restrain 'rogue' labourers. Wages were to return to pre-plague rates, labourers were not to leave their own parish, relief was not to be given to 'able-bodied' beggars, and men who absconded from their workplace could be branded with an 'F' for 'falsity' on their forehead. Although intended to be particularly repressive, these laws were resisted by labourers and employers, and local officials were reluctant to impose the harsh penalties (Webb 1963). In a further effort to regulate the labour market, curb vagrancy and regain order, Richard II introduced the first *Poor Law Act* in 1388 (Garton 1990; Carney & Hanks 1994). Even so, there was little change to the living and labouring conditions of the poor for the next 150 years.

Then in 1536 a new strategy of 'systematic public provision' came into being: '[A] new state-craft ... which sought to harmonise, in one and the same public service, provision for the sick and the aged, education for the children, and the setting to work under discipline of the able-bodied unemployed' (Webb 1963, p 29). This poor law which sought to curtail 'indiscriminate giving' by churches represents the 'first collectivist incursion' into the tradition of administering relief as an individual act of charity (Carney & Hanks 1994, p 27). As a nascent strategy of governmentality, this Act drew administrative links between government agents and paupers, and rendered parishioners accountable to the sovereign, not God, for their charitable actions. Where spiritual ethos had discouraged judgment of recipients, Christians were now required to align faith with legislation, because the state saw unregulated almsgiving as 'socially injurious' (Webb 1963, pp 29-30).

Between 1552 and 1572 further poor laws required parishes to compile an official register of paupers (Bloy, 2002). Those seeking relief were classified according to nine types, and property-owners were obliged to pay a poor tax (Webb 1963). Increasing systems of regulation observed, categorised, incarcerated, criminalised, put to work and punished the poor. Beatrice Webb demonstrates the developing governmental web:

> The Overseers of the Poor in close association with the Churchwardens of the parish; under the direction simultaneously of the Parish Vestry and its chairman the rector or vicar, in some respects also of the archdeacon in his annual visitations, and at all times of the local Justices of the Peace, who appointed the Overseers and passed their accounts; whilst the Quarter Sessions of the County or its Sheriff, the Judges on their circuits, and even the bishop of the diocese would ... be transmitting Orders from the Privy Council of the King. (Webb 1963, p 58).

Between 1597 and 1601 all previous legislation was consolidated in the Elizabethan *Poor Law*. Two forms of assistance were acknowledged: outdoor relief in the form of food, clothing and money, and indoor relief, which provided accommodation in an almshouse, hospital, orphanage or workhouse. Although this legislation established an administrative framework, there was no coordinated, systematic approach. Orders were deployed, but little attention was given to ensuring they were carried out or applied consistently between parishes (Carney & Hanks 1994).

Further Poor Law Acts across the next two centuries continued to prove ineffective in solving the problem of pauperism. In the final decades of the 18th century, high bread prices and food shortages associated with the war with France, consequent riots and exploitation of seasonal labourers, led magistrates in Speenhamland, Berkshire to devise a means of supplementing the wages of the working poor (Carney & Hanks 1994). The Speenhamland system, fundamentally introduced as a safety net, understood poverty as beyond individual control and distributed responsibility among local employers. The system quickly became unmanageable and was heavily criticised for its expense and creation of disincentive (Carney & Hanks 1994). The reaction by Britain's first liberal Parliament was the introduction of the repressive 1834 Poor Law Amendment Act (O'Brien & Penna 1998).

These amendments re-endorsed poverty as a choice and therefore individual responsibility, and the belief that fear of hunger and destitution created work incentive. The principle of 'less eligibility' – requiring that the maximum level of public assistance was below minimum wages – was introduced; it is worth noting this is still a feature of Australian social policy. In addition, poor relief shifted from local parishes to a central commission (Carney & Hanks 1994). Local administrative units were to be established, the work of locally elected guardians of the poor was to be supervised, officials were to be qualified and regulations for administering relief were to be implemented (Bloy 2005). The principle of working for assistance was restored and no supplements were to be provided to the employed. When these amendments were introduced, the Australian penal colonies had been providing another solution to Britain's social and economic problems for 46 years.

Australia's role in relieving Britain of paupers and criminals had resulted from a collection of circumstances. British prisons were so overcrowded that prisoners were incarcerated in hulks on the Thames. Transportation to the Antipodes to relieve 'Britain of its human refuse' (Connell & Irving 1980, p 31) offered a ready solution after American ports were closed to convicts following the American War of Independence (1775-1783). The report of 'The Committee of the House of Commons on the problem of transportation, 1784' claimed that transportees would avoid the poverty, starvation, vagrancy and further crime created by British parishes refusing to receive released convicts. Removal from the temptation caused by 'an aversion to labour, and the inequality of fortunes' and the application of enterprising attributes to establishing and defending a new territory would enable reform. Transportation to an 'uncivilised' land could thus transform the 'lower orders of life' – who were notionally draining private and public resources and creating social disorder – into productive citizens who 'would consider their own happiness as involved in the prosperity of the Settlement' (cited in Clark 1957, p 68).

Colonial contexts

Governor Phillip announced on arrival at Port Jackson that those who did not work would not eat (van Krieken 1992, p 50). The British Government intended to use convict labour, and the reproductive bodies of convict women, to establish a new society and economy driven by patriarchy, enterprise, self-sufficiency and industry. Hard working, married and potentially self-reliant convicts were rewarded with liberties and reduced sentences (Berreen 1994). However, expectations of self-reliance and self-help contradicted the conditions of a penal colony establishing a new settlement in an unfamiliar land and climate (van Krieken 1992). The first years presented life-threatening shortages of survival needs such as food, shelter, clothing and medical supplies. Convicts, free settlers and officers alike were debilitated by diminished rations, exposure and disease, forcing Phillip to reduce work tasks (Clark 1957). In the early 1800s over three-quarters of the women and children existed on government provisions (van Krieken 1992).

Although conditions improved with free enterprise and wage labour becoming established in the 1820s, approximately one-third of the population – including convicts and government employees – remained dependent on government victuals (Berreen 1994). Those who pursued self-sufficiency 'were dependent on the seasons and their own skills to survive and prosper. Not all were successful' (Garton 1990, p 16). Throughout the 19th and early years of the 20th century approximately 10 per cent of Anglo-European settlers lived in permanent poverty and a further 10 per cent lived in temporary poverty (Roe 1975 cited in Garton 1990, p 3).

The arrival of the First Fleet led to the devastation of Indigenous society and culture. In 1788 the 1000 British subjects were outnumbered by between 700,000 and 1.5 million Aborigines. By 1911 this Aboriginal population was reduced to approximately 93,000 by imported disease, disenfranchisement from the land and murder (Jones 1996). Aborigines have been the most disadvantaged population in Australia since British arrival, and their poverty and neglect warrants particular attention. Readers are referred to Chapter 9 for a detailed examination of the poverty imposed on the Indigenous people of Australia since the invasion of 1788. 'Welfare' policy was structured, maintained and progressed by dividing realms of activity into public/private; political/personal; legal/moral; civic/domestic (O'Brien & Penna 1998, pp 21-23). In Australia these oppositional divisions sat within an overarching demarcation between convicts, free settlers and Indigenous people.

Avoiding obligations and dispersing responsibility

The state's obligation to provide against poverty and sickness, except in cases of extreme destitution, was removed in the 1834 British Poor Law amendments. Although no such law existed at the time in Australia, the State governments, in the throes of establishing economic independence, were already committed to this policy of non-responsibility, and even though some attempts were made to institute poor laws, objection far out rode support (Beilharz, Considine & Watts 1992; Berreen 1994). A complex array of reasons associated with moral and cultural values, economic imperatives, administrative efficiency and lack of necessity fuelled resistance to any legislation mirroring the British Poor Law. In one respect, opposition derived from experience in Britain, which caused abhorrence of the workhouse and the harsh attitudes promoted by cruel, soul-destroying laws (Berreen 1994). The administrative brief to establish self-sufficiency also meant colonial governments retracted from any obligation to sustain free settlers. Poor laws would make the state legally responsible, undermine the ethic of self-reliance and potentially impose a poor tax on the propertied classes (Roe 1975).

The absence of a poor law meant the British government and London-based philanthropists took responsibility for sustaining many dependant colonials; it made sound fiscal sense for the colonial governors to supplement scarce financial resources with British subsidies wherever possible (Dickey 1980). Convict status and the want of an hereditary underclass also contributed to a lack of interest, because the section of the population likely to create social disorder was already under state control (Jones 1996). Furthermore, poor laws would require acknowledging poverty, and despite its presence, a collective denial of its existence dominated officialdom. The idea of pauperism 'was peculiarly appalling and undermining' (Roe 1975, p 135); Australia was supposed to offer a solution, not contribute further to the problem.

The constitution of colonial society also meant that poverty in Australia was less visible than Britain (Roe 1975), where the poverty rate was estimated at 30 per cent (Garton 1990). Throughout the 19th century no effort was made to conduct in Australia poverty surveys like those carried out in Britain by Henry Mayhew and Charles Booth (Garton 1990). The first official public inquiry into housing for the poor was instigated and conducted by Henry Parkes in 1860. Although he found living conditions in Sydney were the same as or worse than in London, the government insisted on the responsibility of private enterprise for providing adequate housing (Jones 1972).

In the 50 years between 1820 and 1870 incomes grew by more than twice the average for other Western countries, and during 1850-1890 Australia had the highest per capita income in the Western world (Jones 1996). Although this does not demonstrate wealth distribution, it is not surprising that the attention of Australian governments and capitalist entrepreneurs turned elsewhere. With unemployment considered a non-issue, and despite the many working poor, governments focused instead on providing assisted passages – funded with revenue from land sales – to immigrant labourers who would work harder for cheaper wages (de Lepervanche 1975).

The State governments promoted the attitude that provision for the non self-sufficient should occur as charity through private means, while covertly funding private charities to provide minimal relief. By 1820 a multitude of philanthropic trusts and benevolent societies was dealing with increasing numbers of destitute (Mendes 2003). Across the colonies charity was delivered with varying degrees of generosity, religious moralising and judgmentalism through practices that 'relied on the construction and reproduction of social categories that divided specific people as 'problems' requiring charitable action' (Beilharz, Considine & Watts 1992, p 62).

The dividing practices of the state

Beilharz, Considine and Watts (1992, pp 17-18) argue that the state, not 'the entrepreneurial activity of nascent capitalists', founded Australian society, and that its presence as the structuring principle of colonial administration was never seriously questioned. Rather it was 'the proper role of the state in everyday life' that fuelled debates about freedom from state interference in capitalist enterprise, and the need for intervention to ensure fair access to resources. The state had multiple roles to fulfil, including relieving Britain of paupers and convicts, boosting whale and tea trades and providing an imperialist naval base in South Asia (Connell and Irving 1980). Although the state and the development of the capitalist economy cannot be conflated, they were intertwined. The state assembled and assured the relations of private ownership upon which the labour market and production depended. For example, imprisonment was the main industry for the first 50 years, and the state was the largest customer (Connell & Irving 1980).

As discussed above, governmentality involves more than exercising autocratic power within a structural hierarchy; it constitutes a complex interplay of regulation and resistance. Interpreting state formation purely in terms of social control and economic expansionism obscures the multiple and diffuse actions of power, and how social order and change are actualised (van Krieken 1992). The state is not an independent entity: the relationship between state agents, populations, families and individuals 'is often characterised by osmosis, complex alliances and compromise' (van Krieken 1992, p 7). The knowledge, practices and attitudes of Australia's early charities that classified, normalised and objectified individuals were supported and resisted across all social classes. Robert van Krieken explains:

> The immediate experience working class men, women and children had of their material and social environment explains as much, if not more about the forms that their behaviour, culture and political action took than the regulatory activity of the state … the majority of working class women and men had their very own good reasons to be committed to sobriety, cleanliness, punctuality, orderly behaviour, regular hours, personal hygiene and so on without having to be coerced (1992, p 7).

The culture of inequality, which the British brought to the colonies, was, exercised in the 'art of government' through a web of dividing practices. These were enacted by state institutions and agents, as well as privileged and disadvantaged subjects of the state.

Determining dependencies

The infirm, children, pregnant and nursing women and the aged were the main groups to obtain charitable support in the colonies (Dickey 1980). Conditions for receiving assistance were determined by a plethora of factors including the organisation of individual administering relief, available resources, potential to acquire or regain independence, religious and moral judgments, and beliefs about the causes of poverty. The pervading expectation of self-sufficiency based on labour and enterprise concentrated responsibility for sustaining the state and its subjects on resources produced by able-bodied men and women.

Australia's first charity commenced in 1795 on Norfolk Island when Governor Philip King opened a home for neglected and orphaned female children of convicts (Pownall 1983). Since settlement began there were abandoned children. In Sydney numbers grew at an astounding rate throughout the 1800s (van Krieken 1992), while the 1850s gold rush exacerbated the problem in Melbourne. The 'Royal Commission on Penal and Prison Discipline' reported:

> [F]amilies were broken up by dissolute habits, children were left destitute by the frequent accidents which occurred at the mines, and the bonds of parental obligation were weakened or ruptured by a roving life and fluctuating fortunes. (cited in Jaggs 1986, p 4).

When Victoria introduced the *Neglected and Criminal Children Act* in 1864, 4000 children in Melbourne were being housed in ex-army barracks converted into an Industrial School (Dickey 1980). These institutions had risen in popularity during the mid-1800s, because:

> In full accord with the theories of self-help and industrial improvement, the disadvantaged 'street arabs' could be exposed to organised, disciplined life, regular meals and the opportunity to learn, if not a skilled trade, then at least the rudiments that made them employable on farms, in stables and kitchens. They would be socialised for use in the capitalist economy (Dickey 1980, p 61).

Industrial schools were used to house the neglected, deserted and orphaned, remove children from homes of vice and crime, deflect jail sentences for the delinquent, and control prostitution (Scrivener 2000). By the end of the 19th century, the cost of upkeep and maintenance, ineffectiveness in reforming disorderly children, reports of sub-standard and unhealthy conditions, pressure from middle-class activists and changes in attitude about the causes of poverty, resulted in the closure of many of these institutions. A renewed focus on supporting and reforming families saw the introduction of maintenance payments to widowed and deserted mothers, and revival of boarding out and fostering. Placed in 'good' homes, children would train to be productive, family orientated members of the working class. In practice many children were exploited as cheap labour on farms and in domestic service (Dickey 1980).

Residential institutions and boarding-out arrangements were underwritten by a belief that the transformation of unruly poor children, who it was predicted would become poor, unproductive and socially disruptive adults, required separation from contaminating people and environments. Within the existing social structure, poverty could only be overcome through the acquisition of orderly, disciplined and industrious habits. For this to be achieved, intervention by the state in private and family life was necessary. The trend shifted to greater policing of families unable to establish self-reliance:

> [T]he object of the state was not to consolidate or undermine the family per se, but to support a certain kind of family life by breaking up unacceptable families and redistributing children accordingly' (van Krieken 1992, p 78).

Poor families often participated in these interventions because of the financial benefits, and their own will to divert their children from impoverishment and crime (van Krieken 1992; Twomey 1999; Scrivener 2000).

The aged and infirm also faced destitution from the beginning of settlement. Poor health and incapacity to become productive, self-sufficient workers ensured a different response from that given to children. Governor King's home for girls may have been the first charitable institution; however, the first to receive health care were infirm convicts and members of the British troops disembarking from the First Fleet. The first make-shift hospital was erected on 29 January 1788 (Dickey 1980). In that year 52 convicts were recorded as too old or too infirm to work (Piper 2004).

In general, throughout the 1800s, care for the destitute aged was left to benevolent societies and charitable institutions, and this group comprised the highest proportion of inmates in many asylums and hospitals (Dickey 1980). The overall population of Australia tripled between 1861 and 1900, while the number of aged increased thirteen-fold (Jones 1996). It was a difficult phenomenon to ignore. Aged pensions schemes were introduced in New South Wales and Victoria in 1901 and Queensland in 1908, and the Commonwealth government introduced a national aged pension scheme in 1909 (Jones 1996).

A plethora of events and ideas converged in the decades bridging the turn of the 20th century. Depression, public outcry and pressure from activists and women's groups, the shift from economic to social liberalism – arguing that laissez-faire capitalism needed moderating for the greater good – the influence of the Labour party and the rise of the social sciences contributed to establishing government responsibility for 'protecting the economic welfare of its citizens' (Macintyre cited in Beilharz, Considine & Watts 1992, p 77). These actions were located within wider ideological changes in which the language of 'benevolence' and 'self-help' was replaced by 'rights' and 'citizenship' (Garton 1994, p 55). Scientific knowledge fuelled belief 'that private charities lacked the capacity for systematic administration of important moral reform strategies' (Garton 1994, p 29), while the ever-pressing need for administrative effectiveness further contributed to reorienting how poverty was governed. The result was state intervention in the wage-labour market to protect incomes for the self-sufficient and to secure provision for the dependent. A three-part alliance involving compulsory arbitration, protection and the White Australia policy was set in place, earning Australia an identity as a 'social laboratory' and forming the foundation of a unique welfare state model, described as the wage-earner's welfare state (Mendes 2003, p 12).

The *Harvester* judgement in 1907 was essentially the first social policy legislation to place the needs of (male) workers above employers (Jones 1996). In an effort to protect the working classes against poverty created by an unregulated capitalist market, Justice Higgins determined that a man supporting a wife and three children needed seven shillings a day for a frugal but civilised existence. Higgins insisted that employers 'should go out of business, rather than pay low wages' (Beilharz, Considine & Watts 1992, p 21). The patriarchal values underpinning this ruling established married women and children as the legal dependents of men. A woman employed in the workforce, whether single, married, with or without children, was only to receive a wage based on the cost of supporting herself (Jones 1996). Able-bodied male workers – categorised in charity discourse as 'non-deserving' – were rendered self-sufficient and responsible for their wives and children. Social restructuring was evaded, the need for income supplements was minimised, and the market was made responsible for the well-being of the labour force.

The introduction of the national aged (1909) and invalid (1910) pensions also constituted little more than an administrative reorganisation of how support was provided. The level of provision was determined by the principle of less eligibility and these pensions provided for the non able-bodied deserving poor; the same category given outdoor relief under the British *Poor Law* (Carney and Hanks 1994). The new 'welfare' as opposed to the old 'charity' discourse, in combination with the social policy eruption of the Federation era, divided state constituents into 'responsible providers' and 'dependents'. At the same time, the categories of 'deserving' and 'undeserving' merged with workforce status to yield new categories that defined responsible (deserving) workers: men – who were cared for by wage fixing, employment and worker's compensation schemes, and dependent (undeserving) workers: employed women, children and Aborigines. Added to this list were dependent (deserving) non-workers: invalids, the aged and deserted or neglected children and (undeserving) non-workers, those judged to be of bad character or not deserving of a pension – wife deserters and 'bad' fathers, single mothers, deserted women, and unemployed 'able-bodied' men and women of working age (Carney & Hanks 1994, p 30). Through division, standardisation, protectionism and regulation, the state – in its broadest sense – maximised efficiency and effectiveness while maintaining economic viability. And this was facilitated by the material and dividing effects of poverty.

Conclusion

In examining some of the more pervasive attitudes about and responses towards poverty from settlement to the early decades of Federation, it is evident that the absence of poor laws in Australia did not result in colonials who were in need of material aid escaping either judgment, or exclusion from accessing relief. Many factors were present in early Australian charity practice: the principle of less eligibility, judgment as deserving and undeserving, the attitude that poverty was a choice, fears that relief would create dependency and disincentive, and the condition that public assistance required state intervention in recipients' private lives. Despite shifts in language from 'charity' to 'welfare' and from 'benevolence' to 'rights', as other chapters in this text demonstrate, these ideologies continue to inform the social policies of the present Commonwealth government, and the attitudes and practices of many members of Australian society.

Contemporary Australian society was formed by the diffuse governmental actions of the modern state and structured by its dividing practices. In the present day, accessing social security benefits requires the division of 'welfare' recipients into categories, and their objectification as a 'service-user' or member of a 'target group'. On the basis of various forms of 'assessment', individuals and groups deemed as 'in need' are subject to a range of state-authorised interventions in order to maximise their contribution to the overall productivity of the state. In these ways, poverty – a corollary of the structuring of inequality – continues from its colonial beginnings to be implicated in strategies of governmentality.

Chapter 7

Poverty: The impact of government policy on vulnerable families and older people

Ruth Webber

In Australia over the past 20 years, government policies at both State and federal levels have been increasingly driven by an economic paradigm based on neo-liberalism, which has resulted in some sectors of the population being increasingly disadvantaged. After a brief introduction to neo-liberalism and its relationship to economic rationalism, this chapter examines the impact of government policies on vulnerable families and older people. It would be foolhardy to claim that government policies alone are the cause of increased levels of disadvantage and hardship among Australia's poor. However, particular social policies have made it difficult for some groups to attain a quality of life that includes access to community activities and meets their basic needs. Those with multiple disadvantages experience a cumulative effect of poverty, which can have far-reaching consequences.

This chapter also argues that while governments and big business have embraced neo-liberalism and economic rationalist policies, it would be unfair to see this endorsement as complete indifference to the needs of the poor. Rather, the poor are casualties of this drive to reduce the role of the state in social service provision, in state spending and in taxation. While poverty affects people of all ages, vulnerable families and older people stand out as being particularly disadvantaged, although in different ways. While lack of access to affordable dental and health care affects many people on low incomes, as people age their health declines and their need for health services, hospital attention and medicines increases. Without access to these services, their quality of life declines. Parents with young children generally require fewer health services than the elderly, but face additional financial challenges as they attempt to educate and clothe their children, especially in families receiving welfare benefits or lacking employment or secure housing.

A love affair with neo-liberalism

Because neo-liberalism is the defining political and economic paradigm of our time, a brief consideration of neo-liberalism's theory and practice is needed to put the current Australian situation into context. Two basic assumptions of neo-liberalism are that societies are motivated mainly by economic considerations, and that market competition creates innovation (Stillwell 2000). Adherents of neo-liberalism contend that market inequalities are the necessary by-product of a well functioning economy and are 'just', because what one puts into the market, one gets out of it (Coburn 2000). Neo-liberals advocate deregulation and privatisation, which they believe encourage initiative, enterprise and creativity in meeting the material needs of the community. They also hold that the neo-liberal approach will 'almost of itself, generate the virtues of personal self-discipline and restraint which are required for a liberal society to also be a just society' (Australian Catholic Social Welfare Commission 1997, p 4). They distrust collective mechanisms that limit individual freedoms because they fear that special interest groups will misuse them, and in so doing, prevent competition and economic growth. For example, neo-liberals believe that by representing workers' interests and pressing for a regulated workplace or higher wages and conditions, trade unions may restrict profits and new initiatives.

Neo-liberalism is claimed to be the descendant of the neo-classical economics of Adam Smith, David Ricardo and Thomas Malthus, who advocated the division of labour through specialisation, accumulation of capital, low population, free trade, and income distribution among social classes to enhance a better standard of living (Pusey 1991; 1993). Thus economic goals, which are intended to take primacy over social goals, are best achieved through market forces rather than government intervention (Stillwell 2000). Economic rationalism is based on neo-liberalism, and provides a practical guide to the achievement of the desired outcome of a market-driven economy. For example, commercialisation and privatisation of public sector activities are encouraged and are justified by the concepts of efficiency and competition. The private sector and large corporations are fostered and receive favourable treatment, while government spending is reduced (Goldfinch 2000).

For the past 20 years, public policy in Western countries, including Australia, has been increasingly informed by economic rationalist ideas that see market forces, vigorous competition and a non-collective social framework as keys to national prosperity (Johnson & Taylor 2000). Gamble (2001, p 132) makes the point that:

> [T]he presumption is always in favour of recreating the widest possible conditions for markets to flourish, which means removing as many restrictions to competition as possible and empowering market agents by reducing the burden of taxation.

Within an economic rationalist perspective, market forces drive products and production, with individualism forming a key foundational principle (Neville 1997). In consequence, the Australian Commonwealth and State governments have developed agendas to reduce the role of government in state spending and taxation and to encourage greater reliance on self and less on social protection (Painter 1996).

Critics of economic rationalism claim that the economic consequences of these policies have resulted in increased social and economic inequity and an unprecedented bonanza for the wealthy (McChesney 1999; Cameron & Duncan 2001). Australian welfare organisations such as Anglicare (Neville 2002), the Brotherhood of St Laurence (Perkins & Angley 2003), Mission Australia (Leech 2001), Catholic Social Services Victoria (Cameron & Duncan 2001) and UnitingCare Australia (2000) have published significant accounts of the negative impact of State and Commonwealth government policy changes relating to low-income families, particularly those with multiple disadvantages. The next section describes shifts in community attitudes towards the poor over recent years, moving from compassion to demonisation.

Demonising the poor

The rhetoric about the poor and disadvantaged has become more negative and condemnatory over the past 20 to 30 years in Australia. For example descriptors such as 'dole bludgers', 'welfare dependency', 'welfare cheats', and 'underclass' have entered our lexicon (Johnson & Taylor 2000). A 'blame the victim' discourse has been fanned by influential politicians like the Honourable Tony Abbott, when he was the Commonwealth Minister for Employment, Workplace Relations and Small Business, who consistently attacked the unemployed for being 'lazy' and 'job snobs'. He said on television:

> We can't abolish poverty because poverty, in part, is a part of individual behaviour ... So if you are poor and can't make ends meet, if your children go to school with holes in their shoes and without lunch ... it is not the fault of the employer or economic policies or the social system or the landlord – it is the result of your own 'behaviour' or the fact that you make 'mistakes' (Abbott, 2001b).

Indeed it is difficult to think of a positive term used to describe the poor, either in the media or in everyday conversations. This pervasively negative focus is divisive, and helps to scapegoat those who are most disadvantaged in society. Johnson and Taylor (2000) found that increasingly, many people indict the poor for 'wasting money' on tobacco, alcohol and even, sometimes, on pets. While few would dispute that some poverty is associated with such habits, the reality for many of those living in poverty is a never-ending daily grind to survive, and there is little they can do to get out of the poverty trap. At the same time, the current public language of discourse about the poor contributes to a pervasive negative attitude towards them. The result is that the poor are being increasingly demonised, isolated, and thus disadvantaged.

Locating the poor

It is not a simple matter to establish who the poor are. Although a simple definition is that the poor are those individuals and families whose income falls well below the level considered sufficient to meet living costs, in practice various income measures can be used as indicators of poverty, and the different measures produce differing findings. Most social analysis is based on research into household income, using a poverty line that seeks to categorise households, families, and individuals into satisfactory or unsatisfactory income streams (Bray 2001). Lloyd, Harding and Payne (2004) note that the squeezing of complex social and economic issues into arbitrary benchmarks not only limits the conclusions that can be drawn but also sparks debate among analysts. For example, Peter [Saunders from the Centre for Independent Studies (CIS) challenges published poverty figures and states that poverty rates in Australia are vastly overstated. In particularly he is highly critical of the figures used in the 2004 Senate Report on poverty, and claims that 'the statistics on which this Report is based are seriously flawed' (P Saunders 2004s, p 1). However, it is beyond the scope of this chapter to enter into an examination of the efficacy of how poverty figures are calculated.

The National Centre for Social and Economic Modelling (NATSEM), in its study of Australians in poverty in the 21st century, uses the Organisation for Economic Co-operation and Development (OECD) Half Median Poverty Line, which is based on disposable income. It found that the estimated poverty rate among all Australians was 11 per cent, (Lloyd, Harding & Payne 2004). Thus almost one in every nine people was estimated to be living in poverty in the year 2001. The highest poverty level across the board is among people whose main source of income is government cash benefits (Forster & d'Ercole 2005).

Historically, older people and families with young children stand out as being vulnerable to poverty. In 1991 the poverty rate among children was 9.5 per cent, indicating that almost half a million of Australia's children were poor. In regard to families, poverty rates for single parent families are much higher than for all families with children (Forster & d'Ercole 2005). It is not living in single-parent families per se that increases poverty, but rather the employment status of the parent. Sole-parent families with dependent children are also much more likely to have multiple disadvantages (Bray 2001). In relation to older people, poverty rates among those aged over 65 increased between 1990 and 2000; particularly vulnerable were those in private rental with no private income, women, single people (often women) reliant on the full pension, and those on pensions or allowances for a very long time with no potential for improving their income (Harding, Lloyd & Greenwell 2001).

Impact of poverty for people living on the margins

There is little difference in outcome between those who are a dollar above the poverty line and those who are a dollar below. However those well below the poverty line experience multiple hardships. Understanding this poverty gap is important in trying to understand those who are living on the margins and facing these hardships. Although people from different sectors can experience poverty, two groups have been selected for attention here: families with young children, and older people. 'Poverty is a special concern when it affects individuals who cannot be held responsible for their situation and who are especially vulnerable to its consequences' (Forster & d'Ercole 2005, p 32). Children fall into this category, and to some extent so do the elderly who may not have had the opportunity to provide adequately for their future.

In order to discuss the impact of poverty on families, it is necessary to look first at the impact on children. They are the innocent victims of being in families which lack enough money to enable them to live a fulfilling life; such children inherit marginal living standards, so that such children are rarely able to take part in normal extra-curricular activities such as sport, swimming lessons and movies. In this way poverty can lead to exclusion from mainstream society or minimal interaction with others in the wider society (Leech 2001; Neville 2002). Clearly the impact of marginal living for children can be deleterious and far-reaching, and research has consistently demonstrated a strong positive association between measures of economic stress, reported rates of child abuse and neglect, and juvenile involvement in crime (Weatherburn & Lind 1998). This relationship has been shown to be circular and cumulative, with many interacting factors including quality of parenting, peer influences, social exclusion and resilience. Weatherburn and Lind (1998) reported that economic and social stress exert an indirect influence on juvenile crime by disrupting the quality of parenting and increasing the likelihood of young people being susceptible to peer influence. This relationship between poverty, quality of parenting and child outcomes is disturbing. Poverty strains family relationships: financial hardship generates stress and conflict, creating difficult relationships and poor family cohesion. Many people have been in their present parlous situation for years and see no way out of it, with the result that they become despondent and depressed. In turn this has an effect on the children who may be subject to generational poverty and poor parent-child relationships, leading to further disadvantage.

Low-income families with teenage children face the highest direct cost of raising children but do not receive adequate compensation for these costs (Davidson 2003). Consequently, these families are at risk of deep poverty, even though it is well known that poverty has a negative impact on the physical and mental health of both children and adults. The link between health and socio-economic status is well documented, with lower socio-economic status generally being associated with poorer overall health (Cameron & Duncan 2001; Australian Bureau of Statistics (ABS) 2004a). Poor health can compound poverty because ill health reduces one's capacity to work or to engage in training.

ABS (2004b) reported that those experiencing multiple disadvantages in terms of health, education and training, work, crime, financial hardship and family and community support, have poor outcomes across a range of dimensions of life. For example, people of all ages in fair or poor health, as distinct from excellent health, were much less likely to have a post-school qualification, were more likely to be the victim of an assault or break-in, and to have income in the lowest 20 per cent of all incomes. Compared to those in excellent health, people under 65 in fair or poor health were less likely to feel they could get support in a time of crisis. The ABS report also stated that the effects of several disadvantages acting in tandem can be more difficult to overcome than a single aspect of disadvantage, and can lead to a lack of access to goods, services, activities and resources.

The effect of poverty on people has been well documented since the 1960s (Henderson et al 1970). Much less has been written about the far-reaching economic rationalist changes in government policies, and the extent to which these changes have had negative outcomes for vulnerable people. Policies based on economic rationalism have changed the way welfare and community organisations operate, and have shifted the focus from social responsibility to individual responsibility, which is reflected in a 'user-pays' ideology, as outlined below.

The impact of economic rationalism on social and community services

The welfare system is complex in that there is often no clear interface between various welfare sectors, particularly in areas that fall under different jurisdictions, such as aged care and disability services. During the 1990s, State and Commonwealth governments introduced policies based on economic rationalist principles, which encourage competition rather than cooperation. Reforms brought in during this period concentrated on legislative changes, which endorsed amalgamations, centralisation and other managerial practices including chief executive performance agreements, all of which discouraged cooperation, endorsing a silo mentality. Government departments entrenched an already existing silo approach with clear demarcations between federal and State jurisdictions.

The failure to utilise fully a case management approach to clients has disadvantaged those with multiple difficulties. When people have multiple health and welfare needs, the responsibility for each area may lie in many different places, making coordinated management extremely difficult. For example, an older single man who has a mental illness, a drug habit, poor physical health, a prison record, and is unemployed, is unlikely to find a service set up to look after all his needs. Such a person could have to deal with agencies funded by State, federal, and local governments, all with different criteria for eligibility and funding. The neo-liberal philosophy promotes competition and works against cooperation, even between government departments. This is particularly evident in policies such as compulsory competitive tendering, output-based funding and the application of managerial practices to health and community sectors (Webber & Bessant 2001). Government intent has been to streamline services and to move costs away from the public sector and onto the individual.

Many social and community services provided by the public sector have been reduced, thus compounding the disadvantage for vulnerable groups. Reduced services include health and dental services, migrant support programs, education, housing, childcare and labour market programs (Castles 2004). Through these policies, the safety net that formerly protected the severely disadvantaged has been diminished or undermined. As Perkins and Angley argue:

> [G]overnment protection, in the form of a strong and comprehensive welfare state, has been significantly withdrawn, social reasonability has been pushed from governments back onto individuals and families, and public services have been exposed to market forces and privatisation (Perkins & Angley 2003, p iii).

The scaling down of government protection and the welfare state has had far reaching effects on vulnerable families and older people and has fundamentally changed the way Australian society operates.

Health and welfare policies

Policies based on neo-liberalism are undermining the welfare state, particularly in the area of health (Coburn 2000). Such undermining is partly due to the attempt to move costs to the individual rather than the public sector; one way of achieving this shift has been to encourage people to take out private health insurance and thus bypass the public health system. The private sector can only be used by those who can afford it (Kendig & Duckett 2001), leaving the poor reliant on an increasingly under-funded public health system with its long waiting lists, and in some cases, capping (Smallwood et al 2002). Thus the movement to a 'user pays' system via access to private hospitals is straining the public health system. Neither are public hospitals funded to pay for the growing needs of an ageing population, with the result that there can be inadequate discharge planning and rehabilitation.

In the non-hospital medical system, the poor have been also disadvantaged by the decline in the numbers of doctors who are bulk-billing. This decline is part of the move towards a 'user pays' system, with Medicare being increasingly seen as a safety net for those who cannot afford health insurance. Families with limited incomes, with a member in poor health or with a chronic condition like mental illness, chemical dependency, diabetes, and asthma, or with multiple hardships, can find themselves unable to pay the 'gap' in costs.

Nutrition is a major aspect of ill health; those on low incomes find it difficult to afford the healthiest foods. Poor dental health is another outcome, with restricted access to, and long waiting lists for, free dental services. Thus dental care is beyond the reach for many families and older people, as are prescribed medications. Likewise, meeting the cost of glasses or dentures is beyond the scope of many people living in poverty (Cameron & Duncan 2001.

It is not surprising that the constant grind of poverty has negative outcomes for the whole family. Families must choose between paying for necessities such as food and paying for medication (Smallwood et al 2002). Depression is more prevalent among women in low-income families, and rates of drug dependence, homicide, and suicide are higher among unemployed young people than among those who have a job or are studying (Neville 2002).

Older people are confronted by some additional challenges. Australia's demographic profile shows a rapidly ageing population, linked to declining fertility and mortality rates. There are great concerns in government circles that the high levels of public expenditure needed to cover increased health costs of an ageing population will have to be borne by a relatively shrinking labour force (Gibson & Abello 2005). While trying to maintain high-quality care, the aged care service system has struggled to contain rising costs. In a discussion paper entitled 'World Class Care', The Honourable Bronwyn Bishop MP, Minister for Aged Care (2000), acknowledged that older people on low incomes are significantly disadvantaged in relation to health and are more inclined to suffer disabilities, serious chronic illnesses and/or to report recent illnesses, and that older people on low incomes have more hospital admittances and more out-patient and medical visits. Despite this, the solution is seen as less government intervention, not more, as one might logically assume. She states that the government's aim is to reduce the financial impact on health and allied services associated with an ageing population, by moving some of these costs away from the public purse back to the individual through savings and health insurance (Bishop, 2000).

However, in 2001 about 43 per cent of older Australians had some form of health insurance, while people aged 75-84 years had the lowest rates of coverage of around 36 per cent (ABS 2001a). Health insurance is simply outside the reach of most people in this age group, and government policies promoting it ignore many factors. Current policy does not take into account that when one partner becomes ill and requires assistance, the other partner (frequently the wife) spends their joint resources on that person's care, so that when the remaining spouse becomes frail, there is little money left to take care of his or her needs. A 'user pays' system assumes that most ageing Australians can afford to purchase the extra services that they require and that people are irresponsible if they do not plan adequately for this period of their lives. This assumption disregards the fact that planning is not possible for the many people who lack the resources to plan for the future.

Since the 1950s, long-term aged care has been government funded but privately provided, and most service delivery has been through the private for-profit or voluntary sectors. Since 1985, there has been an increasing policy emphasis on cost containment and efficiency, for example, by increasing home care while reducing the level of institutional care (Gibson & Means 2000). Bronwyn Bishop stated that '[i]f older people have the resources ... to purchase the services they prefer, or to insure for additional or superior support and accommodation services, then markets will respond' (2000, p 52). She went on to suggest that people who are financially secure in their later years will have a wide range of opportunities and care options available to them. In other words, it is up the individual to be thrifty, to ensure good care when older. Those who have not done this will have fewer options. This policy will provide an imbalance of service eligibility that is weighted to the needs of the wealthy; concern then arises about the quality of services available to older people on government payments or low incomes.

Housing policies

Vast areas of public activity, lucrative public enterprises, and basic public services have been privatised, resulting in the poor being further disadvantaged. Government policy on public housing is a case in point. Current policy is based on the assumption that the private sector will invest in a growing market in housing, and that the competition inherent in market forces will ensure housing is affordable and available for each sector of society. This assumption has not been validated in reality, with low-income families and older people who do not own their own home being especially disadvantaged. Over the last ten years there has been a decline in low-cost private rental stock, with rents rising steadily (Cameron & Duncan 2001). Affordable properties are often in poor condition without basic insulation, heating, running water and protection from vermin. In June 2004, the Victorian public housing waiting list stood at 35,025 applicants, and it is projected that this number will increase significantly (Victorian Office of Housing 2004), exacerbating the already often long waiting times.

Many people living in poverty, particularly those without stable accommodation, have a precarious existence. Lack of access to affordable, safe and well-located housing negatively affects families and older people, with 5 per cent of public tenants paying more than 30 per cent of their income on rent (Victorian Council of Social Services (VCOSS) 2005b). Inadequate housing affects health outcomes, particularly for children.

Upgrading accommodation is almost impossible for many people, as paying bonds and rent in advance makes moving extremely difficult.

The unavailability of secure and affordable housing means families are forced to move between private rentals, living with relatives, caravans or boarding houses, or emergency accommodation. Moving also means children have to change schools, make new friends and leave behind supportive networks. Moving makes it harder for the child to succeed academically, because of disruption to schooling, curriculum differences, adapting to new teachers and peers, and coping with different school cultures (Neville 2002).

Homelessness is also an issue for older people, with 8.6 per cent of Supported Accommodation Assistance Program (SAAP) clients being over 50 years of age in 2001-02. Unemployed older single men who previously relied on hostel accommodation face special difficulties, as this type of accommodation is bought up for re-development in inner city areas, and as market forces are let loose without balancing the social effects on the poor.

Thus many people are in tenuous accommodation and need extensive support to remain independently and appropriately housed and to break the housing-homelessness cycle (Commonwealth of Australia 2004). There is an urgent need for greater intervention in the private rental market and increased investment in social housing, especially as the steep rise in the cost of purchasing properties over the past five years means that home ownership is out of the reach of people on low incomes.

Education policies

Historically, education has been viewed as a way to exit poverty. However, this escape is increasingly less likely to occur, leaving many children in low-income families unable to achieve equity. It is no coincidence that this disparity has come at a time when 'user pays' policies are adopted by the federal and State governments in education sectors. Policies designed to shift some education costs onto parents and users of education in the public educational sector have had negative consequences for the poor (Smallwood et al 2002). A Victorian Government report (FitzGerald 2004) found wide disparities in school participation and educational outcomes: children from low-income families had lower participation and attainment rates than did children from homes with satisfactory incomes. One study reported that parents with children of kindergarten age lacked sufficient income to cover kindergarten fees, household bills, and living expenses (Tasmanian Council of Social Service 2001). Similar outcomes are replicated in the primary and secondary school sectors. A 'user pays' system has become entrenched in tertiary education, which is increasingly out of the reach of children from poor families, particularly those from rural areas who cannot afford the accommodation at city universities or face the huge debt arising from university fees and loans.

Employment policies

A key agenda of recent Liberal governments has been to free up workplace relations and to deregulate the sector to increase productivity and to improve competitiveness. Enterprise bargaining and contracts were implemented, award rates abandoned, the role of trade unions reduced, and employers given the freedom to remove restrictive work practices (Kenwood 1995). The effect of these policies has been warmly endorsed by industry, but has made life more precarious for some. The implementation of financial deregulation, competition, efficiency, specific skills requirements and demands for proficiency in the English language have led to higher levels of under-employment and insecure employment, with an increase in casual and part-time workers among the most vulnerable, such as those from migrant or refugee families (Wiseman 1998). In 2000, 44 per cent of employment in Australia (35 per cent for men, 53 per cent for women) qualified as precarious (McBride 2005). The Welfare-to-Work legislation (Commonwealth of Australia 2005a, 2005b) may further erode the ability of workers to obtain secure employment; most affected will be the most vulnerable, who have little bargaining power and could be exposed to offers of reduced employment arrangements and conditions (Ryan 2005).

Unemployment, under-employment, and precarious employment affect all aspects of a person's life and are major stresses on families and family relationships; also affected are physical and emotional wellbeing. While having both parents in some kind of employment might relieve financial difficulty, this is not a viable option for those with pre-school children because of the high cost of childcare. Changes to workplace legislation have had a disastrous effect on children and other family members, and have assisted in the creation of an underclass of people, with the gap between the rich and the poor increasing. 'Long-term unemployment threatens to divide our society. It is creating an underclass of forgotten, underprivileged families and individuals who have little scope to escape dependency' (Cameron & Duncan 2001, p 3).

While Australia has moved with daring speed to deregulate the economy and the workplace, the same has not been the case in the arena of family-friendly public policy. Australia still has no publicly-funded maternity leave schemes,* and still lacks an adequate number of publicly provided childcare places. Public subsidies for childcare are so low that several of the Government's own female members of parliament have urged a radical redesign of the nation's child-care system. Government Senate Whip Jeannie Ferris said, 'The cost of care for a second child makes it marginal for many women to return to work' (Schubert 2006;

---

* Australian Catholic University is the most family-friendly employer with staff given maternity leave of 12 weeks on full pay, followed by 40 weeks part-pay.

p 4). There are long waiting lists for childcare places, which are expensive – with refunds through the taxation system available only after payment.

Households with members in insecure and temporary work situations are increasingly reliant on income support, as their capacity to save and repay long-term mortgage loans diminishes and their credit worthiness is reduced (Wilson 2000; Dalton & Ong 2005). People who try to move to an area where there are more jobs face many obstacles; it costs money to move, particularly interstate, and housing is more expensive in areas of low unemployment.

Many older Australians who wish to continue working cannot find suitable employment. Research indicates that the employment rate is on a downward spiral for some groups, and that although many of those who faced management-initiated retirement wished to keep on working, there was a lack of employment available to them (UnitingCare Australia 2000). If older people are being forced to retire younger and have access only to precarious employment, their ability to enhance their superannuation and savings for the future is extremely limited, if not impossible.

Another burden for older Australians is the lack of employment opportunities for their young adult children, who are staying home longer due to the lack of financial security and increased living expenses (UnitingCare Australia 2000). Many parents of retirement age or already retired are financially supporting their adult children, especially students. In addition, grandparents increasingly are taking on responsibility for their grandchildren because of their adult child's circumstances, which can include the cost of childcare, marital disruption, unemployment, illicit drug use, and physical or mental illness. Therefore older people are dispersing income while being expected to finance not only their own future but that of their children and grandchildren. The 'user pays' system is having intergenerational effects, which to date have not been fully explored (Hills 2004).

Social security policies

Failure to meet the increasing stringent requirements attached to social security benefits can have serious consequences for families, especially in moments of family crises (Curran, 2000). The Australian government has increasingly promoted the virtue of mutual obligation in respect to social security benefits. Tony Abbott, as Minister for Employment, Workplace Relations and Small Business said, in promoting the mutual obligation elements of the 'Work for the Dole' scheme, '[u]nconditional government benefits make as much sense as unconditional pocket money and good governments are no more in the business of just giving than good parents' (Abbott 2001a, p 37). The new Welfare-to-Work legislation (Commonwealth of Australia 2005a) is designed to get the long-term unemployed, single mothers and disabled people off welfare, and therefore is applied to a wider section of the population than just those receiving unemployment benefits. The effects of this legislation mean that single-parent families and people with medical and support needs will face harsh penalties if they breach job search requirements (Australian Council of Social Services 2005). This mutual obligation policy is creating further stress for the most disadvantaged in our community, many of whom would work if jobs were available. Sole parents will be required to actively seek employment, but as no childcare provisions have been put in place to assist in this process; these parents will be in danger of 'breaching' if they refuse a job because of lack of childcare places.

Although the Australian government is increasingly focusing on superannuation funds and retirement planning, there are concerns from welfare sector workers about the government's unrealistic expectations. UnitingCare Australia (2000) responded critically to Bronwyn Bishop's statement that people have a responsibility to save for their own retirement. However, those who spend much of their lives on welfare benefits cannot save for the future or invest in extra superannuation. Female baby boomers are especially disadvantaged, because they spend around 35 per cent less time in paid employment than their male counterparts, due to the unpaid care they provided for their husbands, children and other relatives (Stark 2005). For post-boomers also, there is a similarly large projected average gender gap in compulsory superannuation accumulations (Jefferson & Preston 2005). Many older single or widowed women will be compelled to live on meagre superannuation benefits or aged-care pensions because of these policies.

Conclusion

Some of the practices and policies based on neo-liberal principles have had a negative impact on the wellbeing of a substantial sector of Australian society, exacerbating the disadvantage experienced by low-income families and older people. Governments have removed key elements of social protection that once were part of building and supporting the whole community. As Birrell & Rapson (1997) state, poorer families are shouldering a major part of the burden of raising Australia's children, while middle-class and affluent children are gaining most of the benefits of economic recovery. This ignores social justice and equity principles. Adherents of neo-liberal principles, including senior members of State and Commonwealth go vernments, have promoted an ideology whereby the community does not feel responsible for ensuring that the society spreads its wealth and opportunities among its members. Policies based on neo-liberalism have not resulted in a more just or equitable society, but have had the reverse effect. It is time to re-examine the policies based on economic rationalism with a view to changing those that negatively affect vulnerable people.

Chapter 8

Unemployment at 29-year low: Why unemployment still matters

Margot Rawsthorne

In June, 2005 just over 500,000 people (5 per cent of the Australian workforce) were officially unemployed, a three-decade low (Australian Bureau of Statistics (ABS) 2005a, 2005b). So why is there a chapter on unemployment in a book about poverty in Australia today? Statistics, like the unemployment rate, tell only a partial story. The other part of this story is the individuals, families and communities struggling to cope with marginalisation from the mainstream economy. Official unemployment statistics mask the reality for thousands of Australians, and this chapter will show that unemployment continues to be a significant cause of poverty in Australia. Since the relatively full employment of the 1950s, 1960s and 1970s, unemployment has become a constant feature of the Australian social and political landscape, shaped by global processes. This chapter will argue that unemployment leads not only to material hardship but also erodes community, family and individual well-being. The significance of unemployment is highlighted below from two very different perspectives: the first is that of the Minister responsible for employment and workplace relations, and the second that of a 26-year-old unemployed man:

> Having a job provides far more than financial rewards; it is vital to a person's dignity and sense of worth (Andrews 2005).
>
> It's like being in a prison ... nowhere to go and nothing to do ... (Rawsthorne 1994, p 124).

Current policy approaches to unemployment are shaped by neo-liberal philosophies, which argue that job creation is underpinned by economic growth, fiscal responsibility (balanced budgets and debt reduction), and greater 'flexibility' in the labour market (Mendes 2003; Fenna 2004). Neo-liberalism assumes that once the environment is right for business expansion, new opportunities will be created for the unemployed: that the benefits of greater community wealth will 'trickle down' to those less fortunate in the community. This approach is a move away from earlier interventionist government efforts to create full employment.

However, the politically vaunted fruits of 15 years of 'triumph for the Australian economy' (Fenna 2004, p 279) and community wealth have not been evenly spread throughout our community. The trickle-down effect has done little to address entrenched disadvantage, and despite low official unemployment, the reality is that many people experience unemployment-related poverty. Importantly, international variations in unemployment rates suggest that 'countries do have a choice about the unemployment they are prepared to tolerate' (Peter Saunders 2002a, p 2), and that policy decisions alter the extent of unemployment and its associated poverty.

This chapter first looks at unemployment in Australia, examining the extent of the problem through discussion of current labour market statistics on unemployment and under-employment, the changing nature of the Australian labour force, and the groups most vulnerable to unemployment. It then explores the link between unemployment and poverty, including levels of income support. In its final sections the chapter turns to the costs of unemployment for communities, families and individuals. Suggestions for remedying the situation are made within the sections above, and in the conclusion.

Unemployment in Australia

The extent of the problem

The extent of unemployment in Australia is hidden by three interacting factors: the low official threshold of what constitutes 'employment', the growth in part-time and casual positions, and the significant number of people only marginally attached to the labour force.

First, it can be argued that official statistics underestimate the extent of unemployment, as a result of the definitions adopted. While in Australia the current official full-time working week is 38.5 hours, the Australian Bureau of Statistics (ABS) defines an 'employed person' as someone aged 15 years or over who, during a period of one week, worked for one hour or more for pay, profit, commission or payment in kind, or who worked for one hour or more without pay in a family business or on a family farm (Kryger 1998). The adoption of the one-hour threshold in 1986 has skewed official statistics towards 'counting a person as employed rather than as unemployed' (Kryger 1998, p 1).

At the same time, there has been a shift from full- to part-time employment. Despite 15 years of economic growth, Australia's performance in generating full-time jobs 'has been poor' according to the Australian Catholic Social Justice Council (2004, p 1). Gregory and Sheehan (1998) calculate that one full-time job in five has been lost since 1973, reflecting a decline in manufacturing and utilities sectors (Peter Saunders 1998; Gregory 2002). Employment growth over the past decade has been predominantly part-time or casual, in poorly paid and insecure jobs particularly in retailing and hospitality (Peter Saunders 2002a; Australian Catholic Social Justice Council 2004). Reflecting these trends, casual employment increased by 68 per cent in the 1990s.

The bias caused by the current official definition of employment and the disproportionate growth in part-time work is reflected in the findings of the Senate Community Affairs References Committee (SCARC), which reported that in September 2002, 628,500 people were officially unemployed, 672,100 were under-employed, and a further 808,100 people were marginally attached to the labour force or were discouraged job seekers (2005a, p 57): altogether 2,108,700 people. The term 'under-employment' is used by the ABS to refer to people working less than full-time (1 to 34 hours per week) but wanting to work more hours (Kryger 1998). Discouraged workers are defined by the ABS as those persons who do not satisfy the strict definition of unemployment but who want to work and are available for work but are not actively looking for work due to their age or lack of local jobs (ABS 2005b). The Australian Council of Social Services (ACOSS), a key advocate for the rights of disadvantage people, argues that if the hidden unemployed (including those under-employed or discouraged) are counted, the actual unemployment rate is about double that of official rates (2003a).

Who is affected by unemployment?

Within the overall unemployment figure, there are wide variations in unemployment rates between groups and communities, in that some groups vulnerable to unemployment than others. Reviewing the Australian literature, Taylor (2002) identified the following as important indicators of unemployment:

- having low levels of education;
- being young (aged 15-24 years);
- belonging to specific groups of non-English speaking background people (particularly Vietnamese and Lebanese);
- being Indigenous;
- having large numbers of children;
- having young children;
- being sole parents;
- having health and disability problems;
- living in areas with low socio-economic status;
- living in particular regional or remote areas.

Combinations of these factors (such as being young, Indigenous, and leaving school early) heighten the risks of both immediate and long-term unemployment. Some groups, especially mothers, mature-age people, Indigenous Australians and people with disabilities also have much higher than average rates of hidden unemployment (ACOSS 2003b).

Recent times have also seen three new unemployment phenomena: the emergence of 'workless families' in which no adult is employed, entrenched long-term unemployment, and the emergence of 'job rich' and 'job poor' regions throughout Australia (Gregory & Sheehan 1998; Vinson 2004; Peter Saunders 2005b). These characteristics are widely acknowledged and recognised as contributing to exclusion in a range of spheres, such as education, health, criminal justice, and employment.

The link between unemployment and poverty

Unemployment-related poverty refers not only to reduced income but also to the loss of individual, family and community opportunities. Whether poverty causes unemployment or unemployment causes poverty is a vexed and unanswered issue (Peter Saunders 1998; 2005b), but such academic debate should not draw attention from the harsh reality of life for many of those affected by unemployment.

In the early 1970s, Australia's first major inquiry into poverty highlighted the link between unemployment and poverty. The Commission of Inquiry into Poverty found workforce participation was a dominant and profound factor in determining poverty: only 3.9 per cent of non-aged adults in the workforce were defined as poor, compared to 30.9 per cent of those not in the workforce (Henderson 1975). A similar situation persists today. According to evidence provided to the Senate Poverty Enquiry (SCARC 2004) by the Brotherhood of St Laurence:

> [T]he lack of employment is the biggest single cause of poverty in Australia at the moment. It is a key area that needs to be looked at in any poverty inquiry (2003b, p 55).

Over 30 years after Henderson's work, research by the National Centre for Social and Economic Modelling confirms the continuing relationship between unemployment and poverty (Figure 8.1).

Similarly, recent research by the Smith Family confirms the link between unemployment and poverty, finding that more than half of unemployed Australians live in a family that is poor (Harding, Lloyd & Greenwell 2001, p 12). One critical factor in the poverty-unemployment link is length of unemployment. For example, drawing on unpublished data, Gregory & Sheenan (1998) reported a poverty rate of 13.2 per cent among those unemployed for less than seven weeks, 68.6 per cent for those unemployed between 39 to 51 weeks, and 79 per cent for those unemployed for more than a year.

Figure 8.1. Estimated poverty rates for people aged 15 and over by labour force status, 2001

Source: Lloyd, Harding & Payne 2004, p 15

This evidence suggests that greater attention be paid to unemployment. Current policy approaches to addressing employment have been through fiscal measures, wealth creation and labour market deregulation. However these approaches have not helped those people and communities left at the margins of the workforce, those suffering prolonged unemployment or insecure casual employment. As SCARC (2004) recently recommended, there is an urgent need for pro-active strategies aimed at creating full-time permanent jobs in those communities worst affected by unemployment. The committee drew on numerous overseas examples to recommend that this strategy should include training and long-term support to enable transition into these new jobs. This strategy is not a matter of 'handouts' from the government, but a matter of rights and the type of community in which we wish to live: 'Meaningful employment for the country's citizens is fundamental to their economic and social well-being, and also that of the nation' (SCARC 2004, p 64).

Poverty and income support

Historically, the Australian social security system has provided limited protection against 'life course contingencies, and the vicissitudes of personal life' (Shaver 2001, p 277). Accordingly, income support benefits have been set at levels designed to prevent absolute poverty and homelessness, while not acting as a disincentive to employment or as encouragement to non-productivity (Fenna 2004). Pressure to keep income support payments to a minimum has been increased by neo-liberal concerns about 'welfare dependency' (Mendes 2003, p 92).

In Australia there is no official or consensual view about how poverty should be measured, although over recent years there has been much academic debate about the 'true' level of poverty in Australia, with particular attention given to methods of measurement. While it is important to acknowledge its limitations, the 1970s Henderson Poverty Line measure remains an important indicator of poverty levels in Australia. The Henderson Poverty Line estimates how much money individuals and families of different sizes need to cover essential living costs. It is updated every three months based on figures provided by the Melbourne Institute of Applied Economic and Social Research at the University of Melbourne, and moves in line with average incomes (Brotherhood of St Laurence 2005). As is evident from Table 7.1 below, Social Security payments are considerably less than the current Henderson Poverty Line and are 'insufficient to meet the costs of a minimal standard of living' (Taylor 2002, p 81).

Table 8.1. The Henderson Poverty Line compared with Centrelink income support Australian dollars per week, quarter ending December 2004

Life circumstances Head in the workforce	Centrelink payments	Henderson Poverty Line	Difference	Income as % of poverty line
Single, away from home, 18-20 unemployed	$159.25	$318.48	-$159.23	50.0
Sole parent, unemployed, 1 child	$345.00	$408.87	-$63.87	84.4
Couple, unemployed, 3 children	$593.45	$684.29	-$90.84	86.7

Source: Brotherhood of St. Laurence, Information Sheet No 3, May 2005

As Table 8.1 suggests, life on current levels of income support is extremely difficult. Unemployed people experience financial hardship in meeting even basic costs such as food, while the effects of unemployment can quickly snowball from not having enough to eat, to being unable to pay bills and being unable to pay the rent. In such circumstances many unemployed people use savings (if any), sell assets, increase their debts, and rely on welfare agencies for assistance (Burke 1999; Talbot 1999). Research suggests that families and friends provide a very important 'safety net' for unemployed people (Douglas 2005; Eardley et al 2005). Unemployment for those isolated from families and friends and with few resources to draw on, can lead to homelessness and housing insecurity

(McCaughey 1992; Douglas 2005).The experience of agencies such as The Magdalene Centre highlights the shortcomings of current social security payment: '[M]any families with children view emergency assistance as a necessary survival strategy, in the face of inadequate financial resources to cover the basic cost of living' (Burke 1999, p 47).

The extent and effects of unemployment-related poverty suggest both the need for renewed focus on creating full employment, and the need for increased financial and other support for unemployed people and their families (Mitchell, Cowling & Watts 2003). The Centre for Full Employment and Equity advocates a 'new paradigm in employment policy', and describes current Australian policy approaches as 'roads to nowhere' (Mitchell, Cowling & Watts 2003, p 22). They, like other economists such as Peter Saunders (2005d), point to alternative approaches focusing on job creation in the public sector, approaches which have been adopted successfully in Europe as a means of addressing unemployment-related poverty (Mitchell, Cowling & Watts 2003). Norway, for example, adopted a Job Guarantee policy in 1993 to combat high and persistent levels of youth unemployment. This policy guaranteed young unemployed people six months employment funded by the government. Coupled with other training and education supports, this approach has seen a massive and sustained improvement in long-term unemployment rates among young people (Mitchell, Cowling & Watts 2003).

In recent years concern about 'welfare dependency' has seen progressively increasing obligations placed on income support recipients. Accompanying increased obligations has been increased use of financial penalties (widely known as 'breaching') for those who fail to meet their obligations (Eardley et al 2005). Poverty associated with unemployment and income support has been exacerbated by this expanded use of financial penalties for failure to meet 'participation' obligations (ACOSS 2001a; 2001b). Research by the Social Policy Research Centre found that financial stress was higher among those who had been breached (Eardley et al 2005). One unemployed person, Greg, 32 years old, who had been 'breached' described it this way:

> It's like you are in a hole and you've been given a shovel to dig yourself out and then all of a sudden you don't have the shovel now – here's a spoon (Eardley et al 2005, p 117).

ACOSS (2001a) and the Welfare Rights Network estimate that since 1997 the number of penalties imposed for infringements of social security rules has increased by 250 per cent, reaching 302,000 penalties in the 1999-2000 financial year. Almost 200,000 unemployed people and students were penalised in the year to 30 June 2000, with many being penalised more than once. Penalties range from a 16 per cent reduction of benefits for 13 weeks (administrative breach), to 100 per cent reduction for eight weeks (third activity breach). While more recent policy and procedural changes have slowed the growth of breach-related poverty

(Eardley et al 2005), a breach still has the potential to send individuals and families into severe poverty, as Noel, a 45-year-old Aboriginal man, describes:

> I had to change a lot of things, like you couldn't go out, um you sort of kept quiet you know ... there's not a lot you can do, you either buy meat or veggies or whatever to keep you going for the next fortnight if you can, so that's what I did. Once in a blue moon I would only pay $100 rent per fortnight [rather than $200] and use that to stock up on things like normal groceries and all that. I borrowed a few dollars from my ex, she was alright, like there is no problems or anything like that. A couple of times I even went to [charity], I got a food hamper, no money or nothing like that, just a food hamper, they were pretty good, like ham and little bits of food and that, some of the stuff were out of date by a couple of years and that but apart from that they helped me out at the time so I was grateful for it. (Eardley et al 2005, p 117)

If the dire effects of a 'breach' are to be avoided, much greater discretion and case management should be used by Centrelink, to reduce the likelihood of vulnerable individuals and groups plunging further into poverty.

The costs of unemployment

As discussed above, the costs of unemployment are borne by individuals, families, specific localities, and the broader Australian community. In the 2004-2005 Budget Papers, Treasury noted the multiple short and long-term costs of unemployment:

> [U]nemployment or non-participation in the labour force is a key contributor to relative poverty in the community; employed individuals and households tend to be more actively engaged in society and social activities; and a steady stream of income from regular employment provides individuals and households with greater opportunity to save, borrow and invest for their future and to contribute to the education of their children (Treasury 2005, p 1).

Those agencies providing emergency assistance to the unemployed in Adelaide described the cost of unemployment in terms of vulnerability (Talbot 1999). Unemployment means people have few resources to draw on when things go wrong:

> [Unemployment] progressively moves [people] into situations where they are excluded from, or unable to make use of, opportunities and networks that are available to other citizens (Talbot 1999, p 5).

While the individual and family costs of unemployment are often apparent, it is important that the broader implications of unemployment are not overlooked. These implications include the loss of social cohesion, and loss of a sense of belonging, trust and reciprocity – essential elements of healthy and wealthy democracies (Putnam 2005). Paradoxically, despite the Commonwealth Government's aversion to the notion of poverty in Australia (Peter Saunders 2005b), that government recognises the negative impact of prolonged unemployment on communities and the broader community:

> When people are out of work for long periods they can lose their skills, self-confidence and even their sense of belonging to a community. If this problem is widespread, it creates difficulties for families, neighbourhoods and communities (Commonwealth of Australia 2002a, p i).

The following sections discuss the impact of unemployment on community well-being, family well-being and individual well-being.

Community well-being

Community well-being is undermined by widespread and prolonged unemployment. The broad social effects of unemployment include increasing disparities of wealth and opportunities, under-utilisation of significant amounts of human resources in an economy facing an ageing workforce, and the diminution of social cohesion. The cost of unemployment to the broader community is a fractured society: a society of disparities in both wealth and opportunities. Over the past decade, the gap between those with well paid permanent employment and 'others' has increased (Weeks & Quinn 2000). At a time when many Australians are enjoying a higher quality of life than ever before, others are struggling to meet their basic needs. The social divide created by unemployment-related poverty is highlighted by the experiences of clients of welfare agencies:

> David and Stephanie and their two children need food and financial assistance. One child has a cold, the other an ear infection. All are really run down from not eating well because they have nowhere to cook. The family is living in their car since they were evicted from their private rental accommodation ... Living out of a car mean sustaining themselves on take-away food, and keeping moving around in their car to avoid hassles from the public and police. The family's health suffers greatly because of the poor living conditions, inadequate nutrition and sleep deprivation. The natural energy of small children is difficult to contain when you are living in a car (Burke 1999, p 42).

Government policies and rhetoric have contributed to the perception that unemployment is primarily an individual problem, arising not from structural changes in the labour force but from individual choice (Creed 1998; Mendes 2003). Initiatives such as the 'Fraud Tip-Off Line' and increased surveillance have contributed to a sense of alienation from the mainstream of community for those affected by unemployment (Leahy 2001).

Such a focus on individual responsibility distracts attention from the structural causes of unemployment. Some argue that this distraction inhibits the development of poverty reduction or elimination strategies in Australia, unlike in European countries such as Holland, Ireland and the United Kingdom. Numerous submissions to the Senate Inquiry into

Poverty and Disadvantage noted the importance a national anti-poverty strategy based on job creation and addressing structural issues in the economy (SCARC 2004).

Drawing on in-depth qualitative research into the experiences of people living in three working-class communities, Peel described 'the fathers and mothers of Inala, Broadmeadows and Mount Druitt as *bewildered*' (2003, p 115, emphasis added). They were at a loss to understand what they had done wrong, how their plans of working hard and making a better future for their children had gone so wrong. These were families affected by redundancy, business relocations, company closures, industrial change: changes in the name of efficiency and competitiveness. They were 'angry' about communities with entrenched unemployment (often double the official rate) being forgotten (Peel 2003, p 115). They feared that 'those outside' no longer saw unemployment as 'a shared tragedy ... [but] a necessary, if unfortunate, adjustment' (Peel 2003, p 116). Audrey, a resident of Inala, poignantly describes what it means to lived in a community affected by entrenched unemployment:

> I didn't teach [my kids] how to be poor ... I didn't teach them how to make do with whatever food you could find, didn't tell them to hand down clothes, you know, the things you have to do when you don't have any money. I didn't think they'd need to know. Well, I hoped they wouldn't anyhow. I guess I was wrong. I should have known better (Peel 2003, p 135).

The concept of 'those outside' points to the geographically concentrated nature of economic exclusion (Vinson 2004), with particular communities bearing a disproportionate burden of unemployment-related poverty. As Vinson (2004) and others (for example, ABS 2001b) have shown, rural and regional communities are particularly vulnerable to unemployment arising from changing occupation or industry structures. In these communities a key employer or industry often plays a central role in maintaining employment levels, population numbers and social infrastructure. If this industry withdraws or downsizes, as was the case of the steel industry in Newcastle, community well-being can be significantly affected. The loss of employment opportunities created directly or indirectly by key employers may exacerbate the out-migration of younger people, further reducing the social resilience and regenerative properties of these communities (ABS 2001b). Such structural economic changes are often aptly described as bringing about the death of a community. One consequence of living in a community affected by unemployment is exclusion from a 'word of mouth' employment network (Wilson 1987). Many jobs, particularly those of a short term or casual nature, are filled through personal networks. The loss of opportunity in communities affected by entrenched unemployment was not lost on young people, such as Geraldine's son:

> I sat down with my youngest son and I said to him 'What do you want to do when you leave school?' because he's off to high school next year, and I

figured now is the time he should be working out what he wants to do. He sits there and thinks about it and he goes, 'I'd like to do mechanics, Mum, but by the look of things these days, when I get to 16, 17, I'll be on the dole' (Peel 2003, p 133).

Another consequence of unemployment is the additional stress placed on community and welfare services. Major charities such as St Vincent de Paul, the Smith Family and the Salvation Army regularly report increased demand for emergency relief assistance and the changed nature of the individuals and families seeking this assistance (SCARC 2004). There are also health expenditure implications from unemployment, with international and Australian research documenting higher levels of hospital admissions, doctor visits, outpatient visits, and pharmaceutical use among the unemployed (Mathers & Schofield 1998). Other medical researchers (see, for example, Creed 1998) suggest that current levels of instability and insecurity in the labour market have a more generalised negative health affect, manifested through elevated stress levels.

Family well-being

Family well-being is adversely affected by unemployment. Apart from financial difficulties, the loss of status and identity is associated with high levels of family stress, which impacts in distinct ways, depending on which family member is unemployed. For families reliant on one male wage, unemployment of this breadwinner can have significant material, social and psychological effects on family well-being. Carol spoke of her husband's unemployment:

> My husband had always driven a crane ... he hadn't been unemployed in his life. His self-esteem went down the drain. It's terrible because they think that they're never going to work [again] ... It was really hard, to see a man that age asleep at half past three in the afternoon. He was really depressed. That's terrible. It breaks your heart to see a man who's brought home that amount of money laying on the floor doing nothing. He didn't feel like he wanted to do anything either, because he was depressed. The worst thing was, he felt he was letting *me* down (Peel 2003, p 126).

Clearly then, unemployment and its subsequent financial hardship and anxiety about the future place great strain on family relationships (Rawsthorne 1994; Taylor 2002). For example, a large-scale British study by Lampard in 1994 found a relationship between male unemployment and marital dissolution 'following the negative effects that both the financial and psychological impacts of unemployment have on family life' (cited in Taylor 2002, p 68).

There are also indirect and diffuse health effects of unemployment (Taylor & Morrell 2002). The World Health Organisation (WHO) defines health as 'not merely the absence of disease, but also a positive sense of physical, mental and social well-being' (WHO 2000, p 194). Thus family stress arising from unemployment may produce adverse health outcomes for children, by affecting parenting styles, and by restricting access to high quality child-care and preventive health activities (Vimpani 2001). An unemployed male's mental and physical ill-health is also likely to affect the well-being of his partner:

> My husband's not working, and I'm supporting him. He's going downhill, I can tell you. He's getting all these health problems. I don't want my husband to die, I don't want him to leave me (Peel 2003, p 127).

When the male 'breadwinner' is unemployed, women's experience of unemployment is often overlooked or diminished, including by women themselves. The women in Inala, Broadmeadows and Mt Druitt saw themselves, compared to their husbands, as 'more flexible, more able to adapt' to being part of the hidden unemployed or unemployed and taking whatever part-time casual jobs that were available to them (Peel 2003, p 121). Nevertheless, unemployment among women adds strain to the family, particularly if their employment brought much needed additional income into poor households, or if they were the sole wage earner. Poverty among female-headed sole parent families continues to be associated with unemployment and low paid positions (Shaver 1998). There remain few work opportunities that enable women with sole care of children to reconcile work and family responsibilities (Smyth, Rawsthorne & Siminski 2005). As mentioned previously, unemployment is highest among young people, who are usually part of families. Stress increases for families containing an unemployed young person, who is financially and to some extent emotionally dependent on the family (Taylor 2002). For low-income families in particular, additional financial strain is added to personal and social stresses. For the young people themselves, unemployment means a delay in achieving many of the milestones of adulthood, such as a place of their own, assets (such as cars), and privacy (Rawsthorne 1994; Taylor 2002).

Children growing up in families affected by unemployment-related poverty have been a focus of policy concern due to the short- and long-term impact of prolonged poverty on life opportunities (Peter Saunders 2005b, p 120). The Senate Poverty Enquiry concluded that child poverty 'remains a critical issue in Australia' (2004, p 266). In its submission, Mission Australia stated that in 2001, 7.5 per cent of all children aged under 15 were in families where no one worked: that is, 704,000 Australian children (SCARC 2004, pp 248-249). The Senate Poverty Enquiry also found that children growing up in households where no one works experience great material hardship, including poor access to nutritious food, and to adequate housing, clothing, toys and books. Additionally, children living in families affected by unemployment are often excluded from mainstream childhood experiences such as participating in sports or clubs, having family outings such as going to the movies, or learning skills such as music or dance. Treats or little luxuries that provide much-needed enjoyment or relief for a family under pressure are not an option for a family choosing what bill to pay and what food they can afford to purchase (SCARC 2004). Unemployment leading to food insecurity was highlighted by Julie Douglas' study of the struggles of poor families in the Playford region of Adelaide. One participant, Penny, commented:

> Bills? We never paid them on time because if we didn't have enough for food we had to take some out of the bill money ... After a while you get better at knowing how to do it. How much to pay on the bill to stop them cutting you off. How to talk to those people on the phone to tell them that you have kids you have to feed, how to arrange regular payments, stuff like that. Sometimes they don't listen though (Douglas 2005, p 53).

Current policies and programs that treat unemployed people in isolation from communities and families do little to protect family and community well-being. It follows, then, that support programs, including counselling, should be available to members of families affected by unemployment. These programs should focus on alleviating the health and educational impacts on children and young people living in families affected by unemployment. In the short term such policies could enable vulnerable families to remain intact, and in the longer term could prevent a cycle of poverty shaping the lives of children in poor families.

Individual well-being

Depending on their circumstances, unemployment for an individual can mean loss of income, inability to save, delay in attaining milestones, relationship stress and family stress. For most people, unemployment also has health consequences. The WHO argues that unemployment puts health at risk, and that unemployed people and their families suffer an increased risk of premature death (Vinson 2004). Similarly health researchers and others have shown that unemployment has adverse health effects, 'implying a link between poverty and health that operates via unemployment' (Peter Saunders 2005d, p 123).

For many men, particularly those over 40 years old, unemployment can be enormously distressing because work has played a key role in their identity. Peter Saunders (2005d, p 118) argues that men 'are often incapable of adjusting to the loss of capacity and purpose associated with the joblessness that triggers their poverty'. In Mount Druitt, support groups are run for men who have become too depressed to leave their homes and have developed agoraphobia (Peel 2003). The health worker involved commented that these unemployed men 'felt they had no place in the world any more' (Peel 2003, p 115). Older unemployed men who were aware that their future employment prospects were poor, felt far too 'young' to be retired, and often had previously felt pride in their ability as providers.

One of the most direct health effects associated with unemployment is the increased stress and anxiety, contributing to conditions such as insomnia, serious headaches and depression (Peter Saunders 1996). Research conducted in General Practitioners' waiting rooms (Harris et al 1998) found that compared to the employed, unemployed people were significantly more likely to report poor health, depression, anxiety, and insomnia. The same research also highlighted the limitations to their social activities due to physical and mental health problems. The study called on health workers to become advocates both in relation to the direct impact of unemployment on patients' well-being, and in relation to the indirect impact of stereotypes which contribute to poor self-esteem and mental health.

As argued earlier, current policy approaches do little more than sustain existence, with income support levels set at minimal levels to discourage welfare dependency. This low level of support has direct impact on individual well-being, affecting all levels of existence from access to basic needs such as shelter and food, to problems of emotional, social and physical well-being. Clearly then preventive strategies aimed at minimising the negative health outcomes should be supported and expanded. For example, stronger links between community services and health care providers would enable greater focus on the health outcomes of unemployment.

Conclusion

Unemployment and its associated poverty continue to affect the life opportunities of far too many Australians. More than a decade of economic growth has obscured the harsh reality of those affected by unemployment. The current culture of individual responsibility means that poverty and unemployment are no longer viewed as a 'shared tragedy' (Peel 2003, p 116); this culture has also led to increasing penalties for unemployed people 'breaching' regulations. These changes have undermined notions of community and belonging. It is clear that unemployment and its associated poverty add stress to already stressful lives. Individually the costs are immense in terms of both short-term and long-term material well-being, as well as exclusion from the mainstream of Australian society.

Existing policy approaches to unemployment-related poverty, shaped by concern about welfare dependency and neo-liberal economic theory, do little more than sustain the unemployed at subsistence level. As this chapter has argued, unemployment has broader consequences for community and family well-being. The lack of attention paid to these other consequences means that as a community we have failed to acknowledge the full extent of the damage caused by unemployment. The 'victims' may be the obvious bearers of the burden of unemployment, but the broader society is also burdened by increasing fragmentation.

The creation of full-time permanent jobs remains Australia's greatest policy challenge. Additionally, adopting rights-focused rather than responsibility-focused unemployment policies are more likely to assist individuals affected by unemployment and to build community and family well-being. A rights-focused approach requires comprehensive whole-of-government strategies aimed at preventing the social and economic exclusion of unemployed people and at supporting their transition to permanent full-time employment, thus providing an escape route from poverty.

Chapter 9

Poverty and crime

David Rose

The relationship between poverty and crime has been of critical concern in criminological research (Hale 2005), and has influenced government policy on crime prevention and reduction and the administration of the criminal justice system. Underlying the crime-poverty relationship are broader debates about the extent to which crime is a product of individual characteristics or of social, economic and cultural factors.

This chapter explores these issues, first by considering the extent to which poverty contributes to the commission of crime, and then by discussing the impact of socio-economic factors on people already involved in the criminal justice system. Finally the chapter explores the implications of these issues for policy development and for the implementation of programs to prevent crime and deal with offenders.

The poverty/crime connection

Although much data strongly suggest a relationship between poverty and crime, there is less understanding about the mechanisms of this association (Weatherburn 2004). Because any examination of the impact of poverty on crime is constrained by differing perspectives and political orientations, definitions and measurements of poverty vary and are often highly contested (Peter Saunders 2005b). Further, the term 'crime' encompasses a range of often socially constructed behaviours ranging from minor infringements to lethal acts (Weatherburn 2004). Contemporary examination of the poverty/crime association must also consider the arguments about the extent to which crime is seen as a result of individual factors, of environmental factors, or a combination of both: the extent to which 'nature' and 'nurture' influence crime.

Perspectives on what causes crime

A detailed critique of theories about what causes crime is beyond the scope of this chapter. These theories range from explanations invoking individuals' biological, physical, genetic, characterological and behavioural predispositions, through to environmental-focused explanations based on the impact of culture and economic structure. However, no one perspective can fully explain why people commit crimes, or explain all types of crime, and most recent approaches are multi-factorial, arguing that propensity to crime rests on a combination of factors. Evidence from multi-factorial and longitudinal studies are increasingly providing support for this multi-faceted view. (See, for example, Fergusson et al 2004). For example, meta-reviews of the precursors of anti-social behaviour by young people demonstrate that multiple factors are associated with antisocial behaviour, with different factors associated with different behaviours, and propensity for antisocial behaviour and offending is associated with the numbers and combinations of risk factors, rather than with single factors. Despite many strong associations, however, identifying causal mechanisms is far more difficult and often impossible (Rutter et al 1998).

Patterns of crime and the link to poverty

Areas of high socio-economic disadvantage tend to be more crime-prone (Vinson 2004), and a large proportion of offenders come from disadvantaged backgrounds (Borzycki 2005). However, this observation does not indicate a direct causal relationship: most people living in poverty do not commit crimes, and some people from advantaged socio-economic backgrounds do commit crimes (Hale 2005; White & Habibis 2005).

Before examining the current status of the poverty/crime debate, it is useful to overview the nature of offending in Australia. Data from the Australian criminal justice system indicate that first involvement in crime usually begins at age 12 to 16 years. Of this cohort, one group has one or two contacts with the juvenile justice system then appears to desist from offending, while the other group goes on to commit increasingly serious crimes and ultimately enters the adult criminal justice system (Weatherburn 2004). This pattern is demonstrated in longitudinal studies such as a Queensland project which followed 1,503 young offenders (aged 10 to 17) on supervision orders, starting in 1994-95. At follow-up in 2002, 79 per cent of the sample had progressed to the adult corrections system, with 49 per cent having served at least one term of imprisonment in the adult system (Lynch et al 2003). As many first offences occur prior to legal employment age, it can be seen that a direct causal link between unemployment and crime is problematic.

Nevertheless, unemployment, an element of poverty, is one of the most researched areas of the poverty/crime interface (Weatherburn 2002). Unemployment has been shown in some major studies, mostly in the 1970s and 1980s, to be linked to increased property crime, although this has not been a consistent finding (Box 1987; Chiricos 1987; Land et al 1995). Arguing that much of the inconsistency in findings is because most studies are at the aggregate level, Chapman et al (2002) examined a subgroup of young Australian males who were long-term unemployed (more than 12 months), rather than unemployed per se. Results showed a significant association between long-term unemployment and property crime, and an even stronger association with failure to finish secondary school (Chapman et al 2002).

Despite the evidence of a direct unemployment-crime link for groups such as young unskilled long-term unemployed males, increasing evidence suggests that the indirect impact of unemployment on crime is more critical (Weatherburn 2002). That is, unemployment is a cause of poverty and disadvantage in families, creating a situation that can increase the risk of young people committing crimes (Weatherburn & Lind 1998). Furthermore, Hale (2005) argues that it is now more critical to examine a range of other factors such as inequality in labour market participation. This argument was made in the context of changes in the UK (as could be argued for Australia) in the past three decades of increasing inequality between the richest and the poorest, a rapidly changing labour market with more part-time and temporary positions, and welfare reforms designed to get people off welfare and into work, with sanctions such as loss of benefits for non-compliance.

As Weatherburn (2004) argues, there can now be little doubt that poverty, unemployment and socio-economic disadvantage within families are risk factors for young people first committing crimes and becoming involved in the criminal justice system, but this is not a direct causal link. In a study of the association between economic stress, parenting and juvenile offending in New South Wales, path analysis indicated a very small direct association between parental poverty and juvenile offending, a higher association between parental poverty and neglect of children, and an even higher association between neglect and juvenile offending. The researchers concluded that the likely crime-poverty pathway lies in the impact of poverty on parents' ability to care for their children, which may lead to increased risk of juvenile offending, in the context of a number of other risk factors (Weatherburn & Lind 1998).

One approach to crime prevention is developmental criminology, which focuses on the multiple risk and protective factors that influence young people to first commit crimes and behaviours such as illicit drug use. Research indicates that critical factors include level of parental support and control (Spooner et al 2001; Farrington 2002). That is, families living in poverty are likely to find it more difficult to provide their children with appropriate levels of support and control, and with opportunities to use 'protective' community structures such as school, sport and recreation (Weatherburn 2004). This view is supported by longitudinal studies which have identified both individual and structural precursors to offending (see, for example, Fergusson et al 2004).

Evidence also shows that areas of high poverty, unemployment and income inequality are often associated with higher levels of certain crimes (Stretesky et al 2004). Among several explanations of this link (see, for example, Sampson 1995; Bottoms & Wiles 2002; Weatherburn 2004),

Vinson's (2004) study of postcode areas in Victoria and New South Wales found both geographical pockets of significant disadvantage, and strong correlations between factors such as unemployment and court convictions, and unemployment and imprisonment.

In summary, the historical debates and their supporting data make it difficult to reach firm conclusions about the poverty/crime connection. However, it is known that the majority of people who commence on an offending pathway first commit crimes during their teenage years, and the likelihood of this occurring is linked to a range of risk and protective factors at individual, family and community levels. It is likely that poverty and socio-economic factors impact on juvenile offending via their indirect effect on the family's capacity to provide support and structure to children, and on the ability to access community resources likely to have a protective component.

The criminal justice system

While the extent to which poverty is a factor in people first committing crimes is contested, there is little doubt that being involved with the criminal justice system can result in significant levels of poverty and socio-economic disadvantage. This section examines the situation of people already involved in the criminal justice system. For this group, particularly those who have been in prison, poverty and associated disadvantage is a key issue, either as a risk factor for further crime, or because having a criminal history often leads to exacerbation of poverty, for example, through difficulty obtaining work and adequate housing. This process can lead to a vicious cycle of considerable disadvantage following release from prison, followed by re-offending and imprisonment, further entrenching disadvantage. Although this section focuses on the impact of imprisonment, it is noted that significant numbers of people in Australia are subject to non-custodial sentences, which due to the stigma associated with offending can still affect areas such as capacity gain employment.

Characteristics of prisoners and imprisonment

Recent years have seen substantial increases in the imprisonment rate in most developed countries. In the US at the end of 2004 the imprisonment rate was 724 per 100,000 population, a 17 per cent increase since 1995 (Bureau of Justice Statistics 2005). In England and Wales in 2004, the imprisonment rate was 142 per 100,000, a 52 per cent increase since 1994 (Home Office 2005, pp 97-106). Table 9.1 shows that in Australia the overall imprisonment rate is 162 per 100,000 population, a 45 per cent increase over ten years. Recidivism is high, with 60 per cent of prisoners at 30 June 2005 in Australia having served a prior sentence in an adult prison. Indigenous people are on average 12 times more likely than

Table 9.1. Imprisonment rates & prior imprisonment, Australia 2005

	NSW	Vic	Qld	SA	WA	Tas	NT	ACT	Aust
Rate per 100,000	188	94	178	123	229	150	575	110	162
Previously imprisoned	62%	52%	66%	55%	56%	65%	65%	63%	60%

Source: ABS 2005c, pp 14, 29

non-Indigenous people to be imprisoned, with an overall Aboriginal imprisonment rate of 1560 per 100,000 (Australian Bureau of Statistics (ABS) 2005c).

Prisoners and poverty

Prisoners and ex-prisoners are among the most disadvantaged people in society. Although official socio-economic data for prisoners are limited and some data are anecdotal, it is known that in Victoria in 2004 around 61 per cent of male prisoners and 80 per cent of female prisoners were unemployed at entry into prison. Only 10 per cent of male and 27 per cent of female prisoners had completed secondary education (Department of Justice 2005).

A 2003 Victorian study (Department of Justice 2003) on a representative sample of 500 prisoners showed alarming indicators of disadvantage: 75 per cent were living on a pension or benefit prior to imprisonment; 71 per cent reported having used illicit drugs; 41 per cent met the criteria for alcohol abuse or dependence; before imprisonment about half were living in rented accommodation; 26 per cent met at least one diagnostic criterion for mental illness; 5-7 per cent were living in 'unsettled' lodgings and around 5 per cent had no fixed abode.

Major reviews of the issues for prisoners re-integrating into the community recently completed in the UK (SEU 2002), the US (Re-entry Policy Council 2004) and Australia (Borzycki 2005) have all concluded that most prisoners have low levels of education, poor or non-existent employment histories, significant health issues, histories of unstable housing and/or homelessness, difficulties with attitudes and self-control, poor or no family and social support, financial problems, and inadequate life-skills owing to long/frequent periods of incarceration. Many of these factors pre-dated incarceration, with many prisoners having experienced a lifetime of disadvantage. It is also clear that the imprisonment experience itself can exacerbate many poverty-related factors, such as losing accommodation and employment while in prison (Borzycki 2005).

In summary, imprisonment itself results in significant social and economic disadvantage. With increasing imprisonment rates in many developed countries, increasing numbers of highly disadvantaged people are likely to be caught in a cycle of re-offending and marginalisation from the community.

Policy and program responses

This section examines the crime prevention policy and program responses typically implemented by governments in countries like Australia. Broadly, these initiatives have two aims: to prevent crimes and to reduce recidivism.

Crime prevention

Farrington (2002 pp 657-58) identifies four key approaches to crime prevention:

- *developmental prevention* focuses on preventing the development of criminal tendencies in the young;
- *community prevention* focuses changes to social conditions;
- *situational prevention* focuses on reducing the opportunity for crime;
- *criminal justice prevention* focuses on how people who commit crimes are dealt with by the criminal justice system.

Common policy responses of governments in countries like Australia follow these four approaches. Before examining the Australian government policy responses to crime prevention, however, it is useful to examine policy developments in the UK over the past ten years, as Australia is often influenced by UK developments. In 1999 the Blair Government launched the Crime Reduction Program, which both increased penalties for a range of crimes, and increased funding for crime-reduction activities, focusing on areas such as preventative programs with children and families, and neighbourhood renewal projects (Homel 2004). The Blair Government's mantra 'Tough on Crime, Tough on the Causes of Crime' has been repeated by the Commonwealth and most State governments in Australia (Borzycki 2005).

In 1997 the Blair Government also established the Social Exclusion Unit (SEU), describing social exclusion as 'a shorthand term for what can happen when people or areas suffer from a combination of linked problems such as unemployment, poor skills, low incomes, unfair discrimination, poor housing, high crime, bad health and family breakdown' (SEU 2004, p 4). SEU strategies include employment support and training programs for the unemployed and low-paid, a national minimum wage, financial support to reduce child poverty, early intervention programs for children in high risk situations, and neighbourhood renewal programs (SEU 2004). According to Hale (2005), through such policy directions, the relationship between poverty and crime has re-emerged as an issue of concern.

However, the focus on social exclusion is not without critics. Young (2002) argues that while the concept of social exclusion acknowledges the structural factors that contribute to exclusion, a key driver is also the right-wing influenced notion of the 'underclass' of welfare-dependant people who choose not to work or contribute to society and tend towards crime and drug use (see, for example, IEA 1996). According to Hale (2005), in practice the SEU strategy targets 'inadequate' families and individuals for back-to-work programs, and applies sanctions for non-compliance. While the Commonwealth Government's current Welfare to Work package (DEWR) is not linked to an explicit social exclusion strategy, it shares an emphasis on the need to move people from welfare into work.

In Australia, the Commonwealth Government provides some national leadership in crime prevention initiatives, but primary responsibility rests with the State and Territory governments (Australian Government Attorney-General's Department nd). In general, Commonwealth initiatives tend to focus on 'at risk' populations, for example, by providing parenting support for 'high risk' families, while the State government initiatives tend to focus on making communities safer.

The Commonwealth Government's National Crime Prevention Program, while acknowledging that socio-economic disadvantage can be a risk factor (National Crime Prevention 1999), studied individual child, family, school, critical life events and community factors, and outlined the role of risk and protective factors in early childhood as potential precursors to crime. Programs consistent with this framework include early intervention programs established through State-based crime prevention departments, and initiatives such as the Commonwealth Government's Stronger Families and Communities Strategy (FACS nd). Critics of this approach argue that it has the potential to become a way of monitoring and controlling marginalised families living in poverty (France & Utting 2005).

Major State-based initiatives in Australia have focused on situational prevention, such as educating people on how to make themselves harder targets for crime, and on community prevention activities such as better recreational facilities for young people in crime-prone neighbourhoods (Grant & Grabosky 2000). A typical State policy direction on crime prevention in Victoria (Crime Prevention Victoria 2002) includes three priority areas: improving safety in streets and neighbourhoods, preventing family violence and improving safety in the home; reducing offending and violence by young people; establishing various activities aimed at reducing number of young people who start to commit crimes, including strengthening families at risk.

Thus while government policies acknowledge the socio-economic impacts on offending, crime prevention still mostly focuses on individuals/families at risk and on environmental changes in crime-prone areas. As Weatherburn (2004) points out, while it is justifiable to target interventions towards people or areas 'at risk', the structural factors in society that might be contributing to this risk should not be overlooked.

Prisoner rehabilitation and release

The other key area of government policy and programs is securing and rehabilitating offenders. There are two concurrent trends in how offenders are dealt with in developed countries like Australia. First, aligned with the 'tough on crime' policy, more people are being imprisoned, more prisons are being built, and other community-based options, such as diversion programs and community-based orders, are expanding. Second, there have been increases in psychologically-based treatment programs developed in prisons and the community with the aim or rehabilitating offenders.

As McGuire (2004) contends, the criminal justice pendulum swings between punitive and rehabilitative foci, in co-ordination with community and government views on effectiveness of the criminal justice system. Kendall (2002), a critic of the new focus on individual rehabilitation programs, argues that while initially the two trends may seem incompatible, on closer examination they are consistent with the prevalent political ideologies in countries such as the US, UK and Australia. On the one hand there is a focus on law and order, toughness on crime, and maintaining the social order. On the other hand, the focus on individual treatment programs for offenders perpetuates the notion that people have freewill to make responsible and rational life choices, and therefore that offending can be attributed to faulty thought processes and poor decision-making.

In Australia responsibility for criminal justice administration rests largely with the States, and the Victorian *Corrections Long Term Management Strategy 2001-2006* (OCSC 2002) demonstrates many of the issues raised above. The strategy notes Victoria's increasing prison population, with the prison population rising by 45 per cent from 1996 to 2002, partly due to recidivism rising by 3 per cent per year. It is also notes that:

> [P]risoners are exhibiting an increasingly complex profile. More than 80 per cent have drug or alcohol problems, with backgrounds of social disadvantage, low education, high unemployment, significant health issues (including mental illness) and poor family and social links. The need for new solutions is urgent. (OCSC 2002, p 2)

Consistent with international trends, the OCSC document identifies three key strategies to meet this need: construction of new larger prisons to replace older prisons and increase capacity; an increase in community-based corrections; an expansion of offender behaviour programs to reduce re-offending.

While the centrepiece of the reducing re-offending strategy is psychologically-based behaviour programs (Birgden & McLachlan 2004), some new programs do focus on housing and employment support, which at least acknowledges the impact of these factors. Nevertheless, as already noted, prisoner rehabilitation programs in Australia, New Zealand, the UK, Canada and the US have increasingly moved towards individually-focused, cognitive-behavioural treatment interventions targeting attitudes and thinking patterns, although supporting evidence is variable. For example in the UK Falshaw et al (2003) found no differences in the two-year reconviction rates for prisoners who had been through such programs in 1996-98, compared to a matched comparison group who had not undertaken the programs.

As the rise in the use of such programs goes to the heart of many issues discussed in this chapter, it is useful to examine the precursors to this development. In 1974 a US criminologist, Robert Martinson, made the infamous contention that 'nothing works' in offender rehabilitation (Martinson 1974). In response, from the late 1980s the 'What Works?' movement grew, based on research showing that cognitive-behavioural interventions could reduce some individuals' likelihood of re-offending (McGuire 1995). These programs assess offenders' 'level of risk' of re-offending, by identifying the 'dynamic risk factors' (factors that can be changed) for offending, such as impulsivity or poor problem solving skills. These risk factors are then addressed through cognitive-behavioural therapies (McGuire 1995).

As Hollin (2002) comments, psychology (with its focus usually on the individual) and criminology (with a strong tradition in championing the structural causes of crime) have often been opposed. However the emergence of the 'what works' approach and development criminology, has refocused both psychology and criminology on the traits of individuals as a cause of crime. Kendall (2002) argues that the focus on cognitive deficits discounts the impact of any other factors on crime, stigmatises offenders even further as somehow inherently 'different' from the rest of society, and makes any realistic attention to structural factors unlikely. 'Ultimately, cognitive behaviourism is a government technology which obscures the pains of social exclusion and imprisonment' (Kendall 2002, p 198).

Perhaps in response to such criticisms, there has recently been increased attention on examining post-release factors such as employment and housing, as well as on the prison-based rehabilitation programs (Raynor 2002). For example, the Melbourne Criminology Research and Evaluation Unit suggests in its evaluation of the Victorian Bridging the Gap program (a pilot transitional support program for prisoners) that:

> The provision of material support to people who do not want to change or understand how to change will be ineffective. Encouraging change in people who are bowed down by the struggle to find food and shelter will be ineffective. (2003, p 27)

Approximately 44,000 people are released from prisons in Australia each year (Baldrey et al 2003). Given the profile of prisoner populations, it is critical for the successful transition of prisoners back into the community that they have access to adequate housing, employment, income, and support; these elements are often unavailable to many prisoners released in Australia (Ward 2001). Although what is effective in supporting ex-prisoners has been notoriously difficult to determine, there is increasing evidence that addressing socio-economic factors such as housing and employment can help reduce recidivism. Baldrey et al's (2003) study of the housing experiences of ex-prisoners in New South Wales and Victoria found that a key predictor of re-imprisonment was transient and unstable accommodation. Being homeless (of the sample 17 per cent were homeless before and 21 per cent after release) was also strongly associated with re-offending.

The review of re-offending conducted in the UK by the SEU (2002) found that employment reduces the risk of re-offending by between a third and a half. Closely associated with employment is stable accommodation, which reduces the risk of re-offending by around 20 per cent. Interventions, pre- and post-release, addressing individual thinking patterns and attitudes reduce offending by up to 14 per cent.

Desistance from crime, a recent UK concept receiving increased attention, is concerned with the changes needed in a person's life if he is to desist from offending. This approach recognises that both individual and environmental changes are likely to be needed (Farrall & Maruna 2006; Farrall & Sparks 2006; Maguire & Raynor 2006), so that desistance and rehabilitation efforts must take into account both individual readiness to change and access to social and economic resources and opportunities (Maguire & Raynor 2006). Nevertheless, as Drakeford and Vanstone (2000, p 379) suggest, 'Rehabilitation outside any policy about the redistribution of opportunity of outcome is likely to be seriously flawed'. Dealing with the high levels of socio-economic disadvantage experienced by prisoners/ex-prisoners is beyond the capacity of the criminal justice system alone, and goes to the heart of how society addresses issues such as poverty and access to basic needs such as adequate housing.

In summary, contemporary government crime prevention policies and programs have tended to focus on strategies such as supporting 'high risk' families, making communities safer, and providing rehabilitation for offenders. While most of these initiatives implicitly recognise that poverty, inequality and unemployment are connected to crime and crime prevention, the extent to which these factors are addressed at a structural level is limited. In particular, over the past decade prisoner rehabilitation has moved increasingly towards individual psychological-based interventions, notwithstanding the repeated observation that prisoners often experience substantial and pervasive socio-economic disadvantage.

Conclusions

There is a complex and multi-faceted relationship between poverty and crime. Further, people already involved in the criminal justice system experience high levels of poverty, and such poverty severely limits chances of rehabilitation. While these relationships between poverty and crime are to some extent recognised in government policy, most initiatives target high-risk individual factors rather than overall levels of poverty and inequality in the community. This is not surprising, given the continuing debate in criminology about the extent to which the poverty/crime association is causal, or whether some individuals are more prone to crime and poverty. It can be argued that recent trends have seen the pendulum swinging strongly to the side of an individual deficits approach, resulting in the proliferation of psychologically-based approaches to rehabilitating offenders.

The need for some form of individually-focused interventions, such as the psychological treatment programs, with young people at risk of offending and those people who have offended, is not contested here. However, it is critical that the structural factors that impact on offending do not get lost in this increasing focus on the individual. Many offenders in countries like Australia come from highly disadvantaged backgrounds, and often continue on a cycle of increasing disadvantage and marginalisation due to their imprisonment. While it is clearly important that these factors are recognised in the administration of the criminal justice system, in many respects they traverse the bounds of crime prevention and criminal justice policy to represent the ways the broader society deals with issues of poverty, inequality and disadvantage.

Chapter 10

The impoverishment of a people: The Aboriginal experience in Australia

Sue Green

As Australia is a continent with rich natural resources to distribute among a relatively small population, one would think that no Australians should have to live in poverty. However, poverty continues in Australia today, and the Aboriginal people are the poorest Australians on every socio-economic indicator, and are among the poorest in the world (Brennan 2006). Statistics tell us that a disproportionate percentage of Aboriginal Australians are born into poverty and die in poverty, with little else in between. The chances are high that from the moment an Aboriginal baby is born, his or her life chances and opportunities will be severely limited. Compared to a non-Aboriginal infant, an Aboriginal child has a higher chance of infant mortality and infant illnesses, and a life expectancy approximately 20 years less than the national average (Australian Bureau of Statistics 2001a). It is generally recognised that education improves life chances. An Aboriginal child's likelihood of receiving a basic education, let alone completing high school, is low: Aboriginal children are twice as unlikely as non-Aboriginal children to complete schooling (Australian Bureau of Statistics 2001a). In turn, lack of education reduces their chances of gaining employment – and not just a well-paid job, but any job at all. Aboriginal unemployment rates are many times higher than any other group of Australians (Commonwealth of Australia 2002b). With little prospect of employment, Aboriginal people also face poorer housing and health.

This poverty does not stop with one generation: as parents are unable to move out of poverty, their children continue to suffer it. This means living in inadequate and overcrowded housing (Commonwealth of Australia 2002b), having poor access to services that non-Aboriginal children accept as their right, and living in an environment of apparent hopelessness. In other words, Aboriginal people are continually excluded from the benefits of Australian society. A common rhetoric of many politicians and community commentators paints Aboriginal people as entirely responsible for their situation, and therefore the problem itself: 'the Aboriginal problem'.

Many influential commentators are arguing that the causes of the highly disadvantaged situation that Aboriginal people are in have been created by Aboriginal peoples' dependency. If the problems are to be solved, they say, Aboriginal people have to be forced away from dependency and to become socially responsible citizens – like other Australians. This approach is hailed as welfare reform and Aboriginal people are being invited to take responsibility for these 'problems'. If they do not do so willingly, they should be punished with further exclusion. This so-called reform is not new, but has been revisited upon Aboriginal people a number of times since 1788. With each visitation the poverty of Aboriginal people has become further entrenched.

This chapter will argue that this situation is the result of a long process of dispossession and exclusion, and Aboriginal people continue to experience exclusion from Australian society on every level. This exclusion is nowhere more notable than in their poor economic status. In the current political climate there has been much talk about welfare reform and policy directions that aim to end welfare dependency among Aboriginal people and communities. However, when these policies and programs are considered within a historical context, one has to question whether these so-called new polices are either new or progressive. Many have suggested that the new policies are in fact regressive and represent a return to the not-so-distant past.

It is also argued here that because the experience of poverty for Aboriginal people is different from the experience of other Australians, the way in which poverty is defined needs also to be different. In traditional terms, absolute poverty means lacking the necessities of life, while relative poverty refers to the level to which one is able to participate, within the norms of daily life (Madden 2000; Duclos & Gregorie 2003). Absolute poverty is thus primarily concerned with material deprivation such as inadequate access to food, water and shelter, while relative poverty is non-material in that it relates to inadequate access to normative standards of living (Choo 1990). As the Australian Bureau of Statistics stated:

> To be relatively poor is thus to be forced to live on the margins of society, to be excluded from the normal spheres of consumption and activity which together define social participation and national identity (1996, p 10).

For most Australians poverty is more relative than absolute (Johnson 2002). Unlike most other Australians, many Aboriginal people experience both relative and absolute poverty, unable to access either a decent standard of living or necessities such as food, water and shelter. This chapter will show that the poverty Aboriginal people experience today has its roots in their experience of invasion, colonisation, and dispossession, and will argue that the ensuing government policies ensure that Aboriginal people continue to experience both absolute and relative poverty.

Past policies and Aboriginal poverty

A number of stages can be discerned in the history of Aboriginal poverty: invasion and dispossession, protection, assimilation, integration, the growth of a rights movement, self-determination, and self-management. Each of these stages is discussed below, showing how the poverty enforced on Aboriginal people with the arrival of the First Fleet has remained and even grown throughout all policy changes.

Invasion and dispossession

In January 1788 the Eora people were about to experience a catastrophe on a scale they could have never imagined. Eleven ships arrived in what was to be later called Port Jackson, bringing with them a cargo of humans that was to change the lives of the Eora forever (Day 2005). Within one hundred years the suffering of the Eora had spread across the rest of the continent. While the exact numbers of Aboriginal people on the continent in January 1788 cannot be known, what is known is that the population went into a catastrophic decline that would continue for at least 150 years (Girling 1983; Reynolds 2001). Once Europeans decided to settle the new continent, poverty for the Aboriginal people was inevitable. Indeed even before the British arrived, they had started developing policies about the Aboriginal people. When Phillip set sail for Australia the instructions he received were:

> To endeavour by every possible means to open an intercourse with the natives, and to conciliate their affections, enjoying all our subjects to live in amity and kindness with them. And if any of our subjects shall wantonly destroy them, or give them any unnecessary interruption in the exercise of their several occupations, it is our will and pleasure that you do cause such offenders to be brought to punishment (cited in Egan 1999, p 27).

Although these instructions sound benign, their application was far from benign, and began the long decline of Aborigines into poverty and disadvantage. Certainly Phillip followed instructions and attempted and to some extent developed intercourse with the Aboriginal people. Unfortunately the manner in which he did this showed a complete lack of respect for Aboriginal people. Phillip and his contemporaries demonstrated that they saw Aboriginal people as uncivilised and childlike, needing instructions in how to live and behave (Inglis 1974; Reece 1974; Yarwood 1977). For example, at first Phillip instructed that adult men be captured so that he could engage with them, and when men did not come willingly, they were tied up and held captive until they submitted (Egan 1999). The outcomes for each of these men differed but the results that Phillip had hoped to achieve were not forthcoming. Thus Phillips and others turned their attention to the children, and some Aboriginal schools were established (Yarwood 1997).

However, the schools were deemed failures, because Aboriginal people refused to freely send their children and many of the children who were taken fled back to their families. During this early stage of the colony, Aboriginal people were seen as being somewhat less than human, an attitude used to justify the killing of Aboriginal people (Inglis 1974). Under such an onslaught, Aboriginal people inevitably began their long sojourn in poverty. Inevitable, because the colonial authorities had removed from the Aboriginal people what was essential for their well-being (Baldry & Green 2003). The Aboriginal people's losses included the death of many of their people, access to their traditional lands and sacred sites, and connection with the next generation who would continue the traditions of Aboriginal society. In this way the entire basis of Aboriginal society was fractured, and this cultural fracturing marked the beginnings of the impoverishment of Aboriginal Australian people and society. From the point of dispossession, Australian colonial, State and federal governments have developed and implemented policies that reinforced the dispossession and impoverishment of Aboriginal people.

Protection

During the early colonial period Aboriginal people experienced extreme hardship, including frequent attacks on groups and individuals, new diseases for which they had no immunity, and being forced from their traditional lands and away from sources of food and water. All this resulted in illness, starvation and dehydration, resulting in the death of many people and extreme hardship for the survivors.

As awareness grew of what was happening, many people in Britain and a few within New South Wales and all British colonies were appalled by what was occurring. In response to the outcry, in July 1835 the British Government set up a Select Committee, whose findings resulted in the first official policy pertaining to Aboriginal people: protectorates (Baldry & Green 2003). Every Australian colony set up protectorates as instructed. The protectorate system was, at least in original intent, a humanitarian venture in which the protectors believed that they were positioning themselves between the Aboriginal people and the settlers.

But in Australia the protectorates were never humanitarian ventures: rather than 'protect' Aboriginal people, the protection system simply regulated their lives, herding them onto reserves and missions, with large numbers in rural areas being restricted to pastoral stations. Thus under nineteenth century protection policies Aboriginal people were forced into dependency on the state; their economy consisted of rations handed out by police, missionaries, reserve managers and pastoralists. Contrary to the boasts of the protectorship, conditions for Aboriginal people during this time deteriorated further. Aboriginal health, housing and education were described as abysmal, and employment other than manual labour was non-existent (The Gungil Jindibah

Centre 1994). The system of protectorships did not address the absolute poverty that Aboriginal people experienced because of their dispossession. Instead it further removed Aboriginal people from being able to access the basics of life such as food, water and shelter, and forced them into reliance upon the state and charities for their daily survival. In practice, therefore, the system was a dire failure, and the task of the protectors was as much to protect the white population from the Aboriginal population, as the other way around. The only trace of humanitarianism lay in the protectors' role as agents of 'the pillow under the head of a dying race'. Because this 'dying race' theory was widely held at the time, 'white' society in general felt no need or responsibility for addressing the dismal conditions of the Aboriginal people, who were seen as relics from the past, destined to die out through a Darwinian 'survival of the fittest' process (Haebich 2000). Thus it was seen as natural that Aboriginal people were dying and that they would eventually pass from the face of the earth.

Assimilation

By the 1930s, the Aboriginal people had not died out; indeed numbers were increasing. However it was still widely believed by white society that 'full-blood Aborigines' were dying out and that 'half-castes' and 'mixed bloods' were a growing problem and should be removed from Aboriginal camps and settlements so that they could be made more acceptable to white society (Reynolds 2005). But, as it became evident that Aboriginal people were not going to die out and that the conditions that they were living under were unacceptable for any human, a growing number of Aboriginal people and their non-Aboriginal supporters become more militant with their demands. Thus governments, bureaucrats, anthropologists and others considered yet again how to deal with the 'Aboriginal problem'. Informed by 'scientific' thinking in Britain and Europe, the favoured solution was to absorb Aboriginal people into the general population (Reynolds 2005); if they did not exist, they would no longer be a problem (Baldry & Green 2003). This assimilation policy:

> [S]tated that Aboriginal people 'are expected' to adopt 'the same' manner of living as white Australians, and implicit in its aims was an end to Aboriginal cultural traditions, identity, community and family solidarity and claim to any 'separate' existence in Australian society (The Gungil Jindibah Centre 1994, p 25).

Much of what had occurred under protectionism continued under assimilation. The aim was once again to 'fix' Aboriginal people. Children continued to be removed, as there was a school of thought that if you could remove Aboriginal children at a very young age and place them with non-Aboriginal families, then those children would grow up having no knowledge of or connection with their Aboriginality.

Although policies and practices varied across the States and Territories the aims and impact were much the same in the long term, and New South Wales will be taken as an example of the continuing dissolution of Aboriginal society. Both Aboriginal adults and children were being encouraged to move away from Aboriginality, Aboriginal children through their removal into non-Aboriginal families and institutions, and Aboriginal adults through the granting of exemption certificates. Exemption certificates were introduced in 1943, and to be eligible an Aboriginal person had to show that he or she could behave like a 'white' person and break off any contact with other Aboriginal people including family (Hollinsworth 1998). These certificates claimed to recognise the standards of development and intelligence of the holder and gave the holder the same rights as all other citizens of Australia. Those exempted were not entitled to any rations, payments or support that was provided for the welfare of Aboriginal people. In addition people with exemptions were not allowed to live on or visit missions and reserves for Aboriginal people. For many this requirement meant losing the only places they had ever known as home, and where all their family members lived.

Despite official claims, Aboriginal people granted exemption certificates failed to gain access to the rights and privileges of non-Aboriginal society, in no small part because of entrenched racism and discrimination in non-Aboriginal society (The Gungil Jindibah Centre 1994). Aboriginal people removed from the missions and reserves ended up on the fringes of townships, and access to housing, education and employment was still extremely limited (Baldry & Green 2003). Regardless of exemption certificates, Aboriginal people were largely excluded from social, cultural and political life in Australia (Hollingsworth 1998), thus ensuring that they were highly vulnerable to exploration, including economic exploitation where Aboriginal people were only employed in unpaid or poorly paid work. In addition the Aborigines Welfare Board aimed to make Aboriginal people 'rural workers and domestics', thus locking them out of the economic prosperity enjoyed by other Australians in the post-war years (The Gungil Jindibah Centre 1994). In these ways Aboriginal people were further impoverished, and the NSW government's policies, aims and programs continued to ensure that the poverty was entrenched.

Integration

By the 1960s there was much movement towards a change in political thinking and in attitudes within certain sections of society. In 1967 the Australian population voted at a referendum to change two sections of the Australian Constitution. In addition, in 1969 the Aborigines Welfare Board was abolished, Aboriginal people were no longer wards of the state, and the policy direction moved from assimilation to integration (Baldry & Green 2003). By the 1970s it was recognised that Aboriginal people were full human beings, neither child-like nor less than human, and that Aboriginal people could join Australian society but retain their distinctive identity. This period of integration offered much to Aboriginal peoples, and many thought that the time had come when Indigenous Australians would be able to live in the same manner as other Australians and escape their poverty.

Awareness of rights

However, this hope was not realised, and poverty continued. The failure of the new policies to improve the lot of Aborigines was, in part, because Aboriginal people had suffered generations of disadvantage and had been denied access to resources such as education and employment, resources needed to enable them to share in the benefits enjoyed by other Australians. As well, while some attitudes were changing, societal structures and some entrenched systems of privilege still discriminated against Aboriginal people.

One example is the issue of land and land ownership. The interests of non-Aboriginal Australians and large corporations are placed before those of Aboriginal people and thus limit the rights of Aboriginal people to land and to compensation for stolen land. While at times certain political parties and the Australian High Court have introduced radical initiatives to address the issues of Aboriginal people's rights to land, these are frequently limited by the claims of rights non-Aboriginal people (Hollinsworth 1998). Thus the rights of Aboriginal people appear to remain second to the rights of other Australians and are rarely accommodated when the two are in conflict. This is demonstrated by the Howard Government's amendments to the High Court's *Wik* judgement which found that Aboriginal peoples' rights could co-exist with the rights of land owners (Hollinsworth 1998).

Although by 1969 it was no longer official policy to remove Aboriginal people from society or to force them away from identifying as Aboriginal, in reality Aboriginal people were still expected to aspire to the culture and ways of white society. A person could be Aboriginal, look Aboriginal and call him or herself Aboriginal, but was expected to act 'white' by living in exactly the same way as non-Aboriginal people. Further, services ignored the fact that Aboriginal people were different in their experiences and in their culture, so provided identical services Aboriginal and non-Aboriginal people. One example is child welfare, where policies and practices viewed Aboriginal people as 'no different to anyone else' (D'Souza 1993). Thus resulted in further mistakes being made and Aboriginal people experiencing a system that did not take into account their cultural believes and practices of child rearing.

Despite an air that everyone was equal, Aboriginal people continued to suffer from poverty at a much higher rate than non-Aboriginal Australians. The Henderson poverty report found that Aboriginal people were two to five times more likely to be impoverished than other Australians (cited in Aspalter 2003, p 25). In this climate Aboriginal people and communities continued to demand the right to determine their future and to address the issues faced by Aboriginal people and communities. Many Aboriginal people were disappointed in the limited gains that had been made and were beginning to gain places in government departments where they attempted to make internal changes (Baldry & Green 2003). Aboriginal people and their supporters took the initiative in this battle and established the Aboriginal Legal Service, the Aboriginal Medical Service and numerous other community-controlled organisations (Baldry & Green 2003).

Self-determination

The late 1970s and the 1980s saw self-determination established as the official policy of Aboriginal Affairs (Hollinsworth 1998). Aboriginal people were starting to hold positions within government departments and Aboriginal community-controlled organisations. However the rhetoric and reality were very different. Very few of the Aboriginal people holding government department positions had any significant power, and those who did had to negotiate their way between the expectations of Aboriginal people and communities and the limitations of their roles within the department where they worked. In addition Aboriginal community-controlled organisations were still dependent upon the government for funding, and with that funding came guidelines on how the organisations were to operate. Therefore Aboriginal community-controlled organisations were never in fact fully community-controlled, and while there were some good results such as the Aboriginal Medical Service, the Aboriginal Legal Service and the Aboriginal Children Service, the aspiration of self-determination was never fully recognised.

Furthermore, during the 1990s reports from the Royal Commission into Aboriginal Deaths in Custody (Johnston 1991) and the National Inquiry into the Separation of Aboriginal and Torres Strait Islander children from their families (Wilson 1997) both pointed out the importance of self-determination for Aboriginal people in addressing the impacts of past government policies. Despite laws, inquiries and interventions, the so-called 'Aboriginal problem' never ceased to be a problem and Aboriginal people remained the most disadvantaged, living on the fringes of Australian society. Many non-Aboriginal Australians were horrified with what they saw but were puzzled as to why, after the apparent removal of discriminatory policies and the bringing of Aboriginal people into mainstream society, the 'problem' had not been resolved.

Self-management

Prime Minister Howard and his Cabinet have continued the puzzlement over why Aboriginal issues have not been addressed and continuously announce their concerns about Aboriginal people and the conditions in which they lived. They also made promises to deal with these issues through their policies of welfare reform. Howard and the Liberal Party under his leadership did not believe in self-determination for Aboriginal people, declaring that it was creating two separate groups of people (Dodson 2004). One of the first steps was to cease the policy of self-determination and introduce the policy of self-management. While in practice there was very little difference between self-determination and self-management, there was one very subtle but significant difference. Self-determination was meant to give Aboriginal people the power to determine policies and directions for Aboriginal people and society; self-management holds Aboriginal people responsible for the outcomes of policies without control of those policies. In this way blame for Aboriginal people's poor life circumstances is focused onto Aboriginal people and in particular onto Aboriginal leaders (Bennett in Baldry & Green 2003, p 52). The problems experienced by Aboriginal people were removed from historical to individual responsibility perspectives.

Aboriginal people are again being seen as unable or unwilling to take responsibility for their position, and thus to be in need of correction. Anyone trying to bring the focus back onto the historical perspective and to highlight the role of systemic disadvantaged is called a 'bleeding heart' and as presenting a 'black arm-band' approach (Hiscock 2006). In fact it goes further. The so-called 'bleeding hearts' are actually labelled (Hollinsworth 1998; McCausland 2005a) as being part of the problem and are seen as preventing Aboriginal people from moving out of a self-imposed state of dependency and pauperism. Whether the current policy direction should still be called self-management or whether it would be more appropriately called neo-assimilation is still a debate to be had. However, many of the current policy directions suggest this is so.

New directions or a return to the past

Under the Howard Government, Aboriginal people have experienced great changes in both the type and the amount of services they can access to address their continuing low socio-economic situation. This is despite the fact that Aboriginal people continue to be the most disadvantaged group in Australian society (Trewin & Madden 2005). The Coalition Government's policy for all welfare recipients (not only Aboriginal people) is one of mutual obligation and marks the end of automatic entitlement to any benefit. This has also seen a return to old concepts such as the 'deserving' and the 'undeserving' poor, concepts that existed in welfare policy up until the early 20th century. The old theories that welfare makes paupers and tends to create intergenerational dependency, have also returned. Aboriginal people remain the 'problem' and action needs to be taken to force them into taking their place in society as fully responsible citizens. It is seen that the problem and thus solution are based within Aboriginal communities, as illustrated by the Prime Minister John Howard:

> It is not just a question of money, because a lot more money has been put into Aboriginal health. It is a question of culture. It is a question of practice. It is a question of attitude. It is a question of community responsibility (McCausland 2005b, p 9).

Thus at government level the problem is seen as Aboriginal culture, practice and attitude; therefore the solution is seen as making Aboriginal communities take responsibility. In line with this thinking, the government has recruited Aboriginal people to participate in its processes, thus giving it credibility and making it difficult for anyone to criticise or even question. Anyone who attempts to speak out about what is occurring is accused of being a 'bleeding heart' or 'paternalistic', and is declared to be part of the problem. However, as pointed out by McCausland the government uses such allegations to divert criticism of its new policy (2005a), making any debate or scrutiny difficult.

In its current Indigenous policy the Australian Commonwealth Government states that it has a whole-of-government commitment and changed engagement, which operates on five principles (Office of Indigenous Policy Co-ordination 2006a; 2006b; 2006c) of Collaboration, Regional and Local Need, Flexibility, Accountability and Leadership.

Shared Responsibility Agreements (SRA) are a key component of the government's policy on service provision to Aboriginal communities and people. An SRA places obligations upon communities to undertake certain activities. For example, the Mulan SRA in Western Australia, requires children's faces to be washed before attending in school in return for the provision of non-sniffable petrol. In short, the agreements provide infrastructure and services in a contract that commits the whole community to specific behavioural changes or other actions (McCausland 2005b). While many may see this as empowering communities to take responsibility and ownership for addressing the problems within the community, the reality is different. Aboriginal people are not being empowered by these agreements; they are being kept in a position of subservience and treated once again as needing correction. These corrections to change particular behaviours or engage in particular activities are prescribed by the SRAs. As already stated, this is nothing new, and is very similar to the outcomes of the assimilation policy. Peterson, for example, talks about assimilation being built upon the colonial institutional heritage of rationing: 'they could manage relationships with Aboriginal people by issuing food, clothes, blankets and other necessities and luxuries such as tobacco' (1998, p 81).

Today under SRAs, the government is once again managing its relationship with Aboriginal people within the colonial institutional heritage of rationing. Food, clothes and blankets are no longer being rationed but rather services and infrastructure, which are essential to

Aboriginal community well-being. Peterson also points out that rationing allows the provider to hold considerable power over the recipient in terms of their consumption (1998). By controlling the recipients' consumption, the provider also regulates their behaviour, as SRAs are conditional on 'specific behavioural change in Indigenous communities' (McCausland 2005b, p 10). In drawing parallels from the past with the present, one can only conclude that the government's current Indigenous policy is alarmingly similar to that of assimilation. Given that the assimilation policy and its programs not only did not address Aboriginal poverty but also reinforced it, how can this new policy of shared responsibility result in anything different?

Shared responsibility is based on the concept of mutual obligation which places welfare recipients into a contractual relationship, where they must undertake certain activities in return for welfare payments.

Kinnear sees contractual welfare obligations under mutual obligation as:

> [H]aving all the hallmarks of a 'sink or swim' approach, ie, people learn how to be contractual partners by participating in a contract. In other words, in the full knowledge that they cannot swim they are thrown in the 'deep end' and told they must learn. If they sink, they are then penalized by being thrown in again. (2003, p 112)

Groups who are seen as 'undeserving' – the unemployed, single mothers and Aboriginal Australians – are particularly facing these new conditions. However, it must be noted that Aboriginal Australians are being treated differently. While shared responsibility directly affects income support for other groups, Aboriginal Australians are affected in their lack of access to basic services and infrastructure.

SRAs are coercive as they force Aboriginal people into certain types of behaviours and ways of living. It is reasonable therefore to claim that the government's current Indigenous policy of shared responsibility is the same as the policy of assimilation in practice and intent, if not in name. As with the outcomes of Assimilations, Aboriginal people will continue to be forced to the margins of Australian society with no access to the social, cultural and political life that addresses not just relative but also absolute poverty. These types of policies do nothing to address the structural inequalities within Australian society that prevent Aboriginal people from obtaining the same standards of living as all other Australians. To address the poverty within Aboriginal communities, people must have access to a real economic participation. For this to happen, Aboriginal people need to be able to find employment that is not just within the areas of unskilled labour. However, given the poor health and education levels, it is not easy to address the issue of employment, and without a reasonable income it is very difficult to address the issues of poor health and education. It can seem to be an almost impossible cycle to break out of. However, if a holistic approach is taken within a manner that recognises the needs and desires of Aboriginal people in a manner that does not disempower them, then these issues can be addressed.

Future policy directions

Australian governments and the Australian people need to seriously consider the complex and underlying issues that have resulted in Aboriginal poverty. These issues involve dispossession, marginalisation and exclusion from mainstream social, cultural and political life of Australia. The starting point for such consideration is genuine recognition of the on-going effects of colonisation and dispossession, realistic compensation for the loss of land, the abuses of child removal and enforced labour, and the realisation of legal documents (such as treaties) that set out the rights of Aboriginal Australians and the continuing relationships between them and other Australians. Until the issues of the past are fully dealt with it is difficult for any real change in Aboriginal peoples' position within Australian society.

The area of self-determination is particularly important, as pointed out by Johnson (2002). This ensures that Indigenous people are able to fully and effectively participate at all levels of Australian society on equal terms, without having to give up their distinctive identities. Without full and equal participation of Indigenous people within Australian society, the issues of Indigenous poverty will continue unabated. If Aboriginal people are able to determine the solutions and own the policies and programs that best suit their communities and families, and are able to gain the resources required to implement such programs, the problems can begin to be addressed effectively. Real self-determination lies at the heart of any future policy directions that are serious in addressing the poverty and the disadvantage that Aboriginal people face and experience as part of their daily life.

Finally, it must be realised that the current situation is the result of a complex set of actions and problems that have occurred over a long period of time; thus the required unique and specialised solutions will take time. An equal partnership, where Aboriginal people are not forced into a position or a particular way of doing things, is the way forward in efficiently implementing long-term solutions.

Conclusion

The current policy, set out in the section above entitled 'New directions or a return to the past', is about governing the behaviours of Aboriginal people and communities. It is not about addressing the structural problems that result in the entrenched poverty that Aboriginal people have been experiencing since shortly after the arrival of the first fleet and the beginning of colonisation.

The Commonwealth Government claims that its policies aim to address the disadvantage experienced by Aboriginal people. At best this claim is extremely naïve; at worst it is a continuation of colonial practices that dispossessed Aboriginal people of their rights as the first sovereign peoples in Australia. If the past has shown us anything at all, it is that punitive measures against those living in poverty do not work. What is called for is a new approach. Under the current direction, Aboriginal people will continue to be the poorest in Australia and to live in conditions comparable to those of the 'third world'. It is time for new policies and programs that address dispossession and all that has come with it. Genuine partnerships need to be formed, rather than partnerships where one side has all the resources and the other has all the obligations. The practices of colonisation and government policies have forced Aboriginal people into a poverty that can only be broken with much consultation, consideration, and Aboriginal self-determination.

Chapter 11

Poverty and mental illness

Robert Bland

The Commonwealth Government's decision to target the eligibility arrangements for Disability Support Pension (DSP) as part of the Welfare to Work reforms (Dutton 2005) demands a review of the complex and elusive relationship between mental illness and poverty. The research literature over many decades has affirmed the correlation between mental illness and poverty, yet the directionality of that relationship remains contested and confused (Gomm 1996). Does poverty constitute a form of chronic and severe stress likely to cause mental illness? Is poverty a consequence of mental illness? How are these competing explanations worked out in key related areas such as income security, employment, and social support?

This chapter will briefly examine the competing explanations for the connections between poverty and mental illness. It will then describe the diversity of mental health problems that comprise the spectrum of mental illness, identifying the prevalence and impact of each of these diagnostic groups. The diversity of the phenomenon of mental illness, and consequent disabilities, explains much of the difficulty in establishing the relationship between poverty and mental illness. From here the chapter will consider the nature of economic disadvantage, and concepts of marginalisation, associated with mental illness. An analysis of work and income security provides a focus for understanding the way that poverty and mental illness work together to impact on the lives of individuals and families.

The final section of the chapter examines the implications for social policy, particularly the interface between mental health policy, as expressed in the National Mental Health Strategy, and welfare reform policy. It is clear that welfare reform represents an opportunity for people with mental illness to find work and move off benefits. More likely however, is that the demands of mutual obligation will create new and serious threats to the health and welfare of people with mental health problems.

Poverty and mental health – cause or consequence?

Analysis of the epidemiology of mental illness shows a clear connection between having mental illness and experiencing poverty. Gomm (1996) argues that 'for nearly every kind of illness, disease or disability, 'physical' and 'mental', poorer people are afflicted more than richer people: more often, more seriously, and for longer' (p 110). He argues that poor mental health, poor physical health and poor socio-economic circumstances work together to ensure that rates of mental illness, suicide, use of drugs and alcohol and homelessness are all higher for poor people. Saraceno & Barbui (1997) in their review of the epidemiological data confirm these relationships. They show that people in the lowest socio-economic groups have eight times the relative risk of schizophrenia compared with those in the highest socio-economic group. People with schizophrenia are much more likely to be unemployed, isolated from family, and have poor educational outcomes. Similar higher rates of major depression and other disorders were associated with poverty (Dohrenwend et al 1969).

These socio-genic theories, popular in the 1970s and 1980s, argued that poverty constituted a significant cause of mental illness. The theories claimed that greater environmental adversity such as increased life stressors, poor quality maternal and obstetric care, and scarce social resources, led to a higher risk of psychiatric disorders. These social causation explanations were challenged by other researchers (Mechanic 1971) who argued a 'drift hypothesis'; that people with mental illness fall into poverty as a consequence of their mental illness. More recent studies have tended to recognise the close associations between mental illness and poverty, and the way in which social consequences of illness such as poor employment opportunities, housing, poor services and stigma reinforce the impact of illness (Murali & Oyebode 2004).

Butterworth et al (2004) conclude their review of the literature connecting poverty and mental illness by acknowledging the difficulty of establishing causality in the relationship. Clearly, poverty and financial hardship represent a risk factor for poor mental health. Many welfare recipients have experienced traumatic life events such as unemployment and redundancy, separation and divorce, and disability. These adverse life events are also proven risk factors for poor mental health (Turner et al 1995). Unemployment, for example, might be considered either a cause or a consequence of mental illness. Perhaps mental illness and poverty might also be considered common outcomes of other traumatic life events. Causality remains difficult to establish.

Understanding mental illness

Any analysis of the relationship between poverty and mental illness requires an understanding of the nature and dimensions of mental illness. Butterworth (2003) draws a useful distinction between concepts of mental health and mental disorder. Mental health, he argues, is the general term covering a person's ability to function and undertake productive activities, develop and maintain meaningful relationships and to adapt to change and cope with adversity (p 1). Mental disorders refer to the negative end of the continuum of mental health, and are characterised by alterations in thinking, mood or behaviour associated with distress or impaired functioning (p 1). Mental disorders include schizophrenia, depressions, anxiety disorders, dementia and substance-use abuses. Waghorn & Lloyd (2005) define mental illness as clinically-diagnosed mental disorders such as anxiety, affective and psychotic disorders as defined by the Diagnostic and Statistical Manual of Mental Disorders (DSM-IV) and the International Classification of Disorders (ICD-10) classification systems. These disorders are more serious than 'mental health problems', a term used to refer to short-term adverse mental health states that can occur in response to life stressors and challenging life events (p 5).

A survey of the mental health of the Australian community, the *National Survey of Mental Health and Wellbeing*, has been published in two major reports. *The Mental Health of Australians* (Andrews et al 1999) reports on the high prevalence disorders of anxiety, affective and substance use disorders. *People Living with Psychotic Illness: An Australian Study 1997-98* (Jablensky et al 1999) reports on the low prevalence (psychotic) disorders. It might be helpful to review the nature and impact of mental illness with this distinction between high and low prevalence disorders in mind.

The National Survey was based on lengthy interviews of a large sample of Australian citizens and was designed to answer such questions as:

1. How many Australians have which mental disorders?

2. How disabled are they by these disorders?

The data provide a valuable snapshot of the mental health of Australians. It will be useful to review each of the major sub-groups of mental illness and consequent disability as a context for considering the relationship between poverty and mental illness.

Anxiety disorders

Anxiety disorders comprised the largest single illness group, affecting some 9.7 per cent of the population in the last year, and more common in women (12 per cent) than in men (7.1 per cent) (Andrews et al 1999, p 7). Anxiety represents a continuum from mildly disabling through to the more severe conditions such as obsessive-compulsive disorder, panic disorder and generalised anxiety disorder. Using a measure of disability based on the number of days per month in which the disorder disrupted work and life roles ('days out of role') the survey found that on average a person with anxiety disorder suffered 2.1 days out of role (Andrews et al 1999, p 14). Waghorn & Lloyd (2005) suggest that anxiety disorders are associated with impaired work performance, deflated employment trajectories, and non-participation in employment (p 7). The more extreme forms of the disorder produce severe restrictions on employment. The National Survey also found that, despite the effectiveness of medical and psychological treatments available, people with anxiety were less likely to seek or receive help for the condition.

Substance use disorders

Substance use disorders were found in 7.7 per cent of the sample, much higher in males (11.1 per cent) than in females (4.5 per cent) (Andrews et al 1999, p 17). Alcohol abuse was three times more common than other drug abuse. Substance abuse disorders were higher in younger age groups, and were often found as a co-morbid condition with anxiety or depression. Only 14 per cent of those identified with a substance abuse disorder had sought any help from a treatment service, with males less likely to seek help than females. The level of disability was difficult to calculate for this group but would appear to be greater when substance abuse occurs as a co-morbid condition with another disorder.

Affective disorders

Depression represents a spectrum of disorders from mildly to severely disabling. The National Survey found that if the severe form of bipolar disorder is excluded, affective disorders were found in some 5.8 per cent of the sample, higher for women at 7.4 per cent than for men (4.2 per cent) (Andrews et al 1999, p 23). In more than half the sample, depression was experienced as a co-morbid disorder with other physical and mental health problems. Disability was calculated at an average of 2.7 days out of role, and where linked to other physical health problems, the rate was higher at 6.3 days out of role (Andrew et al 1999, p 26). Waghorn & Lloyd (2005) report that people with depression have reduced labour force participation, work fewer hours and earn less than healthy workers. Depression is associated with impaired motivation and initiative, and workers with depression may be perceived negatively by employers as poor workers. In contrast to other high prevalence disorders, people with depression were more likely to seek help from their general practitioner, though only 40 per cent of the sample had done so in the last year. Depression remained untreated or under-treated, for the majority of the sample (Andrews et al 1999, p 26).

Psychotic disorders

Psychotic disorders, identified in the National Survey as 'low prevalence' disorders, represent the most severe end of the continuum of mental disorders. They form a diverse group of illnesses which have their origins in abnormal brain functioning and are characterised by fundamental distortions of thinking, perception, and emotional response (Jablensky et al 1999). They include schizophrenia, bipolar disorder depression with psychotic features, delusional disorders and other non-affective psychotic illnesses. These psychotic disorders typically start in early adulthood, and their impact on the life trajectory of people who become ill often profoundly affects every aspect of their lives, and the lives of their families (Hatfield & Lefley 1993). Work, life, and educational opportunities are typically disrupted, as is the capacity to establish and maintain close personal relationships.

The National Survey found between 4 and 7 persons per 1000 of their sample suffered from a psychotic disorder and were in treatment with mental health services during any given month because of their disorder. Though the prevalence of these serious disorders is low compared with the anxiety, substance abuse and affective disorders, the impact of the illness is typically severe and life-long. The average length of illness among those interviewed was 15 years and for 43 per cent of the sample, the illness was chronic with no complete recovery between psychotic episodes (Jablensky et al 1999, p 3). The survey revealed a pattern of significant social isolation. Over 80 per cent of the sample were separated, single or widowed. Over 85 per cent relied on social security benefits as their source of income, and 45 per cent lived in some form of supported accommodation or homeless shelter.

Waghorn & Lloyd (2005) identify specific difficulties in managing employment for people suffering from bipolar disorder. People with this disorder may have lengthy periods of time when they are well, and have no difficulty finding and maintaining work during this time. During episodes of mania, or severe depression, they may be unable to work at all.

Recent developments in the mental health services and research areas have emphasised a discourse of recovery as an alternative to what is seen as the excessively negative literature of psychiatry (Pearson 2004). Certainly, there is growing evidence of the value of a recovery focus in employment programs for people who have suffered from psychotic illness (Meadows & Singh 2002). The challenge to employment and rehabilitation services is to address the specific needs of people recovering from severe mental illness so that real employment is an attainable goal of recovery. The statistics drawn from the National Survey, however, leave us in no doubt about the extent of that challenge. Embracing the language of recovery should not obscure the fact that severe mental illness continues to impose significant and persistent barriers to participation in the workforce. Neither is the promotion of a discourse of recovery in policy documents a substitute for the range of specialist services necessary to effect recovery in the lives of people with mental illness.

Dimensions of poverty

As argued in other chapters of this book, poverty remains a complex concept, as broad perhaps as the concept of mental illness. This section will explore some of the dimensions of poverty, focusing particularly on the issues of work, income security and social relationships. It is in these areas that the connections between poverty and mental illness are worked out. It will then address marginalisation and inclusion as an alternative framework for considering the connections between mental illness and poverty.

In their analysis of poverty, social inequality and mental health, Murali & Oyebode (2004) define poverty as a multi-dimensional phenomenon, encompassing inability to satisfy basic needs, lack of control over resources, lack of education and poor health (p 216). They accept the use of a poverty line, based on levels of income and consumption level, as a measure of poverty, but argue that this line will vary from country to country based on community norms. The related concept of 'social inequality' is linked to social stress and poor health outcomes.

In contrast to the quantitative epidemiological studies, a number of recent qualitative studies have given a richer description of the lived experience of poverty and mental illness. Wilton's study of life for mentally ill people living in sheltered accommodation in Canada (Wilton 2003) details the day-to-day hardship experienced by poor people without sufficient income to purchase basic items such as food, clothing and shoes. The people in the study described how they struggled to make their monthly pension last out the four weeks. The cost of public transport worked directly against their participation in a range of social activities such as visiting friends or family. This served to restrict the social support available to them. Their self-image was diminished through an inability to buy new clothes, personal hygiene items like deodorants, or to have a haircut. People felt their obvious appearance as 'poor people' reinforced the powerful stigma of mental illness they already experienced.

Similarly, a qualitative study undertaken by Anglicare Tasmania using focus groups and interviews of people living with long-term mental illness, found a disturbing cycle of poverty and ill-health (Cameron & Flanagan 2004). People reported patterns of unstable housing, inadequate food, a heavy reliance on emergency relief agencies, inadequate clothing, and regular disconnections of electricity and telephone. Many could not afford basic medical, dental and public transport services. A significant finding of the study was the financial impact on family carers – usually the parents of an adult with mental illness. Caregivers were often aged pensioners themselves, surviving on low fixed incomes. Carers identified the need for affordable housing as a long-term solution to the high costs of rent and board.

Work

Access to work, and the financial and social benefits associated with earning a wage, remains a significant mediating variable at the interface of poverty and mental illness. Work as a vehicle for rehabilitation remains a central strategy in the range of psychosocial interventions in mental health services. In summarising the extensive literature on work and rehabilitation, Waghorn & Lloyd (2005) argue that positive work experiences are seen to enhance improved self-concept, self esteem, subjective well-being, and improved personal empowerment. Marrone & Golowka (1999) promoting a consumer perspective on work, advance a number of arguments for work as part of recovery. These include the claim that people should work because unemployment is much worse for one's mental health than the stresses of employment, that work is a way to meet people and expand social networks, and that work gives a higher status than the consumer role.

As argued in previous sections of this chapter, mental disorder threatens the capacity of people to seek, obtain and hold down employment. For the high prevalence disorders of anxiety, substance abuse and affective disorders this appears as a higher than average number of 'days out of role' or lost employment. More seriously though is the widespread exclusion of people with psychotic disorders from the workplace. The psychotic illnesses typically affect young adults through the formative years of education and career seeking, severely restricting opportunities to develop the work skills necessary for steady employment. Despite the obvious benefits of participation in the workplace, significant barriers to employment of people with mental illness remain. These include the presence of active psychiatric symptoms, cognitive impairments, the episodic nature of psychotic disorders, the effect of treatments on work performance, low expectations of mental health workers, and community stigma and discrimination (Waghorn & Lloyd 2005). Discrimination, they argue, is evident in the reluctance of job placement and retraining agencies to take on as clients people recovering from mental illness because they are seen as unlikely to succeed.

Income security

An alternative approach to considering the connection between poverty and mental illness is to examine the connection between dependency on social security benefits and evidence of mental illness. Data from the National Survey of Mental Health and Well-being (Jablensky et al 1999) showed that over 85 per cent of people with a psychotic illness were dependent on social security benefits as their source of income. Other studies have reported on the high level of stress and symptoms of mental illness among those receiving welfare benefits. Butterworth (2003) has analysed data from the National Survey to identify the prevalence of mental disorders among five groups of welfare recipients – the unemployed, students, partnered women with children, unpartnered women with children, and people not in the labour force. The data showed that all mental disorders were much more prevalent among income support recipients than non-recipients (Butterworth 2003, p vii). Almost one in three income support recipients have a diagnosable mental disorder in any 12 month period. He concludes that the poor mental health of welfare recipients is likely to be a barrier to the achievement of social and economic goals.

Recent work by Saunders at the Social Policy Research Centre (Peter Saunders 2005a, 2005c) has further clarified the connections between disability and poverty. Using data from the Household Expenditure Survey 1999 (HES), and applying a number of indicators of poverty, Peter Saunders has identified five dimensions of hardship – financial hardship, restricted social participation, severe financial stress, expressed need, and lack of support. He concludes that having a disability, or a family member with a disability, is associated with substantially poorer measures on all dimensions of poverty. While the identification of having a disability includes people with mental health problems, the results should be cautiously interpreted in relation to the broader group of people with mental illness. The study suggests an alternative approach to exploring the specific nature of poverty and its connection with mental illness. It reminds us that people with mental illness are often experiencing both disability and poverty.

Social relationships

The literature on the experience of mental illness and poverty, particularly the qualitative studies and first person accounts, reinforces the need to recognise the centrality of isolation and loneliness to that experience. As reported, people with psychotic illness interviewed for the National Survey reported high levels of personal isolation. The Thin Ice study (Cameron & Flanagan 2004) showed how difficult it was for people with mental illness to maintain family and community relationships. The lack of supportive relationships exposed people to the worst effects both of poverty and mental illness and limited the resources they had to deal with their difficulties. Similarly, Wilton (2003) showed that social relationships are affected both through direct material constraints and shame associated with poverty. The stigmas of poverty and mental illness reinforce a sense and appearance of 'difference' and compound the isolation for those affected. A focus on social isolation is a helpful reminder that poverty is not simply about a lack of money. Nor is mental illness just about a set of symptoms and treatments: the experience of being poor and mentally ill impacts on every aspect of the person's life.

Social inclusion

An alternative to broad definitions of poverty based on income levels has been the work on social inclusion. Commins (1993) argued that inclusion can be defined in terms of the success of one or more of the systems of 'integration': the democratic and legal system which promotes civil integration; the labour market which promotes economic integration; the welfare system promoting social integration; and the family and community system which promotes interpersonal integration. All four systems are necessary and complementary.

Rather than focus on poverty as an absence of resources, a social inclusion focus seeks to identify the dimensions of the positive and multi-dimensional concept of 'inclusion' and has been applied to a growing body of British research into the social context of mental illness, suggesting both the nature of deprivation and possible ways of addressing the social impact of mental illness. Huxley & Vick (2005) and Huxley et al (2005) have developed the Commins dimensions of inclusion to provide a base for both research and service development. They identify eight dimensions of inclusion, together with objective indicators for measurement. They are:

1. Work and education – educational attainment, training opportunities, adult learning, type of employment, hours worked, reason for not working;
2. Housing – accommodation type, tenure, facilities, neighbourhood;
3. Finances – income, benefit level, financial difficulties;
4. Family relationships – level of contact;
5. Social relationships – social contact, activities;
6. Leisure activities – community participation;
7. Safety – victimisation, personal and neighbourhood safety;
8. Physical and mental health – self-reported health status, contact with primary and secondary care services.

Recognition of the broad domains of inclusion encourages an approach to policy and service response which is multi-factored, allowing us to address the complexities of the relationship between poverty and mental illness at a range of sites.

Policy and the future

Mental illness and poverty represent substantial areas of policy development in the Australian context over the past ten years. The right of people with mental health problems to access an income through the disability support pension is well established as part of the Australian social security system, yet as the research reviewed in this chapter and elsewhere in this book shows, access to the disability support payment is no protection against poverty. The opposite is true. For people with long-term psychotic illness, dependency on the disability support pension as the sole income to support life is a guarantee of poverty. Access to work, and the range of programs to help people prepare for work, find work, and hold work appears to offer the best chance for people to move out of the poverty trap. Butterworth and Berry (2004) review the range of psycho-social interventions available to support the return to work strategy and are cautiously optimistic that enough is known to offer considerable hope for the strategy. Very real barriers to accessing work, however, remain (Waghorn & Lloyd 2004).

The National Mental Health Strategy has emphasised the need for 'inter-sectorial linking' (AHMAC 1992) so that the mental health services will work together with the range of other health and welfare services to support the complex needs of people with mental health problems. There is some evidence that this is happening in the area of housing, where some States have developed detailed working agreements between mental health services and public housing programs to ensure access to affordable housing and support for people with mental health problems in tenancy matters (Seelig et al 2004). There is a real need to extend the concepts of inter-sectorial linking to ensure that people with mental health problems are supported in other poverty related areas such as employment programs, transport policies, and family support programs.

The number of people receiving the DSP increased more than five-fold between 1972 and 2004 and is currently received by some 696,700 people (Peter Saunders 2005a). Many of these recipients are people with mental health problems, either as a primary or secondary disability. Alarmed by this increase, perhaps, the Commonwealth has decided to tighten the eligibility requirements for disability support and extend to this group the principles of mutual obligation recently applied to unemployed people and supporting parents. Administration of the new policy will involve enormous risks for vulnerable people with mental health problems. For the policy to be able to meet the expressed goals of encouraging people to move into the workforce, the following conditions will need to be met:

- People administering the assessments of capacity for work will have knowledge of both mental health matters and vocational rehabilitation principles.
- An appropriate range of programs to prepare and support people for work will be in place.
- Employment and training opportunities will be available to people.
- Employment and training services, and mental health treatment services will work co-operatively to ensure best outcomes for consumers.

- Administration procedures will be flexible enough to cope with fluctuating levels of cognitive and behavioural functioning in people with mental health problems.

Peter Saunders (2005c) acknowledges the potential value of work as a pathway out of dependency on the DSP and poverty. His conclusion about the impact of the changes is, however, pessimistic:

> While there are major uncertainties surrounding their longer-term impact, the short-term consequences of the reforms are more predictable. They will reduce the incomes of many DSP recipients who are already reliant on a poverty level income and produce increased pressures to comply with new mutual obligation requirements. This will only add to the financial and other pressures already known to exist among this vulnerable group. (Peter Saunders 2005c, p 12)

Conclusion

Mental illness and poverty are closely and inextricably linked. At the level of the high incidence disorders, the impact on life circumstances for those affected may be severe. Effective mental health care can reduce the impact of the disorder, yet the evidence suggests that many people do not receive the treatment they need to lead fully productive lives. For the more extremely disabling disorders, the impact on work and life style is often profound, affecting every aspect of life circumstances, and extending beyond the individual to affect families as well. Poverty is a typical outcome of long-term psychotic illness. Yet even for this group there is hope that effective psychosocial interventions can promote a return to the workforce, and to a more integrated life in the community. Access to work and training opportunities for a group largely excluded from these as a result of their illness, may be a positive outcome of the Commonwealth Welfare to Work reforms. More likely, however, is that the coercive aspects of the reforms, including the cancelling or suspending of benefits for failure to meet obligations, will result in increased hardship and despair for this very vulnerable group. Mental health services and consumer and family advocacy groups will need to exercise a vigilant monitoring role to prevent abuse and suffering.

Chapter 12

Poverty and people with a disability

David Sykes

> People with a disability and their families are more likely to live in poverty; disability adds to the risk of poverty and poverty adds to the risk of disability; people with a disability have lower education and employment rates than the general population (Elwin 1999, p 27).

Whether they live in industrialised countries or countries in transition, people who have a disability and their families are consistently among the world's poorest (Inclusion International 2005). Using even fairly crude measures of poverty such as income, which does not take into account the costs of disability and the reliance on cash (Peter Saunders 2005b), in Australia a significant number of people with a disability live at or below the poverty line. Recipients of the Disability Support Pension have an income about $20 per week below the poverty line (Bradbury et al 2001; Brotherhood of St Laurence (BSL) 2005).

There is limited discussion on the association between poverty and people with a disability in the social policy discourse in Australia, with the exception of the need for greater access of people with a disability to open employment. When issues of social or economic disadvantage are raised, scant attention is given to the fact that people with a disability are over-represented among those living on the margins of our community: they are hidden poor (Gleeson 1998). Where there *is* policy debate around this issue, it is generally in relation to the funding and nature of the service system which supports the more significantly impaired of those with a disability. Indeed much of the focus of disability advocacy has been on seeking improvements in specific support systems such as the mental health or disability services. The broader socio-economic problems confronting many people with a disability, such as access to education and employment, tend to be the focus of smaller advocacy efforts. This failure to adequately address broader socio-economic factors occurs despite shifts in disability policy, which have seen greater emphasis on fostering a more inclusive community. This notion of inclusion goes beyond simple employment opportunity, and challenges us to consider inclusion beyond narrow concepts of economic contributions; instead inclusion is focused on the individual's needs and preferences.

This approach seeks to offer people with a disability more choice in determining how they will participate and contribute to society. This approach also raises the challenge of providing an appropriate pension so that those who choose to contribute in ways other than paid employment (for example volunteering) are not forced to live in poverty.

This chapter therefore explores the relationship between current policy debates about disability and poverty, at both federal and State levels in Australia. In the process of this exploration, we first define 'disability', then consider key policy challenges needed for improving the quality of life of people with a disability.

Defining disability

The term 'disability' is used to describe both the person's impairment and the disabling nature of others' reactions to the person and his/her impairment. Each of these components rests on a different explanatory model, although both tend to use the terms 'disability' and 'impairment' interchangeably.

The first is the medical model, which is concerned with the actual impairment, so that here 'disability' means having impairment in one or more of the intellectual, psychiatric, sensory or physical domains. Each domain has sub-categories; for example, the impairments in the sensory domain are subdivided into disabilities such as deafness or visual impairment. The medical model therefore sets out a detailed classification system of impairment and disability, and fits individuals and their deficits into this system. Eligibility for welfare services and benefits is decided on the basis of this fit between the classification system and the person.

In 1980 the World Health Organisation (WHO) defined 'disability' in terms of three dimensions: impairment, disability and handicap. This definition is problematic, because 'disability' is used both as a general condition, and as a subset of itself, while 'impairment' is also a subset of 'disability'. To aid the application of this definition, the WHO also developed a system of disability classification.

However, with time these terms were seen increasingly as stigmatising, so in 2001 the WHO endorsed the International Classification of Functioning, Disability and Health (ICIDH) developed by the WHO (2000). In this system the term 'disability' has been replaced by the neutral term 'activity', with negative circumstances described as 'activity limitation'. 'Handicap' has been replaced by 'participation', and negative circumstances in this dimension are described as 'participation restriction'. 'Disablement' has been included as an umbrella term to cover all the negative dimensions of the ICIDH-2 (that is, impairments, activity limitations, and participation restrictions), either together or separately. In turn, 'disability' is defined through three dimensions: impairment, disability and handicap, each described from body, individual, and societal perspectives by two basic lists: (1) body functions and structure; (2) activities and participation. 'Functioning' refers to all body functions, activities and participation as an umbrella term.

The aim of the ICIDH-2 is to provide a definition of disability that facilitates consistent classification, recognising that disability is the result of the interaction between health and health-related domains. Within this system factors such as education are systematically grouped; for example a given health condition is considered from the perspective of what a person with a disease or disorder does do or can do. It also lists environmental factors that interact with all these constructs. In this way, ICIDH-2 provides a useful profile of individuals' functioning, disability and health in various domains (WHO 2000, p 8).

This ICIDH-2 definition has been widely accepted by the international community as a framework for conceptualising disability, and has influenced the Australian Bureau of Statistics (ABS 1999) disability survey which is carried out every five years.

The following diagram by the WHO (Figure 12.1) outlines how the concept of disability now recognises that the components of functioning and disability—body functions and structures, activities and participation—reflect an interaction between health conditions and the person's environment (WHO 2000). The environmental, personal and health factors are all important considerations when reviewing the person's level of participation in the wider community. This conceptual framework underpins much of the Australian data on disability.

Figure 12.1: International classification of functioning, disability and health

```
                    Health condition
                  (disorder or disease)
                          │
        ┌─────────────────┼─────────────────┐
        ▼                 ▼                 ▼
  Body Functions ◄──► Activity ◄──────► Participation
   & Structure
        ▲                 ▲
        │                 │
        └────────┬────────┴────────┐
                 ▼                 ▼
           Environmental       Personal
              Factors           Factors
```

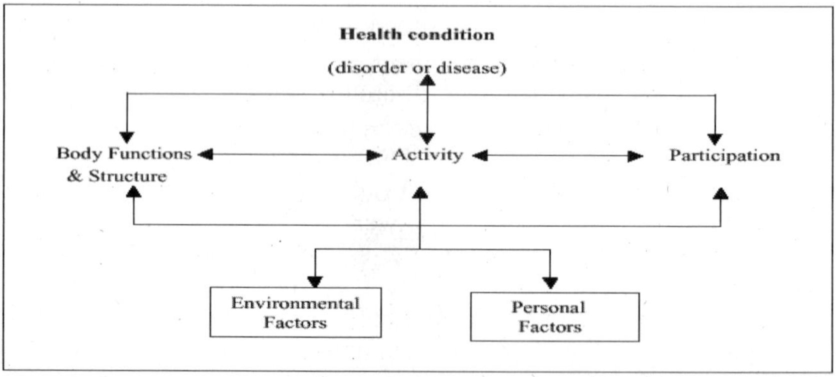

Source: World Health Organisation (2000, p 21)

The second description of disability rests on the social model, which holds that the capacity of a person to contribute to the community can be determined by the community's attitudes towards that person. This social approach is incompatible with the categorisation of individual deficits, and raises a moral objection to the classification process, which it sees as labelling and potentially discriminatory (Mabbett & Bolderson 2000). A development of the social model assumes that if community perceptions about people with a disability can be changed, then it is possible to change the notion of disability (Shakespeare & Corker 2002). However, this more recent debate has acknowledged that impairments can still create difficulties for some people even if the community is not stigmatising the person.

While each of these approaches reflects efforts by the wider community to understand the position of people with a disability, the experience of the person with a disability can also influence whether one defines oneself as having a disability. For example, a person with a chronic back injury may feel that she is restricted in what she can do, because she knows what she used to be able to do. Conversely, a person with cerebral palsy may not consider himself 'disabled' because his life is organised in a way which limits the adverse impact of the disability upon his daily life.

Extent of disability in Australia

In 2003 in Australia, the lives of 3.9 million people (20 per cent of the population) were affected by an impairment, activity limitation or participation restriction; 2.5 million were aged under 65 years. The overall 2 per cent increase since 1993 is largely due to the ageing population (Otis & Howe 1991; Australian Institute of Health and Welfare (AIHW) 2005). These estimates cover a broad range of disabilities, in terms of both the nature of the disability and effect upon the person. For example, 6.3 per cent of the population had a profound or severe core activity limitation, meaning that they always or sometimes needed assistance with activities of self-care, mobility and communication (AIHW 2005, p 210). Of this section of the population, 677,700 were aged under 65, and 560,900 were 65 or older, indicating that 3.9 per cent of the population aged under 65, and 22.5 per cent of those 65 and over were classified as having severe or profound core activity limitation (AIHW 2005, p 211). The figure relating to those under the age of 65 years with a profound core restriction closely approximates the 700,000 people currently in receipt of the Disability Support Pension (DSP) (*The Australian*, 2006).

Poverty and disability

Although past definitions of poverty have been dominated by the use of income-based measures, there is growing recognition of the need to define poverty in relative terms (Gleeson 1998, p 323). Our understanding of poverty has progressed to mean more than simply the deprivation which results from financial hardship, to include 'an inability to participate in community life' (Peter Saunders 2005a, p 2). Indeed in a review of the international literature by Alcock (1993), four main dimensions linking poverty and people with a disability were identified: employment exclusion and exploitation; social service inadequacy; income deprivation; and inaccessibility of the built environment and workplace. The choice of these dimensions acknowledges the importance of the interaction between health and environment, in understanding people's experience of poverty.

The following discussion of poverty and disability uses these four main dimensions to consider in a more comprehensive way the impact of poverty on people with a disability.

Employment exclusion and exploitation

For people with a disability, obstacles to employment often start not with the job application, but with the earlier years of education and training. Physical access can be an issue, as educational institutions have rarely been designed with the needs of people with a disability at the forefront, thus potentially limiting their opportunities. Further, because of limited funding, children at mainstream schools may not receive the level of support and assistance they require (Department of Education, Science and Training (DEST) 2003).When people with a disability do attend further education such as university or vocational education and training (VET) courses, they are less likely than their non-disabled peers to gain employment. A survey of the destination of university graduates in 1999 revealed that 'at the bachelor level, of those students with a disability available for employment, 31.7 per cent were unemployed', nearly four times the unemployment rate for non-disabled graduates (DEST 2003, p 3). For VET courses, less than 50 per cent of graduates with a disability find employment upon completing their course, compared to 74 per cent of all graduates (Australian National Training Authority (ANTA) 2000). At least a large part of this disparity of outcomes can be attributed to access (see later section) and attitudinal barriers. These barriers impede employment success upon graduation, and contribute to the low levels of work experience common to graduates with a disability, which places them at a disadvantage to their peers who do have work experience (DEST 2003, p 3).*

Exclusion from employment occurs through a number of direct and indirect means. The attitude of open labour market employers towards people with disabilities as potential employees is one element. The attitudes of many employers reflect the unfounded yet traditional perceptions of poor productivity and dependability, safety concerns, and lack of social aptitude (DEST 2003). Interestingly the most effective way

---

* The author wishes to thank Janine Dillon for contributing the information on education.

to challenge some of these common myths is through direct personal contact with and knowledge of a person with a disability (Department of Human Services 2000), and it is this personal knowledge that most affects an employer's decision to hire a person with a disability (Weston 2002).

From the 1 July 2006 the Commonwealth Government will create an additional 101,000 employment assistance places to help more people with a disability to move into open employment (Dutton 2005). However, this commitment reflects a mere $500 million spent on targeted measures to increase employment for people with disabilities (Ozdowski 2004; Department of Family & Community Services 2003 cited in BSL 2005, p 3). This amounts to the government spending five cents on disability employment assistance for every dollar spent on the Disability Support Pension payments (Department of Family & Community Services 2003 cited in BSL 2005). Under the Hawke-Keating and Howard Governments, the market has been seen as the key to reform initiatives. Market deregulation has brought about an increase in real wages, but has not led to a decline in unemployment. Consequently Commonwealth government policies remain focused on getting welfare recipients to work (Peter Saunders 2005b, p 2). The effects of this emphasis on the market as the key instrument of reform are magnified by the government's use of limited aggregated economic indicators of unemployment, inflation and interest rates to measure the impact of their policies (Swan 2005). The broad nature of such indicators means that the Howard Government does not fully realise the impact of such policies on people whose disability significantly limits their capacity to work.

In summary, there is a need for increased funding support for students with a disability across all levels of the education system, greater resourcing of targeted measures to increase employment for people with a disability, and mutual obligation requirements for employers. Together these actions could be more effective in producing increased education and workforce participation rates for people with a disability. However, care needs to be exercised not to see people with a disability as a cheap labour force that can be easily exploited and paid below the minimum wage (Gleeson 1998).

Social service inadequacy

The extent to which people with a disability are adequately supported can be critical to the extent to which they are able to participate in education, the workforce and community. The level of both mainstream and specialist support services can contribute to the poverty experienced by people with a disability and their families for a number of reasons.

First, many people with a disability people incur non-discretionary out-of-pocket expenses for goods and services. The fundamental aspect of service funding is affected by two factors: the numbers receiving such services, and the per capita costs of furnishing these services (Smith et al

2000). Thus if service costs are not managed effectively, then either total expenditure increases sharply, or costs are controlled by introducing restrictive eligibility criteria to limit access to services (Stancliffe & Lakin 2005). Consequently careful management of costs and cost effectiveness are important elements of equitable and sustainable service provision. The growth in the number of people with a disability, combined with the ageing of the population, means that it has been difficult for government spending on disability support services to keep up with demand.

According to Davis & George (1993), the International Year of Disabled Persons in 1981 raised awareness among policy-makers and the public of the inequities facing people with a disability. This awareness coincided with growing support by both government and non-government sectors of disability services for the principle of normalisation, which emerged from Scandinavia in the late 1960s and started to have an impact globally by the early 1970s. Simply stated, the principle is that people with a disability should be enabled to lead lives like those of the rest of the population (Cocks 2001).

Consequently, since the early 1980s community-based, user-oriented models of service provision have been preferred by public and non-government agencies, leading to the progressive closure of many large residential institutions for people with a disability. In keeping with this, the introduction of the Home and Community Care (HACC) program in 1985 and the enactment of the Commonwealth *Disability Services Act* 1986 were landmarks in legislative and service reform. Both of these developments acknowledged the importance of people being supported in the community.

The first Commonwealth/State Disability Agreement in 1991 was designed to rationalise and integrate federal and State responsibilities for disability services. In broad terms the agreement gave the Commonwealth responsibility for employment services and the States for providing accommodation and other support services (AIHW 1995, p 330). This was the first national framework for the provision of disability services, and had a clear focus on the human rights of service recipients (Yeatman 1996). This Agreement still holds today, despite being a regular source of conflict between the State and Federal Governments over the levels of funding provided to the States by the Commonwealth.

Between 1983 and 1991, the Commonwealth increased expenditure on disability services by 58 per cent in real terms (Minister for Health, Housing and Community Services 1991), followed by increases of 6.8 per cent in 2000, 5.3 per cent in 2001, and 7.9 per cent in 2002 (AIHW 2003, p 36). Nevertheless significant levels of unmet need remain across Australia: 12,500 people need accommodation and respite services, 8,200 places are required for community access for people not in the labour force, and 5,400 people need employment support (AIHW 2003, p 380). Indeed most new services were being provided to people with very urgent needs. However, it also needs to be kept in perspective that in

2003-04 a total of 187,806 people accessed services funded under the Commonwealth State and Territory Disability Agreement (AIHW 2005, p 237). This represents only 27 per cent of the total number of people under the age of 65 with a profound or severe core activity limitation.

At State level, using Victoria as an example, there has been an increase in funding from $910.4 million in 2004-05 to $987.6 million in 2005-06. When this is adjusted for CPI (2.75) and population (1.0), and comparing the revised budget of $926 million against 2005-06 estimates, the overall increase is 2.77 per cent (Victorian Council of Social Services (VCOSS) 2005c). However, there are still high levels of unmet need, with average case management waiting time rising from 32 days in 2003-04 to an estimated 50 days in 2005-06. There are also 3,262 urgent and high priority cases waiting for accommodation and support. At the current funding rate it will take nearly 19 years to clear the current waiting lists alone (VCOSS 2005b).

The move towards models of individualised funding, where government provides the funds directly to family and people with a disability, has the potential to enable services to be more responsive to their needs. This system will require people with a disability and their families to be better informed of the range of options open to them, so that they can make sound decisions. To achieve this outcome, the assistance of a facilitator to assist may be necessary. The process will also require a fair and transparent process of individual resource allocation, and sound monitoring approaches (Stancliffe & Lakin 2005). Evaluating the effectiveness of these more individualised service responses will require examination of the services provided against those sought by the individual. These services will be challenged to become increasingly cost effective (Stancliffe & Lakin 2005).

In Victoria, a policy was released to address the disadvantage experienced by sections of the community – including people with a disability – by removing barriers to opportunity and providing access and choice for all (Minister for Community Services 2005). Interestingly, the strategy of creating new opportunities for people with a disability is primarily focused upon using $119.5 million over four years to improve the disability and mental health support systems. This targeting of funds acknowledges the important role these services play in maximising the inclusion of people with a disability in our community.

In summary, the costs associated with the management of services need to be reviewed to ensure that the bulk of the resources allocated for services reach the intended recipients. The move towards individualised funding is an important step towards reducing the amount paid towards co-ordinating the delivery of the service. Governments also need to make some important decisions about how much resourcing should be allocated to services in this area if current unmet demand is to be reduced. This goal would be assisted by current funds being used more flexibly.

While the role of the formal service system is important, unpaid carers remain the mainstay of the support system for people with a disability. In 2003 there were 202,000 primary carers of people aged under 65, living with the main recipient of care, usually their son or daughter (AIHW 2005). The extent to which the wider community provides the majority of support for such people is a point increasingly being impressed upon governments by carer groups lobbying for greater support. Families and carers of the person with a disability often receive less income because their caring role places limits placed on their capacity to earn. For example, carers may trade income for flexibility to help a person with a disability. While many authors have pointed out the crucial role played by family in caring for other family members, few studies have comprehensively examined the financial burden involved (Lewis & Johnson 2005). Indeed the caring role can place additional costs on the carers. Fujiura et al (1994) estimated the extra non-reimbursed spending by families supporting an adult with an intellectual disability as at least US$6,300 in additional expenditure each year. This works out to be at least a 60 per cent increase in family costs for raising a child with disabilities.

However, care must be taken not to view costs in purely economic terms. Baldwin (1985), for example, drew a distinction between direct financial costs (for example loss of earnings) and psychological costs (for example, restricted social life, raised stress levels). There is a clear need for government to ensure that both formal disability services and informal carers are sufficiently resourced and supported in a way which recognises the additional costs of disability, so as to improve the capacity of people with a disability and their carers to participate in our society (Lewis & Johnson 2005).

Income deprivation

The income deprivation experienced by people with a disability results from their exclusion from the labour market and to the additional expenses associated with having a disability. Australia has the lowest average personal income for people with disabilities of any Organisation for Economic Co-operation and Development (OECD) country: Australians with a disability have an income level 44 per cent of that of people without disabilities (OECD 2003). Peter Saunders (2005a) recently reported that the median after-tax income of households where a person has a disability is 14.9 per cent below that of non-disability households.

Nearly half of all people with a disability exhibit a high rate of social dependency compared with less than one quarter of all Australians, because their main source of income is government pensions or cash benefits. People with a disability aged between 15 and 64 have a participation in the workforce rate of 53 per cent, compared to 81 per cent for people without a disability (AIHW 2005). Moreover, as the severity of handicap increases, the reliance on government pensions or benefits also increases (AIHW 2005), and it follows that the greater the severity of impairment, the greater the potential depth of poverty (Gleeson 1998). The additional costs associated with having a disability were a critical factor identified during the Henderson Inquiry, and he recommended that supplementary payments or services in kind be made available to people with a disability to help them to participate in key activities such as paid work (ibid).

A number of recent Australian surveys provide an overview of the association between disability and standard of living (Peter Saunders 2005a). Using these data the following findings emerged:

1. Having a household member with a disability is associated with a substantial increase in the incidence of financial hardship, a higher probability of experiencing severe financial stress, and is more likely to result in having to seek help from others. Disability also leads to less social participation, and to being more likely to report not having access to external financial support if required (Peter Saunders 2005a).

2. Where the poverty line is set at 50 per cent of the median (adjusted) income, disability is associated with a two percentage point increase in the risk of poverty where it affects an adult, and a five percentage point increase where it affects children (Peter Saunders 2005c). These findings appear to support the view that the welfare system provides a comprehensive but modest income safety net that protects most people from extreme income poverty (Peter Saunders 2005c).

3. Among disability households, unemployment is approximately 2.5 times higher than average. Household employment rates are lower where there is an adult with a disability, particularly in relation to full time employment (ibid). Unemployment rates are higher for those with severe or profound disabilities (BSL 2005).

4. People with a disability are more likely to have health problems that significantly affect their quality of life (Bradbury et al 2001).

Any one of these indicators may pose a significant barrier to a person with a disability being included in our community. Further, the multiplier effect means that households with a person with a disability can be among the most disadvantaged groups. Thus as Swan (2005) has argued, if we are going to find effective solutions to poverty, we need to move beyond the narrow definition of poverty centred on 'lack of resources', to a definition that encompasses all the factors that prevent people from participating in the community.

Given this brief introduction to disability theory and its intersection with debates on poverty, let us now consider current policy developments at both federal and State levels. The Commonwealth government income support for people with a disability and their carers has changed significantly over the past 20 years. Most notably, the 1991 Disability Reform Package heralded a raft of changes, including the introduction of the Disability Support Pension (DSP) to replace the Invalid Pension and Sheltered Employment Allowance. This change raised the eligibility threshold level, enabling people with a disability to earn more income through employment without threat to their benefit amount (Disability Task Force 1995, in Gleeson 1998). The number of people receiving the DSP increased more than five-fold between 1972 and 2004, from 138,800 to 696,700, by 5.2 per cent a year on average, well above the increase in both the disability population and the total working-age population.

Following the 2005 federal budget, reforms were announced linking DSP eligibility to mutual obligation activities designed to facilitate the Welfare to Work transition (Peter Saunders 2005a). The key feature of these changes is a reduction from 30 to 15 hours a week in the 'capacity to work' requirement. This change means that people with a disability coming into the benefit system will be ineligible for DSP if they are capable of working more than 15 hours, forcing them onto the lower Newstart Allowance (Peter Saunders 2005a). This policy effectively removes choice for many people with a disability who are willing and able to work on a part-time or casual basis. These changes appear to be premised upon a medical model of disability, as no acknowledgment is given to the significant barriers to workforce participation which confront people with a disability. Indeed the creation of a work capacity assessment process seems to consider the capacity of the person to work over the barriers others may place in the way of this capacity (Dutton 2005).

While the level of financial support and services to people with a disability have improved significantly since the Henderson Inquiry, it is difficult to determine how much this has alleviated the poverty levels within the population of people with a disability. This poverty level also relates to the extent to which they need to meet their own costs of support thereby increasing the costs of disability. Moreover if the Disability Support Pension (DSP) is insufficient to cover the additional costs of disability then this can also contribute to the additional hardship experienced.

In the context of income deprivation we can see not only the consequences of the various issues outlined in the area of employment exclusion and exploitation, but can also understand the associated costs of disability. As the issues of employment exclusion are not going to be addressed immediately, the mutual obligations being placed on job seekers alone will only serve to push more people with a disability into greater levels of poverty. There is a need to broaden this notion of mutual obligation to apply to employers, and to provide more adequate pension levels which recognise the true costs of disability. There is also a need to review whether current pension levels are providing sufficient support to people.

Inaccessibility of the built environment and workplace

Transport inadequacies and inaccessible buildings and workplaces also act as barriers for potential employees with a disability, particularly those with a physical disability. Efforts to improve the accessibility of the built environment, whether in relation to workplaces, public spaces or housing, are politically highly sensitive. For example, governments do not want to place extra demands upon employers in a global marketplace where many governments are seeking ways to entice business to their corner of the globe. In relation to housing, increased regulation around accessible housing is seen as potentially limiting on developers whom governments are keen to attract.

The concern in relation to building codes has been that the small business sector may be disproportionately hit with compliance costs to strengthened building standards which place a greater emphasis on accessibility and at a broader level may adversely affect building activity and the wider economy (Australian Government Productivity Commission (AGPC) 2004).

In public transport, the transport disability standards have been criticised by disability advocates because they give transport operators and providers up to 30 years to comply (AGPC 2004). In 1998, the Human Rights and Equal Opportunity Commission issued an exemption to the Victorian Government in regard to certain aspects of the public transport system not being required to meet full compliance with the federal Disability Standards. The commission ruled that the transport system must be 100 per cent compliant within 20 years or by 2022, with the exclusion of trains and trams. These would need to be 100 per cent compliant within 30 years or by 2032 (Department of Infrastructure 2006). This delay has been largely because of the costs of upgrading many of these services. Given that the infrastructure is aging, there is an opportunity for our built environment and transport infrastructure to be made more accessible to the wider community.

Conclusion

The concept of social exclusion is just starting to enter the lexicon of modern Australian social policy. Much of Australia's social and economic policy has been based on this concept, with ideas of mateship and looking after each other having been very influential in shaping a unique Australian way (Swan 2005). Historically, this 'fair go' principle has enabled the negotiation of compromise between government and the market, ensuring our relative prosperity and delivering opportunities to the majority (Swan 2005). A minimum wage and collective rights in the workplace, universal education, universal health services and a modest safety net have been part of this approach (Swan 2005). However, the dominance of market-led reforms has resulted in progressive policy changes which have impacted adversely upon all these areas. Changes such as those recently proposed to industrial relations legislation, together with changes to education funding and growing pressures on the health system increasingly challenge this egalitarian ethos.

The introduction of inclusion into social policy discourse has been an important development for disability policy. However, the fact that the market continues to be the main driver behind any social reforms has resulted in undue emphasis on employment as the key to greater inclusion of people with a disability in our community. This limited focus prevents adequate addressing of the fundamental barriers to effective participation of people with a disability in our community. This is particularly the case for those people with high support needs who may find it difficult to access open employment, and so need to be able to be included in our community in other ways of their own choosing. The proposed changes to the DSP highlight the flaws in an employment-focused approach to inclusion, unless there is an accompanying rigorous address of barriers to employment.

Social inclusion needs to be person-centred in its approach and requires a move beyond the narrow concept of productivity and economic imperatives. We need to embrace this philosophy in order to redefine how our society is constructed so as to be genuinely inclusive of people with a disability. This will only occur when we know them as a work colleague, a member of our local sporting group, local church, or as a neighbour. Ideally, there will be greater leadership from people with disabilities in this process of community capacity building. Indeed the current generation of young people with disabilities and their families has different lifestyle expectations and aspirations from those of 20 years ago.

Considering social inclusion from a human rights rather than economic framework opens up the choices of people with a disability, giving legitimacy to both social and economic participation in the community. While having a choice to work is certainly an important aspect of this, there must be a simultaneous focus on the benefits of social inclusion and the ways to achieve this. Such an inclusive culture would acknowledge the significance of the values of social justice, relationships, choice and human rights.

Chapter 13

Government anti-poverty strategies in Australia

Benno Engels & Gavin Dufty

As the preceding chapters reveal, poverty engenders heated debate over its conceptualisation, measurement and causes. These debates have necessarily spilled over into the practice domain, which identifies who needs assistance and what form this assistance should take. So far in this book little has been said about existing anti-poverty strategies aimed at ameliorating the impact of poverty on individuals and households in Australia. In fact, little has been written on this topic because in Australia anti-poverty strategies are uncoordinated and dispersed across several tiers of government (for exceptions see Hollingworth 1972; Mendelsohn 1979; Emery 1983; Graycar & Jamrozik 1989, 1993).

This chapter therefore provides an overview of what the three levels of government – federal, State and local – are doing to counteract poverty in a number of key areas. The chapter focuses on the government sector because governments direct substantial public resources into programs to help reduce poverty. This choice of focus should not suggest that the non-government sector is inconsequential, as it too makes an important contribution to reducing poverty. However, it is beyond the scope of this chapter to examine the many initiatives undertaken by the non-government sector.

Anti-poverty strategies and the government sector

A review of the literature reveals no universal agreement on what an anti-poverty strategy should or should not encompass, probably a symptom of the conceptual difficulties that beleaguer this field. In the early 1940s William Beveridge, the architect of the modern British welfare state, proposed a very practical conception of what such a strategy might constitute for governments. He argued that a comprehensive anti-poverty strategy had to address what he called the 'five giant evils' of poverty – want, disease, ignorance, squalor, and idleness (Beveridge 1943, pp 42-44). Following this conception, post-World War II government spending in the UK and Australia was expanded in five social welfare areas – income support, health, education, housing and employment services – as it was believed that these were the areas most capable of making a contribution to raising the living standard of poor individuals and families (Bryson 1992; Graycar & Jamrozik 1993).

More contemporary research has suggested that government-funded anti-poverty strategies can be extended beyond these classic forms to include community development, labour market programs, emergency relief, recreation, counselling for alcohol, gambling and drug addiction, travel concessions, legal aid, consumer protection, anti-discrimination, and affirmative action (Graycar & Jamrozik 1993; Alcock 1997). It is beyond the scope of this chapter to consider all these forms of poverty alleviation, so the discussion will focus on government programs concerned with income support, health care, housing, and some personal social services.

Government spending on social welfare takes two main forms: direct and indirect. With direct assistance, cash goes directly to eligible individuals or families, via a wide variety of pensions and allowances. Indirect assistance includes a wide array of benefits and price concessions that reduce the cost of living, and may be targeted to the poor alone or to the broader community. When assistance occurs at the community level, provisions are made not to disadvantage the poor through access and cost thresholds, as the poor often make greater use of these services and facilities. The Pharmaceutical Benefit Scheme (PBS) is a good example.

To complicate matters, in Australia anti-poverty programs are not always delivered by the level of government that funds them. Certain indirect forms of assistance can be funded and delivered exclusively by one level of government, while other programs can be funded by one but delivered by another level of government, or by non-government organisations. There are also examples where two levels of government are the funding sources, with program delivery handed over to a third level of government or to non-government organisations. Such complex funding and delivery arrangements can be confusing and are evident within the activities of the Commonwealth government, to which the discussion now turns.

The Commonwealth government:
Income support, concessions, and fiscal federalism

The ability of the Commonwealth government to reduce poverty is delimited by two provisions in the Commonwealth Constitution (Mendelsohn 1979; Jamrozik 2001). Section 51 originally permitted the government to legislate only with regard to the provision of invalid and old-age pensions, but a referendum to amend the Constitution in 1946 extended its authority to provide a broader range of income support plus a number of social services (Sawer 1963; Kewley 1973). Over time, the income support responsibilities of the Commonwealth government have expanded further, with the approval of the States, partly because the Commonwealth has greater revenue-raising capacity to finance such services.

In contrast, s 96 of the Constitution restricts the Commonwealth government to supplying financial assistance to the States and Territories (hereafter simply referred to as the States) for the provision of health care, education, housing and social services. The Commonwealth government cannot dictate how these general purpose grants are to be used. However, under s 96, the Commonwealth can also provide specific purpose grants to the States, and thereby influence how these funds are to be spent. It can also offer grants directly to organisations such as local government, community groups and welfare agencies, should a State government not wish to support a social welfare initiative of the Commonwealth Government (Emery 1983; Mendelsohn 1983).

To support the anti-poverty initiatives of the government, a number of departments and statutory authorities have been formed at the federal level, and perform a wide range of functions including research, policy formulation, distribution of funds, program monitoring, and some service delivery. These include Centrelink, the Department of Family and Community Services, and the Department of Employment and Work Place Relations. Hence the Commonwealth Government is a crucial public agent in the fight against poverty, as the following discussion illustrates in greater detail.

Probably the most significant anti-poverty strategy of the Commonwealth government is its provision of income support, which in 2003 benefited more than 6 million Australians (Senate Community Affairs References Committee (SCARC) 2004). Income support refers 'to the provision of cash payments to persons who, for one reason or another, do not have access to an adequate income' to cover basic living costs (Jamrozik 2001, p 112). Clearly, if income support were not provided by the Commonwealth government, many Australians would be living in poverty.

Income support can take several forms: pension, allowance, payment, or benefit. They are differentiated by their legislative intent, eligibility conditions, dollar value, and whether recipients are obliged to do something in return for their receipt (Jamrozik 2001). Table 13.1 shows a variety of pensions, allowances, payments, and benefits.

In addition to the direct payment of income support, the Commonwealth government also provides some indirect assistance in the form of price concessions, in an attempt to reduce the cost of living. Concessions provide governments with another tool to target assistance precisely to those in need, and include the Health Care Card, Foster Child Health Care Card, Low Income Health Care Card, Pensioner Concession Card, Commonwealth Seniors Health Card, and an Interim Card. Table 13.2 lists the differing conditions of each concession card type. Such concessions make a significant contribution to reducing the cost of living for the poor, especially in accessing health care and medicines. The provision of such concessions is another important component of the fight against poverty by the Commonwealth government.

Table 13.1. Main income support payments and allowances

Types of income support	Eligibility requirements	Recipients at Sept 2005*
Age Pension	Men aged over 65 and women aged over 62*, subject to residency, income and asset tests.	1,904,823
Disability Support Pension	People with a physical, intellectual or psychiatric impairment that prevents them from working full time (30 hours per week) for the next 2 years.	702,836
Widow Allowance	Women aged over 50 who become widowed, divorced or separated and have no recent workforce experience.	35,363
Parenting Payment	Carers of children under 16 years, primarily in single income families with low income. It is paid for single and partnered parents.	593,574
Newstart Allowance	Unemployed persons aged over 21 and actively looking for work.	424,988
Youth Allowance	Full-time students under 25 and unemployed people aged 16-20 years. Income tested on both individual and parental incomes.	360,988
Austudy	Students aged 25 years and over engaged in full time study.	22,407
Carer Payment	People who provide full-time care to someone with a severe physical, intellectual or psychiatric disability who is expected to receive this care for at least 6 months.	89,544
Sickness Allowance	People aged over 21 who are temporarily unable to work or study because of illness, injury or disability.	1,473
Family Tax Benefit A	Families with children under 16 or full-time dependent students aged 16-24. Income tested on family income.	Paid to 1.8 million for nearly 3.5 million children#
Family Tax Benefit B	Single income and sole parent families. Income tested on second earner's income only in two-parent families.	Benefits around 550,000 families##

Sources: * Centrelink, Populations 2004 Qtr 3 (05-09-03) Ver-01, Postcode by Payment Type; # Key demographic and income features of the Family Tax Benefit Part A customer population, Paper presented to the 9th Australian Institute of Family Studies Conference, 9-11 February 2005, Melbourne, Australia, By Amanda Robertson and Jianfei Gong; ## Australian Budget papers 2004-2005, more help for families, http://www.budget.gov.au/2004-05/bp2/html/revenue-02.htm

Table 13.2. Commonwealth concession cards and eligibility requirements

Concession card types	Eligibility requirements
Health Care Card (HCC) Automatically issued every 3 to 12 months	Meet the residency requirements and be in Australia to retain the card
	Be in receipt of a qualifying social security benefit, or
	Be receiving certain social security supplementary payments, or
	Be in specific circumstances such as receiving the fortnightly maximum rate of Family Tax Benefit A by instalments, a parent caring for disabled children and receiving Carer Allowance (child), etc
Pensioner Concession Card (PCC) Automatically re-issued on the person's birthday	Meet the residency requirements and be in Australia to retain the card
	Be receiving a social security pension
	Over 60 years of age
	Available to certain other Centrelink programs
Foster Child Health Care Card (FCHCC) Automatically re-issued every 6 months	A child must be in foster care
	Be living in Australia with an Australian resident or a special category via holder
	Meet the definition of family tax benefit child
Low Income Health Care Card (LIHCC) Must be applied for every 6 months	Meet the income test
	Meet the residency requirements and be an Australian citizen
	Meet the requirements of special benefit via holder
Commonwealth Seniors Health Card (CSHC) Automatically re issued each year in August	Meet the residency requirements and be in Australia to retain the card
	Not be receiving a social security pension or benefit, or a service pension
	Be of Age Pension age
	Meet an annual adjusted taxable income test (there is no asset test)
Interim Card Issued after a needs assessment	Valid only for two weeks
	Issued to persons entitled to concessions who have an urgent need while waiting for the mail delivery of their normal card

Source: Centrelink (2005b)

Table 13.3. Other Commonwealth Funded Programs in Australia, 2005

Program areas	Program description
Health	
Medicare	Universal health care system
Pharmaceutical Benefit Scheme	Subsidised prescribed medicines
Aboriginal Health Strategy	Funding for housing and infrastructure projects in rural and remote communities
Education	
Assistance for Isolated Children Scheme	Improving learning outcomes for children from isolated communities
Country Area Program	Assist with literacy, numeracy and special learning needs of children with disabilities and educationally disadvantaged
Disability Funding	Funding for students with disabilities
English as a Second Language Program	Provide assistance to newly arrived migrant children
Housing	
Rent Assistance Program	Provide supplementary payment for all eligible recipients renting privately
The Commonwealth-State Housing Agreement	Funding is supplied to the states and territories to provide public housing and other support services
Support Accommodation Assistance Program	Designed to tackle homeless and provide crisis accommodation for victims of domestic violence
Community Housing Infra-structure Program	Seeks to improve the housing and related infrastructure needs of aboriginal people
Social Services	
Independent Living Allowance	Assistance to young people who have difficulties with the transition to their own independent living.
Home and Community Care Program	Funding community support program for the aged and disabled who wish to remain living in their own accommodation
Child Care Benefit	Payment made to families in order to help with the expense of child care
Emergency Relief Program	Funds distributed to welfare organisations for emergency relief assistance

Source: Centrelink (2005a)

The Commonwealth government also funds major programs in health, education, housing and social services that make an important contribution to the well-being of the entire community, as well as the poor (see Table 13.3). One of the main health initiatives is Medicare, introduced in 1984 by a federal Labor government. Medicare was designed to provide all Australians with rebates for fees paid to privately practising doctors, and free treatment within public hospitals. In addition, the PBS gives patients access to a broad range of subsidised medicines, with Commonwealth concession card holders paying a discounted fee for each prescription item. Moreover, once the card holders' expenditure exceeds a threshold within a single year, further prescriptions are free (ABS 2004a).

The Commonwealth government also funds two very important housing programs which assist the poor. Probably the more important is Rent Assistance, a supplementary payment to income support recipients renting in the private housing market. In 2002-03 the Commonwealth government spent $1.8 billion assisting 940,708 persons unable to secure public housing (SCARC 2004). The other key housing program is the Supported Accommodation Assistance Program (SAAP). Funded jointly by State and federal governments, it provides crisis accommodation to people who are homeless or at risk of becoming homeless, and to women and children escaping domestic violence. In 2001-02, it has been estimated that SAAP assisted on average 20,000 people per day, many of whom were experiencing extreme poverty (SCARC 2004). Some of those persons are able to get additional assistance from the federally-funded Emergency Relief Program (see Chapter 14). Lastly, the Commonwealth government also co-funds with the States the Home and Community Care Program (HACC), a vital social service for the elderly and disabled who prefer to reside in their own home. The details of this program are discussed below.

The States and Territories: Concessions and welfare services

The second tier of governance in Australia consists of the States and Territories. Assisted by federal funding, the States provide a wide range of social welfare programs and services in education, health, child protection, youth, family support, the aged, disabled, criminal offenders, drug treatment, crisis accommodation, public housing, emergency relief, public transport, and community services (see Emery 1983; Bowman and Healy 1988; Graycar & Jamrozik 1993). Most of these programs and services are delivered as indirect assistance to individuals and households, with only a small number being targeted for the poor.

The States' reliance upon indirect forms of assistance can be attributed to two factors. First, income support is a constitutional responsibility of the Commonwealth government. Second, the States do not wish to introduce any form of cash assistance that could encourage the Commonwealth government to reduce its provision of income support.

There are the odd exceptions to this rule, such as the Victorian Educational Maintenance Allowance paid to low income families to help with a child's educational expenses during primary and secondary schooling.

Any discussion of welfare at this level of government is especially complex, because programs and services differ significantly between States, due to the political and policy orientation of former and current governments. Each State has its own departments of education, health, transport and human services, with the latter usually focused on social welfare services to children, families, aged, disabled, the homeless and the broader community. Service delivery can vary enormously, as the States may contract the services out to local government and community sector agencies, or deliver them themselves (Steering Committee Report 2005).

Despite these differences, all State governments attempt to tackle poverty by lowering living costs via price concessions to eligible residents. Table 13.4 summarises the range of concessions offered by the States in the following areas: utilities, health, hardship, transport, education and local government rates. Several patterns emerge from these data. First, not all States offer concessions in identical areas, but electricity, water, public transport, visual impairment assistance and taxi travel for the disabled are supplied across the board. Victoria, ACT and New South Wales are the most generous, and the Northern Territory is the least generous in providing concessions. Second, not all concessions are made available to low income people and the poor. For example, electricity concessions in Queensland, Tasmania and the Northern Territory are restricted to aged pensioners, war veterans and war widows. Travel on private bus routes is only subsidised for the poor and income support recipients in Victoria, Western Australia, ACT and the Northern Territory. Third, concession levels also vary across Australia. For example, the electricity rebate for eligible persons in New South Wales is $112 per annum, $115 in Queensland, $120 in South Australia and $146 in the ACT. These figures suggest that some States are more actively engaged in the alleviation of poverty than others. It is beyond the scope of this section to undertake a detailed assessment of what else the various States are doing to reduce poverty, so the remainder of this section will concentrate on one State: Victoria.

The decision to focus on Victoria was made partly because Victoria has a recent history of Labor governments that have tried to implement programs to tackle poverty. In the 1980s, the Cain Government adopted a social justice strategy that sought to redress disadvantage, especially among the long-term unemployed, the aged, and children from poor families (Wiseman 1992). This political era was followed by seven years of austere Coalition administration, until the late 1990s brought a new Labor Government that sought economic and social reform. In 2005 the Bracks Labor Government released 'Challenges in Addressing Disadvantage in Victoria', and 'A Fairer Victoria', which take a whole-of-government approach to tackling disadvantage in Victoria. These initiatives propose

Table 13.4. State and Territory based concessions, 2005

Concessions	Types	NSW	VIC	QLD	WA	SA	TAS	ACT	NT
Utilities	Electricity	√	√	√	√	√	√	√	√
	Gas	√	√	X	X	X	X	√	X
	Water	√	√	√	√	√	√	√	√
Health	Life support	√	√	√	√	X	√	√	X
	Dental treatment	√	√	√	√	√	√	√	X
	Patient travel	√	√	√	√	√	√	√	X
	Glasses	X	√	√	√	X	√	√	√
Hardship	Emergency relief	√	√	X	X	√	X	√	X
Transport	Public transport	√	√	√	√	√	√	√	√
	Private bus	√	√	√	√	√	√	√	√
	Visual impaired	√	√	√	√	√	√	√	√
	Seniors travel	√	√	√	√	X	√	√	√
	Taxi for disabled	√	√	√	√	√	√	√	√
	Car registration	√	√	√	√	√	√	√	√
	Drivers licence	√	√	X	√	√	√	√	√
Education	School fee relief	√	√	X	√	√	√	√	X
	TAFE	√	√	√	X	√	√	√	X
	Training programs	X	X	√	X	X	X	X	X
Local government rates		√	√	√	√	√	√	√	√

Note: a √ *signifies the provision of a concession and a shaded* √ *indicates that the concession is available to anybody including all holders of Commonwealth Health Care Cards (which includes foster child care and low income card recipients). An X indicates that a concession is not provided.*

Source: complied from Victorian Concession Unit (2005) Interstate Concessions, unpublished report, Department of Human Services, Melbourne.

to target groups including children, youth, aged, disabled, the mentally ill, Aborigines, and people who live in disadvantaged places with access problems to key services such as public transport, schools, ambulances, hospitals and affordable housing (Victorian State Government 2005). Almost half a billion dollars has been budgeted for this anti-poverty strategy over the next five years. From these programs, the housing initiative is now considered in more detail.

The Victorian anti-poverty initiative targets access to affordable housing because extensive research links housing and poverty. The poor usually expend proportionally more of their income on housing, than do middle and upper income households, and many are unable to access suitable private housing because they have special needs (SCARC 2004; Yates et al 2004). Several housing programs are designed to help reduce housing poverty in Victoria. For example, via the Commonwealth-State Housing Agreement, public housing is supplied at below-market rates to low-income individuals and families in crisis, identified via a number of assessment and referral services. Unfortunately the demand for public housing continues to exceed its availability, leading housing advocacy groups to lobby the Victorian Government to accelerate its building program (VCOSS 2005a). For low-income households unable to secure public housing, rental bond loans and home purchase schemes aim to reduce the cost burden of private market accommodation. In addition, a number of community housing programs provide subsidised rental housing for persons with special needs, including the disabled, elderly, mentally ill and the homeless. As well as participating in the joint Commonwealth- and State-funded SAAP for homeless persons, Victoria has developed its own Homelessness Strategy.

Homeless and low-income individuals can also secure emergency relief assistance in Victoria. As Table 13.4 shows, Victoria is one of the few States to fund a hardship program. Emergency relief usually takes the form of food and clothing, distributed through local charities and welfare agencies (see Chapter 14). Emergency assistance with unpaid utility accounts and free financial counselling is also provided by the Victorian Concession Unit, within the Department of Human Services. Finally, the Victorian Government in conjunction with the Commonwealth also funds the HACC program which provides a range of support services to elderly and disabled persons in their homes, although delivery of the service is often undertaken by local government or contracted agencies. The discussion will now briefly turn to local government and some specific examples from Victoria.

Local government: Rates and welfare support

Local government in Australia is not fully autonomous, but falls within the constitutional jurisdiction of the States and Territories (Power et al 1981; Jones 1993). With the exception of the ACT, each of the six States and the Northern Territory has its own system of local government, but they do share a number of things in common. They have roughly the same limited powers and functions which include the provision and maintenance of roads, garbage collection, public health, libraries, infant health, child care, building regulations, land use zoning, upkeep of parks and sporting facilities, social planning, community development and the delivery of a small range of social services. Program funds are largely derived from state and commonwealth grants, with some revenue also raised from local land rates, service charges, fines, and business undertakings. As a result, the capacity of local government to undertake anti-poverty programs is largely restricted to offering individual and household waivers or discounts from local rates and charges (see Table 13.4). Only New South Wales and South Australia extend these discounts to the poor and low income, while the other States and Territories restrict them to aged pensioners, veterans and war widows.

The HACC Program, begun in 1985, reinforces the provision of local welfare assistance to the 'deserving' poor – the aged and disabled. This program has two main purposes. First, it provides support in the form of personal home care, meals, property maintenance, respite care and planned group activities, to the elderly and disabled who wish to live independently. Second, supporting such persons in their own accommodation helps to reduce the need for governments to build extra institutional residential care facilities (Howe 2000). This program does, however, have one other outcome. All these support services are provided at subsidised rates and help to reduce living costs of eligible recipients, although low-income individuals and families cannot access these services unless they share accommodation with an eligible recipient. Clearly, the HACC program helps to reduce poverty among the aged and disabled population, even if local government or contracted agencies do little more than deliver these services on behalf of the Commonwealth and State governments.

However, municipal councils and shires are not entirely under the control of State governments. They do have some discretionary capacity to decide where their resources will be directed and what policy agendas are prioritised, in accordance with community need. For example, two Victorian municipalities – Darebin and Hume – have directed resources to tackling poverty by undertaking studies into its extent within their communities (City of Darebin 2001; Hume City Council 2003). Both studies make recommendations that neither council will be able to fully implement due to resource constraints and to the broader structural nature of poverty emanating from outside their municipal boundaries. Fortunately, Hume City Council was able to secure funding from the Victorian Government's Neighbourhood Renewal Program in 2003 and 2005, to provide unemployed persons with an opportunity to escape poverty by offering them paid work and training to help upgrade local public housing in Broadmeadows (Broad 2005). Such community-based initiatives offer some potential for participants, who can apply for other paid work once the project has finished.

In contrast, Knox City Council, also in Victoria, channels its discretionary resources into a very different anti-poverty strategy. It provides to the poor a range of support services, including assessment and referral, financial counselling, emergency relief, no-interest loans, and help with problem gambling (SCARC 2004, p.407). All three councils work closely with religious and welfare agencies in their municipalities to help alleviate the impact of poverty upon their communities. Unfortunately, the level of need is much greater than their discretionary resources, so poverty continues in these three Victorian municipalities.

Problems and possible remedies

Despite anti-poverty strategies at the federal, State and local government levels, poverty has not been eliminated in Australia. In fact, there is evidence that poverty has increased over the past two or three decades (SCARC 2004; Jamrozik 2005; Peter Saunders 2005b). How could this be possible? A number of reasons can be advanced to account for this apparent anomaly.

First, the existence of anti-poverty strategies such as a national income support system seems to suggest that federal governments over the past 100 years have been committed to the goal of eliminating poverty in this country. However, this is not the case. Rather, Commonwealth governments, whether Labor or Coalition, have only ever sought to 'relieve poverty, rather than eliminate it' (Jamrozik 2005, pp.132-33). This assertion is borne out by the fact that there has only been one official Commonwealth government investigation into poverty – the Commission of Inquiry into Poverty (Henderson 1975). Moreover, the federal Coalition Government has recently rejected the findings of an 18-month poverty inquiry by the Australian Senate completed in 2004, on the grounds that it was a political attempt to condemn the government (Topsfield 2006). Inter-party politics has been and continues to be a major impediment to the development of a bipartisan commitment to eliminate poverty in Australia.

Secondly, income support varies in terms of how much cash assistance is provided to different types of recipients. Pensions are set at 25 per cent of male total average weekly earnings, adjusted twice yearly for changes in the CPI. By contrast, benefits are only adjusted annually to the CPI (SCARC 2004). Thus benefits are generally worth less than pensions, as they are supposed to be only temporary assistance. This position is evident in Table 13.5. The only recipient type to not be worse off than an aged pensioner is the single parent with a child under the age of 16 years. So why are the other income support recipients not provided with more adequate cash assistance? This deficit can be attributed to a deep-seated

Table 13.5. Payment differentials between the aged pension and a sample of benefits, September- December 2005

Pension or benefit recipient types	$ per fortnight basic payment	Additional payments	Total payments (Columns 2 + 3)	$ Amount above or below the Aged Pension
Single Aged Pensioner > 65 yrs	$488.90 +	$608.74 (#%$&^)	$1,097.64	$0
Single Parent with 1 Child <16 yrs	$488.90 +	$731.66 (* #)	$1,200.56	$122.92 extra
Single Disabled living away from home 18–20 yrs	$418.90 @	$523.90 (# %)	$ 942.80	$ 84.84 less
Single unemployed away from home > 20 yrs	$404.50	$503.70 (#)	$ 908.30	$105.04 less
Single Student away from home >18 yrs	$326.50	$425.70 (#)	$ 752.30	$183.40 less

Notes:
*Family Tax Benefit Part A and B (an additional $161.70 per fortnight if child is under 5 and an additional $126.14 if child is between 5 and 15 years of age)
\# rent assistance maximum rate $99.20 pf or $116.62 pf for single parent
% Pharmaceutical benefit $5.80 pf
$ Telephone Allowance $81.60 per annum (that is. $3.14 pf)
& Utility allowance $3.90
^ Seniors concession $7.80. In addition, since July 2000 there has been a pension supplement. of $17.50 for elderly single persons
@ Youth Disability Supplement of $92.40 pf is payable to DSP customers aged under 21 and is included in the above rates

Source: Complied from Centrelink (2005)

belief within government and the community that the aged, severely disabled, orphans and veterans, are more deserving than the unemployed, mildly disabled, students, carers, and people with illness. This belief stems from the assumption that these pensioner groups have already made a contribution to society, or are victims of circumstances beyond their control. Far less compassion is exhibited towards those labelled as undeserving poor, who continue to be the largest group suffering poverty in this country.

Thirdly, income support payments are inadequate, especially for recipients with complex needs. For example, disabled persons have extra living costs such as a greater than average need to use a taxi, telephone, medicine, and home heating. Indeed ACOSS (2003c, 2003d) found that the most frequent users of emergency relief were disabled pensioners and persons on the lower-valued benefits (see Chapter 14). In late 2005 the

Commonwealth Government introduced changes to transfer single parents and the mildly disabled onto less generous benefits. This move could lead to an even higher level of demand for emergency relief from these income support recipients. These legislative changes have been introduced because it is believed that the income support system has begun to spawn a culture of inter-generational welfare dependency (Newman 1999; Wroe 2005). Whether this is true or not remains unclear. To compound matters, groups such as asylum seekers, newly-arrived migrants, and 'breached' unemployed, are excluded from income support for varying periods of time (Noble & Wroe 2005). Thus poverty continues to be fuelled in Australia by inadequate levels of support and temporary exclusion from income support assistance.

Fourthly, although price concessions offered by the States help reduce living costs for the low income and poor, again the 'deserving poor' have preferential access to these concessions, ahead of the 'undeserving poor'. Even when these concessions are provided, they can vary in value, so that some people can be further disadvantaged simply because of their place of residence.

So what could be done to overcome these problems? Several remedies have been proposed in the recent Senate Enquiry (SCARC 2004) on poverty and financial hardship. First, it recommends the development of a national strategy to alleviate poverty, involving all three levels of government and the non-government sector, necessary to foster better cooperation and thus better coordination of programs. In turn, and irrespective of their political orientation, all States would offer the same range of concessions. Secondly, such nationwide coordination is best handled through the establishment of a national anti-poverty authority or agency which would also engage in program evaluation across all levels of funding and delivery. This agency would need to be independent of government, and it could report annually to the existing Council of Australian Governments. Thirdly, a coordinated national anti-poverty strategy should ensure that government programs in key social policy areas such as education, employment, health care, housing and personal services, across all three levels of government, are targeted to tackle poverty. In addition, other major policy areas, such as justice, industry, training, energy, and the environment, would be required to demonstrate how they could contribute to the alleviation of poverty; that is, a whole-of-government approach is needed. Fourthly, the different levels of government and the non-government sector must reach agreement on how to define and measure poverty. Once a national measure has been developed, it will be possible to set national poverty reduction targets. Such national targets would help to de-politicise the ongoing debates about whether certain income support benefits should be more generous or not. Finally, all of these remedies are only possible if the community and government acknowledge that poverty deserves to be prioritised as our principal social problem in this country. Unless there is this heightened level of awareness, the goodwill and cooperation needed between the three levels of government will never occur.

Conclusion

This chapter has provided an overview of the different kinds of anti-poverty strategies currently implemented by federal, State and local governments in Australia. A number of findings have emerged. First, a wide variety of anti-poverty strategies are being employed, including income support, concessions, subsidised use of services or goods, and emergency relief. No attempt was made here to suggest that one type is more important than another at alleviating poverty, as it is assumed that they all make an important contribution. Secondly, constitutional constraints compel the different levels of government to adopt different types of anti-poverty strategy. Thirdly, the funding and delivery arrangements that underpin anti-poverty strategies in this country are extremely complex and multi-layered, reflecting the influence of federalism. This situation raises questions about possible wastage of resources on the administration of a single program at all three levels of government. The funds spent on such administration are probably better spent on helping the poor. Fourthly, although there is Australia-wide consistency in the level of income support from the Commonwealth government, access to and levels of price concessions vary among States. This is a perfect example of why we need a co-ordinated national strategy to eradicate poverty in this country. Fifthly, a more coordinated and comprehensive strategy for alleviating poverty can be developed only if it is prioritised as our most serious social problem that demands a whole-of-government response across all three levels. Finally, the differences between relieving and eliminating poverty should be articulated, and specific programs developed to redress both the experiences and the causes of poverty.

Chapter 14

The funding and provision of emergency relief in Australia

Benno Engels

In January 2003, the Australian Council of Social Services (ACOSS) reported a substantial rise in the number of people seeking emergency relief (ER) from welfare agencies across Australia. The survey found that almost 200,000 people had to be turned away because of the agencies' increased operating and insurance costs, an increase in the number of people seeking assistance, plus the complexity of client need (ACOSS 2003b).

One year later, a follow-up ACOSS (2004) survey reported a steady growth in the demand for financial and material assistance across Australia, leading it to conclude that the welfare sector remained unable to cope with the level of demand. Both the 2003 and 2004 reports confirm the stories of financial hardship and suffering given as testimony by individuals and welfare workers who appeared before or made written submissions to the Senate Poverty Inquiry (Senate Community Affairs Reference Committee (SCARC) 2004) into poverty. For many community welfare agencies and their frontline employees, it is apparent that more and more Australians are simply not able to make ends meet, even among those who are employed in full-time low paid occupations (see Wynhausen 2005). For such individuals and families, ER has become a survival strategy against descending into further poverty.

Emergency relief assistance is defined here as 'the provision of financial ... [and material] assistance to those persons who find themselves in financial crisis' (ACOSS 2003a, p iii). The provision of ER has a long tradition in Australian social welfare history, and can be traced back to the colonial period (Dickey 1980; Kennedy 1985; Cage 1992). Surprisingly, Australian researchers interested in poverty alleviation have done only a limited amount of work on ER, despite its importance in relieving poverty (Henderson 1975; Spenceley 1980, 1986; Thornton 1987). The last detailed Australia-wide study into providers and users of ER was done 28 years ago (DSS and ACOSS 1978). In an attempt to overcome this information gap, this chapter examines the current system of ER provision at its various levels.

The first section of the chapter considers the role played by the Commonwealth Department of Family and Community Services (FaCS), a key funding source for ER across Australia. The second section reviews the different funding and delivery arrangements within the States and Territories, with a special emphasis on Victoria. The third section reports some of the key findings from a recent study of 60 ER providers in metropolitan Melbourne, as an illustration of the kinds of organisations involved and the kinds of issues they confront in their efforts to assist some of our most needy. Finally, the concluding section suggests where and why reforms are urgently needed, if ER is to be provided in the coming years.

The Commonwealth level:
Contracts and the funding of emergency relief

Since the late 1970s the Commonwealth government has contributed to the funding of ER, after two commissioned reports revealed considerable variability among States and Territories in their funding and delivery of ER programs. This variability gave rise to serious inequities (Department of Social Services (DSS) and ACOSS 1978). Rising levels of unemployment and economic hardship during this period also contributed to the decision by the Commonwealth to take on this responsibility, which had previously belonged to the States and Territories. Although the federal Hawke Labor Government tried to hand back this responsibility in 1988 as part of its attempt to reduce federal budget outlays, the States and Territories refused this proposal (Dunn 1988; Palmer 1988; Ryan 1988). As a result, the Commonwealth remains a key funding source. However it has refused to be involved in the delivery of ER, which is left to State- and Territory-based organisations.

Following the election of the federal Howard Coalition in early 1996, a review of the funding agreement with the States and Territories was undertaken to address problems with how the Commonwealth was calculating and distributing its grants. After consultations with the States and the community sector in late 1996, a new funding formula was introduced in the 1997 federal budget. This formula remains the basis for funding allocation and distribution to ER providers at State and Territory level (see Department of Health and Family Services 1996). A brief outline of how this formula works is given below.

Annual grants are determined within the federal budget, and grants have increased each year in line with the Consumer Price Index (CPI). The distribution of Commonwealth funding to the States and Territories is constrained by a number of factors. The first constraint is the set proportional allocations. The funds are divided into three areas designated to specific users:

Table 14.1. Commonwealth government emergency relief allocations to States and Territories, 1999-2000 to 2005/06, in AU$

States	1999-2000	2000-2001	2001-2002	2002-2003	2003-2004	2004-2005	2005-2006
NSW	7,737,372	8,217,128	8,226,264	8,768,933	9,004,065	9,221,844	9,616,307
VIC	5,383,343	5,717,137	5,719,073	6,006,712	6,158,766	6,345,662	6,695,178
QLD	5,034,446	5,385,648	5,637,132	5,925,129	6,15,7088	6,146,670	6,223,097
SA	2,059,325	2,19,1979	2,241,972	2,343,717	2,387,493	2,396,810	2,476,522
WA	2,309,147	2,452,326	2,556,528	2,759,694	2,901,013	2,893,773	2,969,478
TAS	816,694	867,333	868,581	934,274	943,488	974,257	995,321
NT	622,988	622,988	686,071	736,686	750,647	776,688	795,083
ACT	281,760	299,230	299,491	296,335	303,489	307,725	315,115
Total	24,253,000	25,756,830	26,235,122	27,771,480	28,606,049	29,063,429	30,086,100

Source: FaCS Annual Reports and Budget Statements, 1999/2000 to 2005/06

1. 91 per cent is distributed to organisations that deal directly with the general population seeking ER;

2. 8 per cent goes to organisations servicing the Aboriginal and Torres Strait Islander population, and

3. 1 per cent is allocated for the development of training and support for ER workers (FaCS 2005).

The second constraint involves the distribution between the States and Territories, which receive funds in proportion to the number of recipients registered for specific Centrelink benefits, including Disability Support, Newstart Allowance, Parenting Payment Single, Youth Allowance, Family Tax Benefit A, and the Community Development Employment Program (McNaughton & Hansen 2005). Table 14.1 shows the Commonwealth funds allocated to the States and Territories over the seven budgets since 1999/2000. The most populous States – New South Wales, Victoria and Queensland – receive the largest shares of the annual allocation, as they have more Centrelink benefits recipients, while the Northern Territory and the Australian Capital Territory receive the smallest grants. The distribution of funds is performed by the State- and Territory-based offices of FaCS; these offices oversee all the funding agreements with contracted ER organisations. In 2005, approximately 900 organisations operating from 1400 outlets received funding via this source (FaCS 2005). Some organisations are entirely dependent upon the Commonwealth, whereas others supplement these funds with other sources. Normally two payments are made each year, in July and December, to contracted organisations (FaCS 2003).

Several constraints are imposed on contracted organisations. First, they must distribute ER in the form of cash, cheques or food vouchers (ACOSS 2003a). Recent changes permit organisations to use up to 25 per cent of their allocated funds to purchase food or in-kind goods (McNaughton & Hansen 2005). Secondly, 85 per cent of annual funds must be allocated to ER, while the remaining 15 per cent can be used to meet administration costs, but not staff salaries (ACOSS 2003a). Thirdly, organisations are required to report annually to FaCS on how they spent their allocated funds, with an independent audit required for all grants over $10,000 (ACOSS 2003a). Fourthly, organisations are required to re-apply each year for Commonwealth funding, to enable FaCS to respond to shifts in ER within and between States and Territories (ACOSS 2003a).

Although the Commonwealth ER program seeks to assist people in 'crisis' in a way that maintains their dignity and ensures an equitable distribution of funds between the various States and Territories, a number of problems persist with the current situation. The most notable problem is that the amount of ER funding does not reflect the true level of need in the community (ACOSS 2003b; Penter 2005).

One reason for this funding shortfall is that the Commonwealth formula relies upon the registered number of Centrelink clients receiving certain benefits. However, these benefits do not include persons on the aged pension, carers' payment, tertiary students on Austudy, and newly-arrived migrants who are ineligible to access social security assistance for two years. In addition, it is accepted within parts of the welfare sector that the number of officially registered unemployed persons on Youth and Newstart allowances underestimates the true level of unemployment, thereby masking a higher level of need (Mitchell & Carlson 2001). Moreover, tying the Emergency Relief Program to the CPI is fraught with problems. For example, there are continuing disagreements about the method of calculating the CPI and its accuracy in reflecting the rising cost of living (Dufty 2000). Finally, funding to individual agencies can be reduced because the state and territory yearly allocation is fixed, while the number of agencies is not. Thus the grant might have to be divided among more organisations than had been funded the previous year. Some of these issues receive further attention in the Melbourne-based case study below, but the discussion will first turn to the role that the States and Territories play in the provision of ER.

The States and Territories: Concessions and the COSS network

As the previous section shows, in Australia ER is funded at the national level but delivered at State and Territory level. Pre-federation, responsibility for both funding and provision of ER was held by the various colonies. When the colonies became State and Territories within the Commonwealth of Australia, ER services remained their responsibility. Interestingly, not all the States and Territories have chosen to co-ordinate the distribution of ER within their administrative boundaries, despite their legal capacity to do so, preferring to leave this responsibility to their respective state-based Council of Social Service (COSS). However COSS possesses very limited capacity to coordinate organisations delivering ER, because COSS membership is voluntarily, and many ER organisations are not members. For example, the Victorian Council of Social Services (VCOSS) auspices the Emergency Relief Victoria Forum, where ER providers gather every second calendar month to share information, discuss issues and formulate policies. However, in 2005 only 49 out of a possible 553 organisations were registered members of VCOSS. Even for member organisations, the decisions made by their State-based COSS are not binding on them. Hence, the distribution of ER inside the States and Territories remains largely uncoordinated.

Another distinctive feature of ER provision is the dominance of religious and community-based organisations, as shown in Table 14.2. Large organisations with multiple outlets in a single state or territory had each outlet counted separately. Even so, these figures probably underestimate the number of organisations providing ER across Australia.

Table 14.2. Type and number of emergency relief providers by State and Territory, Australia, 2005

Types	NSW	Vic	Qld	SA	WA	TAS	NT	ACT	Total
Religious	263	249	66	119	228	14	16	14	969
Community	145	141	42	35	119	7	14	5	508
Welfare	51	56	5	9	34	2	7	4	168
Local govt	0	7	0	0	4	3	0	0	14
Aboriginal	23	28	9	0	31	3	12	0	106
CALD	14	19	1	1	17	2	2	0	56
Other	37	55	3	10	50	0	1	0	156
Total	533	555	126	174	483	29	52	23	1977

Sources:
NSW: Foodbank NSW, NSW Community Services Directory, NSW Citizens Advice Bureau;
VIC: Foodbank Vic, Victoria Relief;
QLD: Foodbank Townsville, Brisbane Life Line Directory, Internet agency search;
SA: Foodbank SA, South Australia's Health and Community Services Directory;
WA: Foodbank WA, WACOSS Community Services Directory;
TAS: TACOSS Communication, Internet agency search;
NT: NTCOSS Community Services Directory of the Northern Territory;
ACT: ACTCOSS Communication, ACT Citizen Advice Bureau Community Directory

A religious provider is defined as any organisation whose ER activities are guided by religious principles; included are Anglicare, the Salvation Army, St Vincent de Paul Society, Mission Australia, and a raft of parish churches and faith-based organisations. Community-oriented organisations are defined as serving local communities; examples are the Citizens Advice Bureau and community and neighbourhood centres. Welfare providers are defined as non-religious and non-local organisations set up to deliver ER according to charitable principles; examples are the Smith Family, Red Cross, and Travellers Aid Society of Victoria. Culturally and Linguistically Diverse (CALD) organisations cater exclusively for ethnic groups via migrant resource and welfare centres. Surprisingly, this ER type was reasonably small in number, despite Australia's growing multicultural character. They were more strongly represented in New South Wales, Victoria and Western Australia, the States with the largest share of the post-1960s wave of migration. There are also government and non-government funded ER providers catering solely for Aboriginal and Torres Strait Islanders. Local government is also active in ER provision, especially in Victoria. The 'others' category includes the service clubs such as Lions, Rotary and Returned Soldiers League, and schools, hospitals, foundations, fire and police stations. Notably, the data in Table 14.2 show an almost identical pattern of ER provider types and sector proportions across the States and Territories, despite the absence of any deliberate Government intervention.

Most States and Territories have developed concession programs giving ER to persons unable to pay their utility bills. Table 14.3 (p 176) lists the major utility concessions available. For those States and Territories that do not directly offer assistance there are a number of alternate payment arrangements for eligible applicants. In New South Wales, applicants can contact their utility provider or the government department and be referred on to designated ER providers, who are authorised to issue payment vouchers. In the ACT, applications are referred to the ACT Essential Services Consumer Council which interviews each applicant in 'hardship hearings', to decide whether an outstanding debt will be discharged on the clients' behalf or partially repaid through the Incentive Discharge Scheme. In Victoria, applicants are referred by their utility distributor or local ER provider to the Victorian Concessions Unit which assesses each application for eligibility for the Utility Relief Grant Scheme (URGS).

Table 14.4 (p 176) shows the ratio of processed and approved applications for the URGS from 1999 to 2004. The approval ratio and the total sum allocated to this program have been rising, suggesting an increasing level of need. The URGS provides once-off assistance to persons temporarily suffering financial hardship and at risk of being disconnected. Applicants are also offered financial counselling. The URGS is funded annually out of the state budget allocation to the Victorian Department of Human Services, which also funds Victoria Relief.

Table 14.3. State and Territory government concessions for low income and income support applicants, 2005

State / Territory	Electricity	Water	Gas	Other
New South Wales	X*	X*	X*	√ #
Victoria	√	√	√	√
Queensland	X	X	X	√
South Australia	√ +	√ +	X	√
Western Australia	√	X	X	√
Tasmania	√	X	X	√
Australian Capital Territory	√	X	X	√
Northern Territory	X	X	X	√

Note:
* Low income individuals and households are able to gain some ER assistance via the NSW Energy Accounts Payment Assistance scheme which is administered by a number of nominated welfare agencies;
+ Some single persons without dependents might not be eligible for these concessions in South Australia;
# Concessions provided in other social support service areas such as dental treatment, patient travel, taxi transport for the disabled, etc.

Sources: NSW Department of Energy, Utilities and Sustainability: Utilities Concessions; Victorian Department of Human Services: Victorian State Concessions; Queensland Department of Communities: Concessions Made Easy; SACOSS, The Concessions Handbook; Western Australian Department of Community Development: Guide to State Concessions; Tasmanian Government Concessions: Investing in People; ACTCOSS personal communication and the ACOSS ER Handbook, 3rd edn; ACOSS ER Handbook, 3rd edn

Table 14.4. Victorian Utility Relief Grant Scheme: Ratio of processed and approved applications, 1999-2004

Years	Number of applicants	Number approved	Approval ratio
1999-2000	10,346	7,450	72%
2000-2001	12,438	9,989	80%
2001-2002	12,888	8,496	66%
2002-2003	11,448	8,051	70%
2003-2004	11,402	9,709	85%

Source: Victorian Concession Unit (2005, p 24)

Established by an Act of the Victorian Parliament in 1958, Victoria Relief is a centralised collection and distribution point of food and material aid for ER and natural disaster relief within Victoria (Victorian Relief Committee 2005). Until recently, food and material aid were distributed to ER providers for a nominal donation to assist with the cost of storage and handling, but rising operational costs necessitated the introduction of a standard fee in mid 2005, and a merger with the already fee-charging Foodbank Victoria in 2006. The charging of fees is generating considerable concern within the Victorian ER sector.

There were other funding options available to the Victorian Government. In Western Australia, the State electricity concession program and some ER activities by the Western Australian COSS are subsidised by grants from the State gambling authority, Lotterywest (Penter 2005). The other States and Territories, including Victoria, could similarly re-direct some of their gambling taxes towards ER programs. In fact, findings from some ER providers in different parts of metropolitan Melbourne, clearly indicate that they cannot absorb a handling fee from the merged Victoria Relief and Food Bank Victoria. To better understand the process of ER provision and its precarious nature, one needs to look at the agencies distributing ER. The chapter now turns to a case study.

The provision of emergency relief at the local level

The bulk of ER distributed in Australia occurs at the local level via the activities of small agencies and organisations. This section of the chapter reports on the findings of a study conducted by the author in early 2004 into the activities of 60 ER providers in different parts of metropolitan Melbourne (Engels 2005). The data in Table 14.5 reveal the dominance of community- and religious-oriented organisations in this random survey (see Table 14.2).

Not surprisingly, the survey secured fewer responses from less prominent ER provider types such as welfare, CALD and local government, and no responses from any Aboriginal-oriented provider. The 'others' category consisted of a variety of organisational types which provided ER to a clientele not ordinarily covered by conventional ER providers, such as persons seeking specialist health care, political asylum and protection from domestic violence.

Despite these specialist ER providers, ER providers who responded to the survey were proportionally representative of the ER sector in the rest of Victoria and in Australia. Providers varied in size from the very large religious-oriented organisations like the St Vincent de Paul Society and the Salvation Army, to very small parish churches, welfare agencies and community support centres. For some the provision of ER was their primary focus; for others ER was just one responsibility among many others. Variability in size and operational intent also often translated into differences in organisational philosophies used to justify the

Table 14.5. Type of ER provider organisations surveyed in metropolitan Melbourne, 2004

Organisation type	Number	Percentage
Community	28	46.7
Religious	20	33.3
Welfare	4	6.7
Local government	2	3.3
CALD	1	1.7
Aboriginal	0	0.0
Others	5	8.3
TOTAL	60	100.0

Source: Engels (2005)

distribution to ER (Engels 2005). It was not uncommon for clients to be referred to an organisation by a Centrelink office, a local government authority, or another ER provider. All the surveyed organisations interviewed clients before ER was provided, with the assessment often performed by an untrained volunteer because FaCS guidelines prohibit the use of its grant to meet staffing costs. Professionally trained staff – social, welfare and community workers – performed this task only in the larger organisations with the funding capacity to employ them (Engels 2005).

Figure 14.1 (p 179) summarises the forms of ER supplied by the 60 surveyed providers. If we disregard for a moment the 'Others' category, then food vouchers redeemable at approved supermarkets accounted for 14 per cent of emergency relief distributed. Cash cheques for specific purposes and cash itself – $30 on average – were the next most frequently issued forms of relief, accounting for 12.9 per cent and 11.7 per cent of the total emergency relief distributed. Food parcels and vouchers to pay for outstanding utility bills were the next most frequently issued forms of emergency relief, accounting for 9.9 per cent and 9.6 per cent of total distributed relief respectively. Many organisations are reluctant to hand out food parcels because of storage and handling issues. Perishable foods must be kept in specialised storage space, and even long-lasting food such as canned and dried foods take up a large amount of storage space (Savage 2004).

Table 14.6 (p 180) summarise how the surveyed ER organisations fund their ER activities. In total, 38.9 per cent of funds received by the sampled ER providers came from government sources, whether Commonwealth, State or local. Thus 61.1 per cent of total funding came from non-government sources. This disparity between government and non-government funding highlights the precariousness of the organisations, and of the provision of ER itself. Gaining government funding is no

THE FUNDING AND PROVISION OF EMERGENCY RELIEF

Figure 14.1. Types of emergency relief distributed by organisations in metropolitan Melbourne, 2004

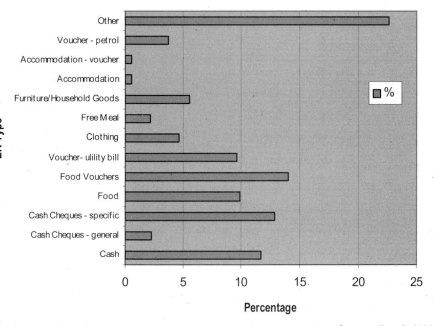

Source: Engels (2005)

guarantee of financial security. As shown earlier, funding from the Commonwealth is assured only for 12 months, after which organisations must re-apply. Even if an organisation secures a renewal of its funding, there is no guarantee that it will be granted the same amount. Funding from State and local government is even more insecure, due to the absence of any formal commitment or funding agreement to support ER, and funds from non-government sources can also fluctuate from one year to the next. Of all the funding used by sampled ER providers, 74.5 per cent came from sources that are non-recurrent and unpredictable, not just from one year to the next but also during the year. This funding situation prevents organisations from being able to engage in forward planning to meet the changing level of client demand. In fact, an overwhelming majority of the organisations indicated in the survey that they had to ration ER assistance to their clients, in an attempt to ensure that they have enough for the 12 month period. This rationing is done in several ways: by limiting how often clients can seek assistance in a specified time period; by limiting how much is handed out; and by limiting the number of days the organisation is open to distribute ER (Engels 2005).

Table 14.6. Sources of funding to ER providers, metropolitan Melbourne, 2004

Source of funding	Percentage
Commonwealth government	25.5
Trusts	23.8
Victorian State government	12.8
Personal donations	7.6
Magistrate Court Fund	7.6
Church donations	6.9
Private businesses	3.8
Op shops	2.8
Fund raising	2.6
Agency funds	2.6
RSL/Rotary Clubs	2.2
Victoria Relief	0.8
Local government	0.6
Charities	0.4
TOTAL	100.0

Source: Engels (2005)

Table 14.7 (p 181) shows who the various organisations identified as their main clientele. The main user groups were single parent families of which the majority were headed by women, and poor families. Lone males were a significant user group but were only ranked as sixth; probably many lone males were also counted in the unemployed and renter groups. The most significant new user group was refugees, whether with permanent residency or on temporary protection visas. Traditional social security recipients – the unemployed, elderly and disabled – were also frequently identified as users. Lone women and tertiary students were two other small user groups on the rise over the last few years. Finally, many of the surveyed organisations indicated that they are struggling to assist the poor within the current climate of funding vulnerability, suggesting that reforms are needed if the provision of ER is to continue.

Table 14.7. Receivers of ER assistance in metropolitan Melbourne, 2003-04

Users of ER assistance	Number of times	Percentage
Single parents	34	14.7
Poor families	21	9.1
Renters (private and public)	18	7.8
Refugees	16	6.9
Unemployed	16	6.9
Lone males (16-25 yrs)	15	6.5
Disabled persons	14	6.1
Aged pensioners	10	4.3
Lone women	10	4.3
Newly-arrived migrants	10	4.3
Homeless (youth)	9	3.9
Persons with mental illness	8	3.5
Drug users	7	3.0
Lone males (50-65 yrs)	5	2.2
Gamblers	3	1.3
Alcoholics	3	1.3
Students (post-secondary)	3	1.3
Family breakdown victims	3	1.3
Carers	1	0.4
All of the above	25	10.8
TOTAL	231	100.0

Note: The figures in this above table do not represent the total number of clients assisted in a designated time period, but denote the different type of clients assessed for ER assistance by the surveyed 60 organisations during 2003 and 2004.

Source: Engels (2005)

The need for urgent reform

The preceding discussion has revealed a number of problems with the funding and provision of ER, and if it is to remain an effective way of dealing with poverty, there needs to be reform. Several areas of reform are suggested. First, there needs to be a national summit on the funding of ER, bringing together all levels of government and community-based organisations in Australia. A central issue for the summit is the need to establish an appropriate level of funding. Such a decision is possible only if a national strategy is devised to collect data on ER demand. Secondly, a summit should also consider the need to co-ordinate the ER sector on a national basis, rather than leave it to the under resourced States and Territories. Thirdly, a decision must be made to either better resource the ER sector, or to enhance Commonwealth benefits paid to income support recipients. At present, the Commonwealth is using ER as a cheap solution to helping those individuals and families who have fallen through its social security safety net, but it is unwilling to meet the major operational expenses of the distributing organisations. Fourthly, if ER is to continue, there needs to be greater consistency with how it is distributed, in what proportions and forms. It makes no sense that an ER applicant should be denied a concession in one State but be eligible in another. Nor does it make any sense that an ER applicant should be able to secure a $30 food voucher from one agency, whereas another agency elsewhere in Melbourne will issue the same person with $50 cash. Local disparities must be eliminated if we believe that people in need should all be treated in an equitable way. Finally, the ER sector can no longer rely upon volunteers to staff the organisations distributing ER, because they are ageing and fewer younger volunteers are replacing them. Formal training and some remuneration are necessary if the next generation of ER workers is to be found.

Conclusions

This chapter has sought to reveal the main features of a social support system that is largely invisible and unknown to many Australians. It has shown that the provision of ER is a nation-wide undertaking supported by Commonwealth, State and Territory governments. The funding of ER programs varies between these tiers of government, with the Commonwealth being the major contributor. Findings from a survey of ER providers in Melbourne, however, revealed that the amount of government supplied funds was both insufficient and restrictive. Many organisations distributing ER are compelled to raise funds from non-government sources that are becoming increasingly unreliable. As a result, almost a quarter of the organisations surveyed believed that a shortage of funds and the continued rise in client demand would contribute to their decision to discontinue providing ER within the next five years. Should this indeed occur then it will be disastrous for the poor, as neither the States nor the Commonwealth wish to become involved in the delivery of ER. Changes are needed if this situation is to be averted, and the discussion made a number of suggestions about where reforms should occur.

Chapter 15

Moving forward: Alternative anti-poverty strategies

Klaus Serr

Earlier chapters in this book have demonstrated that many problems arise from the implementation of neo-liberal principles, and that there is a crisis of poverty affecting billions of people globally, including many Australians. As indicated in chapter one, mainstream development based on economic growth has largely failed to alleviate poverty in both underdeveloped and developed nations. While Marxist-inspired criticisms have provided many insights into the failings of capitalism, Marxist models have not given better practical answers than have the neo-liberal approaches. This chapter therefore chooses a different focus: alternative economic principles which have led to models of community-based development. After a brief history of alternative thought and movements, this chapter looks at concepts of community and how economic principles generated outside the orthodoxy have influenced the model of self-reliance and participation to build distinct anti-poverty strategies. In this context the chapter examines the values of cooperatives/social enterprises, social capital and capacity building for anti-poverty work.

Historical context

In the 18th and 19th centuries the industrial revolution created material wealth, but also inequality, poverty and social dislocation on an unprecedented scale (Geremek 1997). In response to these developments, contemporary thinkers sought new answers about how best to organise society and deal with poverty. The two main theoretical positions arising from this challenge are neo-classicism and Marxism/socialism. Classical and neo-classical economists, often labelled 'capitalist' and 'mainstream', argued for laissez-faire management in the pursuit of ever-increasing economic growth and free market policies, as do mainstream prescriptions today. Marxists/socialists criticised these mainstream principles, pointing out the exploitative and alienating nature of capitalism, and arguing for radical social and economic change in the service of equality.

While seemingly in conflict, these two orientations share a number of things in common (Handa 1985). For example, Marxist models do not question the maximisation of production and accumulation of capital, as long as these are distributed equally. Both paradigms are progressionist, sharing a linear and material view of life and society, where man is seen as the conqueror of nature; both lead to large centralist and bureaucratic economic and social systems (Hettne 1995; Korten 1995).

A third group of thinkers, often called 'utopian socialists', presented alternative visions of the economy and society. Sismondi (1773-1842), Saint Simon (1760-1825), Fourier (1772-1837) and Owen (1771-1858) condemned both laissez-faire doctrines and the massive human costs of industrialisation, exploitative accumulation of capital, and unequal distribution of wealth and power (Buber 1958). Utopian socialists also argued for the importance of the common good over self-interest (see Nitsch 1990). In contrast to Marxist socialism, however, they believed in meeting people's needs via small-scale development and participatory social relationships based on cooperation (Serr 2001). Proponents of alternative models therefore stressed the importance of structural transformation of societies through the renewal and the building of local communities and organisations (see Ife 1995; Campfens 1997). They also identified capitalism's destruction of local communities, involving what German sociologist Tönnies (1963) later called the major transition from Gemeinschaft (community) to Gesellschaft (society).

Importance of community

For Tönnies, community is a natural state consisting of a small group bound together by a common culture, neighbourhood and village life. In this natural state a limited number of people interacted and were bonded together by a common kinship, place and beliefs, enabling a life richer in real experiences and with a deeper level of meaning, than in the modern society that replaced it. Tönnies argued that industrial capitalism increasingly weakened and destroyed these bonds and the relationships built on them. The process towards 'society' was thus characterised by modern contractual arrangements which led to impersonal and legalistic relationships between people who lived in modern cities without communal spirit. Here people no longer had a sense of belonging, were alienated and socially isolated, and did not know many of the individuals they came in contact with, apart from knowing the different roles these people played in society (Tönnies 1963).

This kind of analysis was foreshadowed by Saint Simon, Fourier and Owen who were pivotal in inspiring the principles and structures of alternative development and cooperative movements. They offered comprehensive systems of thought which aimed to address poverty-related issues and the societal structures responsible for poverty. As Taylor points out, these principles are of:

> [D]irect relevance to the problems which confront men in modern industrial societies, particularly the problems ... which ... are unlikely to be solved unless we are able to develop that same sense of vision, of enthusiasm for an alternative form of social life, which motivated the utopians. (Taylor 1992, p viii)

The ideas of the utopians have influenced modern alternative economic visions, variously described as 'new economics' (see Ekins 1986, 1992), 'living economics' (Ekins & Max-Neef 1992), 'socio-economics' (see Nitsch 1990), 'human economics' (see Lutz 1999), 'social economics' (Etzioni 1991), 'another development' (see Hettne 1995). These visions include forms of community development as developed by Ife (1995). The dream of living in communal arrangements has transcended the centuries, and there is a long history of alternative communities, often established with social, religious and environmental aims. They can be called communes, intentional communities, cooperatives or grassroots organisations (see Metcalf 1996; Serr 2000).

Inspired by utopian socialist ideas, the many orientations found useful in developing community-based anti-poverty strategies include self-reliance (SR) and participation. The importance of community values and principles is also acknowledged in the formation of businesses such as cooperatives and 'social enterprises' and the more recent concepts of 'social capital' and 'capacity building' To ascertain their potential for anti-poverty work these approaches are briefly reviewed below. As self-reliance and participation relate to each other conceptually, they are grouped together for the purpose of the discussion. The same applies to cooperatives and social enterprise, both of which are business-style models. This is then followed by the last group consisting of social capital and capacity building, both of which are relatively new concepts and focus less on holistic developments than the other approaches.

Self-reliance and participation

Proponents of an alternative model saw SR as the 'antitheses' of economic globalisation (Dag Hammarskjold Foundation 1977; Galtung 1986; Burkey 1993; Serr, 2001). SR, often misinterpreted as meaning 'self-sufficiency', was part of an attempt by the poorer nations in the 1970s to break the cycle of dependency created by the wealthy countries, by trying to lessen exploitative practices (Hettne 1995). Galtung (1986) provides a theoretical framework and principles:

> 1. [S]elf reliance concentrates on the fulfilment of basic human needs rather than on generating, artificially, needs based on material things, often associated with money;
>
> 2. [W]e have to ask how we can produce what is needed, relying on ourselves, on our own production factors, meaning nature (land, raw materials, energy); labour, skilled and unskilled; capital, liquid and fixed; research, basic and applied; and administration.

3. [S]elf reliance implies a total rejection of this 'division of labour', a rejection of the use of others as an external sector for the dumping the negative externalities and the denying them the positive externalities in the production process. It means treating others like an internal sector.

4. Trade is possible under SR when something can not be produced at the local level. In this case exchange and trade will go beyond the local level into the neighbouring spheres and regions. However, trade should at least be at about the same level in both directions without exporting negative externalities to somebody else's locality. (Galtung 1986, pp 101-03)

In order to reduce dependency on the global economic system, SR advocates self-sufficiency at least in fulfilling a country's basic needs, such as the production of food, clothing, shelter, energy, and whatever is needed for health, education and home defence.

The many interpretations of SR (Hettne 1995; Ife 1995; Serr 2000) share a development strategy chosen to minimise or prevent excessive impact of the mainstream market on the community. This is accompanied by what Ife (1995) conceptualises as holistic community development: that is, social, economic, political, cultural, environmental, and personal/spiritual development. This approach deserves much attention as its principles can help to establish a model for social change and poverty reduction in both under-developed and developed communities. Using some of these principles, many grassroots organisations have built successful small community-based development projects (Ekins 1992; Metcalf 1995, 1996). For example, The International Institute for Sustainable Development (IISD) (2000a) lists more than 50 successful organisations around the world. These projects were honoured by the United Nations in 1995 for their initiative and success in developing:

> [A] sense of community at a local, regional or global level ... [and] each one demonstrates positive and practical solutions to difficult problems and has inspiring lessons to offer to other communities and to the United Nations. (IISD, 2000b)

Under SR development, people try to develop democratic communal processes of self-determination based on what they perceive their needs to be (Ife 1995). The aim is to limit exploitative practices, in contrast to mainstream development where the entrepreneur and market determine peoples' needs, and implement global and centralised processes based on a division of labour.

As one of its main aims is addressing the fulfilment of basis needs, SR could make an important contribution in the development of a national anti-poverty strategy. It is also well suited to build holistic communities and provide people with the necessary choices for building better lives. However, SR requires people to work together and participate at all levels of society, and with the loss of community structures as found by Putnam (2000) and others, people are ill-equipped for such a process. In many ways this kind of development needs people to be empowered again so that they can participate in their local community and make the appropriate choices. While the current poor have most to benefit from SR projects, without appropriate assistance they may lack the skills and attributes to be part of the process. Developing participatory processes where the poor benefit is difficult, as the next section demonstrates.

Participation

SR is linked with the empowerment of people and encourages participation in the decision-making process of development. Participation gives control to the poor to influence their situation (Ife 1995; Trainer 1996; Serr 1998). As the United Nations Development Programme (UNDP) notes:

> The important thing is that people have constant access to decision-making and power. Participation in this sense is an essential element of human development. (UNDP 1993, p 21)

Invariably this means small-scale development with decentralised economic and socio-political structures (see Schumacher 1973; Hettne 1995; Lutz 1999). However, setting up an alternative system based on participation is not easy. According to Burkey (1993, pp 59-60), in relation to participation four difficult issues need to be taken into consideration. First, participation will develop in different ways and situations, depending on the problems faced by specific groups of the poor. Promoting participation according to neatly defined standard 'development objectives' may thus inhibit rather than promote people's initiatives. Secondly, for participation to be successful the situation of the poor must be improved, although such success may generate conflict with more affluent sections in society. Thirdly, participatory development needs to be linked to self-reliance but often requires initial outside assistance. Care must thus be taken to ensure such assistance does not undermine self-reliance and create long-term dependency. Fourthly, as the organisational structures required in participation can easily be controlled by a few, the poor need retain genuine control over their own organisations. As noted above, participatory processes seldom begin spontaneously, but are generally initiated by a leadership whose vision is external to the perceptions and aspirations of the people concerned.

In Australia, such a model is difficult to employ, particularly with disadvantaged people (Serr 1998, 2000, 2006). For example, a New Work Opportunity Project funded by the then Department of Employment and Training (DEET) in 1996 aimed to employ 16 people for six months who had been unemployed for at least five years (Serr, 1996, 1998). While this project was part of a welfare program, it aimed to implement a structure based on SR and participatory development ideas. Many difficulties were involved:

> Many [members] showed signs of low self-esteem, depression and social isolation. Lack of social skills and in some cases mental illness, made work with participants difficult, especially at the beginning. There was much potential for conflict and challenging behaviours to jeopardise the work and very tight time-lines. (Serr 1998, p 8)

Lessons were learned from this program. It was shown that, with a great deal of welfare-style support, a group like this can gradually achieve a good level of participation and improve the lives of group members. Further, after six months a remarkable transformation could be noted: most participants' personal problems had decreased, and their self-image, social interactions and abilities had improved. This group was now much more able to work towards a community-based poverty alleviation project.

The model of self-reliance/participation has a great deal of potential for structural change and renewal in society. Its principles flow directly from some of the alternative economic principles of the past. This approach is holistic in that it aims to address peoples' basic and other needs. While trade is seen as important, community values such as participatory processes are viewed as equally significant. SR could therefore make an important contribution to a national strategy for poverty reduction. However, the practice of real participation and democracy can present many challenges which can undermine the success of community projects based on this strategy.

Cooperatives and social enterprise

Owen (1966) is often seen as a founding father of the cooperative movement, and his work in Scotland led to one of the first cooperatives in England, where 28 poor weavers formed the Rochdale Pioneers Society in 1844 (see Birchall 2003). These Rochdale Pioneers developed the cooperative principles which were adopted by the International Cooperative Alliance (ICA) in 1937 and still largely form the bases for cooperatives today. The now re-drafted principles include voluntary and open membership, democratic member control, members' economic participation, autonomy and independence, education, training, and information, cooperation among cooperatives, and concern for community.

Since then, many cooperatives have been started around the world, with varying success. In general, cooperatives operate as workers' cooperatives, consumer and housing cooperatives and have been defined by the International Co-operative Alliance (ICA) as:

> An autonomous association of persons united voluntarily to meet their common economic, social and cultural needs and aspirations through a jointly owned and democratically controlled enterprise. (ICA 1995, p 4)

The aims of the cooperative movement lend themselves to the fight against poverty. There is growing interest around the world in setting up cooperatives, because of their perceived potential in broader anti-poverty strategies (ILO 2003). As Birchall (2003) notes, by benefiting the lower and middle strata of society, cooperatives have:

> [R]aised whole classes of people out of poverty and prevented them from slipping back into it, which is in its own terms an achievement ... Cooperatives were not designed as tools of poverty reduction, but were a means by which groups of people could gain economic advantages that individually they could not achieve. (Birchall 2003, p 7)

Despite these possibilities, cooperatives do tend to exclude certain people, particularly poorer members of a community. As with self-reliance and participation, developing a cooperative with the very poor is problematic and there is little evidence that such a strategy can work for very disadvantaged people, who may have personal issues such emotional/psychological problems and substance abuse, and lack relevant skills, education and financial capital (see Birchall 2003; Rose & Serr 2006; Serr 2006). While these difficulties sometimes meant that the poor did not benefit from the cooperative movement as much as they should, cooperatives still have the potential to become a preventative anti-poverty strategy for its members, especially when the membership is large enough to be self-sustaining.

In many countries, cooperatives have made important contributions as worker and consumer organisations, benefiting both members and society. According to the ICA:

> [T]he co-operative movement brings together over 800 million people around the world ... Co-operatives provide over 100 million jobs around the world, 20 per cent more than multinational enterprises. (ICA 2006)

While many have failed, the successes are impressive. For example, Mondragon Corporacion Cooperativa (MCC) in Spain is one of the largest and most successful organisations, having provided to its members with about 70,000 jobs and numerous benefits such as employment and social security benefits. It has also benefited the surrounding community, with the creation of affordable housing and education (see Mathews 1987; Whyte & Whyte 1988; MCC 2005). In Europe there are about 4,500 cooperative banks with 700,000 staff members and 130 million customers (European Association of Co-operative Banks 2004, p 2), representing about 17 per cent of the market share in terms of deposits in the European financial sector. These cooperatives make a significant contribution to human development of their regions. Although it has lost its original aim and become like a normal business, the Co-op Group in the UK remains the largest consumer cooperative in the world, demonstrating the potential of the cooperative idea.

In the US, about 30 per cent of all agricultural products are marketed through cooperatives, providing enormous benefits to members and local communities. By the mid-2000s the 100 largest cooperatives had an annual turnover of over US$ 117 billion (ICA 2006). Japan has also developed an extensive cooperative network with more than 14 million members, involving cooperatives for teachers, universities and various sectors such as retail, medical, housing, and insurance. The retail sector alone has a combined turnover of 2.519 trillion Yen (US$21.184 billion) (ICA 2006).

Australia has a long history of cooperatives since the 1900s, operating in a variety of sectors such as social clubs, agriculture, wholesale and retail, transport, childcare, housing and banking. By the mid-1990s the largest agricultural cooperatives had a combined turnover of $6.5 billion, and by the early 2000s there were about 2,400 registered cooperatives nationwide, with about 1.4 million members in New South Wales alone (Lyons 2001).

Cooperatives cannot change the forces of the global economy but by providing jobs and services that members otherwise might lack, they can make communities less vulnerable to the potential risks of economic globalisation. Despite some of their limitations in reaching the very poor who may lack appropriate skills and capital to take full advantage of this strategy, cooperatives can help to build better communities for all:

> Cooperatives and similar organisations can help reduce the risks to whole *communities*, through connecting them up to wider markets, and diversifying sources of income ... Cooperatives cannot do much about the macro-level man-made risks such as the overthrow of elected governments or civil war, but they can contribute to the kind of civil society that makes these risks less likely. (Birchall 2003, p 25)

Social enterprise

Since the 1990s many developed countries have shown an increasing interest in the notions of 'social enterprise' and 'social entrepreneurship' (Gray et al 2003). Similarly, associated terms such as 'venture philanthropy' and 'strategic philanthropy', which denote programs in which foundations and businesses to provide seed funding for social ventures that will become self sufficient have also attracted attention.

Definitions of social enterprise (SE) vary considerably between commentators and contexts (Barraket 2004), and a literature review by the OECD (1999) found no coherent conceptualisation of SE across a number of countries. There is also some confusion in use of terms; for example, a cooperative can be called a SE (Barraket 2004). While the types of entities described as SEs vary, most incorporate some commercial/business principles to achieve social goals. Social Enterprise London, established to support the development of SEs in London, defines SEs as having three key attributes. First, SEs have an enterprise orientation, producing goods or services and seeking to be viable entities that make an operating surplus. Secondly, SEs have ethical values and social aims such as job creation, and aim to build community capacity. Thirdly, SEs have social ownership, facilitated through structures based on participation by stakeholder groups or trustees, and profits shared by the stakeholders or used for community benefit (SEL nd, p 7). This definition is consistent with notions of SE in Australia. For example, the Adelaide Central Mission holds that SEs exist to operate as sound businesses, creating benefits for the community. By increasing opportunities for people it builds the notion of self-help (Talbot et al 2002). There is some disagreement, however. Some argue that many existing Australian not-for-profit welfare services that undertake commercial activities to support their operations are SEs (Simons 2000). Others argue that the only true SEs are fully self-funding through their commercial activities (Boschee & McClurg 2003).

The current rise of interest in SE in countries like Australia needs to be seen in the context of changing government policy. Most Western countries including Australia have traditionally been strong welfare states; in such countries governments have focused increasingly on the failure of traditional welfare, the problems of social exclusion, and the need to invest in social capital and community building in areas of entrenched disadvantage. In Britain this focus is reflected in the 'Third Way' politics of New Labour, and in Australia in developments such as government increasingly moving away from service provision and into 'partnering' with the community sector to provide health and welfare services (Mission Australia 2002; Gray et al 2003).

Gray et al (2003) argue that there are three distinct drivers for the increased government interest in SE. First, governments are moving away from providing services towards the contracting out and privatisation of services. At the same time government policy is challenging individuals' rights to welfare provision, advocating for community responsibilities such as mutual obligation. Secondly, there are resource constraints on the not-for-profit sector and increasing accountability through reporting, resulting in services seeking untied resources from social enterprises, by choice or necessity. Thirdly, some sections of the social welfare sector argue that traditional welfare provision is limited in its capacity to empower people and truly improve their lives, believing SE has the capacity to achieve better outcomes for the disadvantaged.

While government interest in SE has been increasing, only very recently is there evidence of explicit government support for the development of SEs. This interest has been particularly apparent in Britain where in 2002 the government established an action plan for the development of SEs. *Social Enterprise: A Strategy for Success* (DTI 2002) incorporates regular reviews of the strategy and the extent of SE development (DTI 2003). A specific unit within the Department of Trade and Industry was also established to support SE development, and has undertaken projects such as reviewing how SEs are financed, the impact of government regulations on development of enterprises and mapping and research programs (SEU 2005). These government initiatives have been supported by the establishment of a national peak body, the Social Enterprise

Coalition (SEC 2005), and regional bodies to support and resource the establishment of SEs within their regions. Some examples are SE London (SEL 2005), North East SE Partnership (NESEP 2005), Cumbria (Enterprising Communities 2005), and Scotland (SenScot 2005).

For the Victorian Department of Communities, Barraket (2004) reviewed the role of government in the development of community and SEs, and found that while the level of government support for SE development was limited, there were signs of an increasing emphasis in government policy and funding. This interest is demonstrated by Commonwealth strategies such as the Prime Minister's Community Business awards for partnerships between business and not-for-profits, and a focus on SE and grant programs as part of the community building strategies of Department for Victorian Communities, established in 2002 (DVC 2005).

Criticism of the SE approach

There has been considerable criticism of the approach. Some criticism claims that SE is part of what has traditionally been practised as social and economic community development, but has been 'hijacked' by business, 'entrepreneurs', and government (McArdle 1999; Gray et al 2003). It is clear that some commentators present SE as the 'answer' to unemployment, poverty and social disadvantage (Seelos & Mair 2005). In response, critics have argued that the SE movement is based on false premises concerning the true structural causes of mass unemployment, and assumptions about the constraints on government capacity to support people through benefits (Cook et al 2003). There are also concerns about the potential consequences of widespread development of SE, for the provision of universal services and social justice (Cook et al 2003; Gray et al 2003). In addition, as with cooperatives, it is not easy for poor people to set up SEs independently without adequate support (Rose & Serr 2006).

Further, in Australia, even within groups supportive of SE development, there has been considerable debate about the way it should be approached. For example, in 2001 the Social Entrepreneurs Network (SEN) was established to support SE development, but was disbanded in 2003 for a variety of reasons, including conceptual differences on how to approach the development of SEs in Australia (Barraket 2004). To a great extent the SE development in Australia to date has been mostly focused on further service expansion for large welfare services, rather than on true new enterprise development. Indeed, Mission Australia, a large national welfare service which has implemented several SE projects around the country, notes that two of the key challenges for the not-for-profit sector in implementing SEs are:

- To engage in community capacity-building activities and avoid the promotion of further service dependency among clients;

- To support genuine community ownership of organisations, not looking to community capacity-building activities as a means of growing the organisation. (Mission Australia, 2002, p 30)

This section has shown that while cooperatives have a demonstrated record of building organisations that can benefit millions of members around the world, they also have limitations as an anti-poverty strategy. Shortcomings include difficulties in getting poor people involved in such groups, partly because the success of cooperatives requires capital and skills, which the very poor often lack. Nevertheless, cooperative principles are linked with successful alternative economic development in the past, and their operations do contribute to better communities around the world. The case of SEs is less clear. Although SEs could function like cooperatives, there are uncertainties about how they are defined in the current political climate. SEs may be used for political purposes in order to avoid the structural issues of poverty and inequality, and may also be used as an excuse for not funding adequate welfare support for the poor. As the move towards SEs often concentrates on economic development rather than on holistic community improvement, it has less social value than cooperative ventures. Similar limitations can also be noted in the notions of social capital and capacity building discussed in the next section.

Social capital and capacity building

Since the 1990s the trend towards social capital (SC) has been influenced by writers such as Bourdieu (1983), Coleman (1988), and most importantly by Putnam (1993, 1995, 2000). SC has also been taken up by international organisations like the World Bank (1999) and in Australia by writers such as Cox (1995). All these sources identified SC as one of the strategies for increasing the chance of local economic and social development.

According to Putnam, SC is a set of social relationships that can either strengthen or weaken communities; thus the extent to which people are involved in communal activities such as sports clubs, church groups is more important than participation in political processes such as elections. Putnam believes that he found evidence of a decline in SC in the US, where he noticed a reduction in associational activity and a growing alienation from family, friends, and neighbours. Social capital therefore refers to:

[C]onnections among individuals – social networks and the norms of reciprocity and trustworthiness that arise from them. In that sense social capital is closely related to what some have called 'civic virtue'. The difference is that 'social capital' calls attention to the fact that civic virtue is most powerful when embedded in a sense network of reciprocal social relations. A society of many virtuous but isolated individuals is not necessarily rich in social capital. (Putnam 2000, p 19)

Putnam's work seems to appeal to many economists because it appears to promote economic growth. The World Bank (1999) for instance cites statistics to show the value of the concept for economic and social progress. In Putnam's view, community, shared values, reciprocity and so on are all good and necessary ingredients for the economic development he claims to have found in his work in Italy, where SC is seen as 'strong society, strong economy; strong society, strong state'. It therefore 'helps explain why social capital, as embodied in horizontal networks of civic engagement, bolsters the performance of state and economy' (Putnam 1993, p 176).

While the importance of community relationships is clear enough, the breakdown of community has already been noted as part of the effect of industrialisation, as previously discussed. There seems to be little new in the concept of SC, leaving out important factors of culture, political activism, environmental issues and so on. Concentration on social networks means that important structural issues of the political economy can be avoided and do not have to be considered in policy making. The SC conceptualisation thus attracts criticism because it seems to promote economic rather than the much broader and real community development (see Fine 2000; Hickey & Mohan 2004).

The extent of general poverty among 17 of the 24 most wealthy OECD countries suggests that meeting basic needs, so important in the reduction of poverty, is not considered in the US, the UK, and Australia. As UNICEF (2005) and UNDP (2005) demonstrate, this situation is especially unacceptable when it comes to the deprivation experienced by those '40–50 million children ... growing up in poverty in the world's richest countries' (UNDP 2005, p 69). Another example is increasing inequalities in wealth and resources on national, regional and global levels. And while Putnam (2000, p 19) calls for 'connections among individuals' and 'social networks and the norms of reciprocity', SC building exercises can do little to address the fundamental structural arrangement which are at the heart of such complex issues. Its application will therefore not help those poor US families who receive only 5 per cent of the nation's income and have a 25 per cent lower life span than those in the top 5 per cent income bracket. Nor will it provide health care to the 45 million Americans who have no health insurance (UNDP 2005, p 58).

Capacity building

As policy makers moved away from a more holistic approach of community development during the 1980s and 1990s, the term 'capacity building' entered the development discourse, particularly in the developing nations (see Eade 1997; Skinner 1997; Lopes & Theisohn 2003; Blagescu & Young 2006). Capacity building (CB) has also been embraced by international organisations in the attempt to reduce global poverty. A good definition is:

> Development work that strengthens the ability of community organisations and groups to build their structures, systems, people and skills so that they are better able to define and achieve their objectives and engage in consultation and planning, manage community projects and take part in partnerships and community enterprises. It includes aspects of training, organizational and personal development and resource building, organized in a planned and self-conscious manner, reflecting the principles of empowerment and equality. (Skinner 1997, pp 1-2)

Though this definition is detailed, the concept remains vague and flawed:

> A difficulty remains, however, in pinning down what it actually implies in practical terms. This may be due to the fact that the discussion often relies upon abstract notions that are hard to translate into actions and objectives. (Lopes & Theisohn 2003, p 1)

Notwithstanding some acknowledgment of and initial interest in fostering local networks to develop better functioning communities, much of the work and the ideas behind CB relate to economic and technocratic notions of economic development, such as investment and competency-based resource management. As the UNDP suggests, rich nations developed a 'capacity-building aid agenda' where:

> [T]here is an unhealthy concentration on building capacity in areas that rich countries consider strategically useful. (UNDP 2005, pp 10-11)

Like its counterpart SC, CB can circumvent structural issues such as crippling foreign debt, and unfair trade practices where commodity prices (income for poor nations) fall and rich countries benefit from unfair import taxes they impose on developing nations. The UNDP cites Ethiopia, one of the poorest countries in the world, as an example, where the annual income for a coffee-producing household has decreased by $200 since the late 1990s. Ethiopia, like many African and other developing nations, is a good example of where a reliance on the CB strategy has failed to reduce poverty. While there are hundreds of NGOs working in the country, many of which believe in CB strategies, Ethiopia has an estimated 50 per cent absolute poverty rate (Ethiopian Catholic Church (ECC) 2004; UNDP 2004). Especially in the cities, there seems little focus on meeting the basic needs of people living in absolute deprivation. In the capital of Addis Ababa, for example, thousands of beggars roam the streets, including an estimated 150,000 street children (ECC 2004), and poverty-stricken men, women and children huddle around church walls at night without food, shelter or basic sanitation.

While organisations such as Oxfam are aware of these limitations and make laudable attempts to improve the situation (see Eade 1997) it is not clear how the structural issues or even the very urgent and immediate basic needs can be met by the CB method. As notions of social capital and capacity building bring out the importance of community and the necessity to develop people's potential, they are not holistic strategies. They tend to concentrate more or less on economic development, falsely assuming that this will automatically lead to social cohesion and a better society. To increase their potential, these approaches need to take a more holistic perspective and learn lessons from alternative economics in the past.

Conclusion

This chapter briefly explored the notions of self-reliance and participation, cooperatives and social enterprises, and social capital and capacity building, and their potential for community-based anti-poverty strategies. By providing a historical context, the chapter showed how alternative economic principles have influenced the model of self-reliance and participation. Learning from the past, SR advocates holistic development and structural change in society. While there are difficulties and challenges with implementing participatory processes, the SR model has the greatest potential for community renewal and anti-poverty work as it focuses on meeting peoples' needs. This strategy can apply at both national and local levels.

Cooperatives have proved themselves able to make enormous contributions to communities around the world, including Australia. By providing members with employment and many services they may otherwise not be able to access, cooperatives can shield communities from some of the negative processes of economic globalisation. However, bringing benefits to members and communities does not necessarily include the very disadvantaged, who can easily be excluded from cooperatives. Further, setting up a cooperative structure may not be an option for those lacking the skills and capital needed to take advantage of this strategy.

Finally, the chapter argues that the concepts of social capital and capacity building are positive developments in that they recognise the value of social relationships, community and capacity-building of individuals. However, these concepts seem to be furthest removed from holistic community development, and too narrowly focused on economic development. Their implementation in terms of policy and practice lacks the structural and societal considerations necessary for successful anti-poverty action. Community projects that do not follow holistic principles are destined to fail, as they will not be able to meet the complexities of human needs. As Ife argues:

> Such one-dimensional community development is highly likely to fail. It derives from linear thinking, rather than adopting the holistic approach ... By concentrating only on one dimension, it ignores the richness and complexity of human life and of the experience of community. (Ife 1995, p 131)

Chapter 16

Conclusion

Klaus Serr

> At the start of the twenty-first century we live in a divided world. The size of the divide poses a fundamental challenge to the global human community. ... The twin scourges of poverty and inequality can be defeated – but progress has been faltering and uneven. (UNDP 2005, p 4)

As we enter the new millennium, the world is facing unprecedented challenges. The crisis faced by humanity involves increasing disparities between poverty and wealth, life-threatening environmental destruction, an senseless arms race, and worrisome human right abuses. As these issues are global, engulfing all societies, this book sets the crisis of poverty into the global context. This situation is the starting point for *Thinking about Poverty* and the reason for questioning the wisdom of current neo-liberal economic polices and principles, which are very much at the heart of today's Australian policy makers.

Contributions in this book have therefore explored various aspects of poverty and how they have been influenced by neo-liberal policies in Australia. The exploration of these topics relates to the recent public debate on the nature and the extent of poverty in this country. The issues in this debate and in this book are vital to our understanding of what constitutes a functioning society, and in which direction Australia should be heading. Effective actions will require a partnership between the different stakeholders in the community. As government is integral to society, politicians need to acknowledge the existence of poverty and be willing to be persuaded by the evidence at hand.

The current poverty dispute is therefore significant and at the forefront of our perception of issues of social justice, egalitarianism and what it is to be fair, just and democratic. In this context the key questions are: Is Australia to become just 'an economy' which organises its institutions, social and other arrangements exclusively to serve the interest of a few wealthy actors based economic principles? Do we want to develop a more functional society which shares in the benefits of the nation, with all the social, cultural and political complexities, most of which cannot be measured by economic indicators. As pointed out by the United Nations Development Programme (UNDP):

> If people's interests are to guide both the market and the state, actions must be taken to allow people to participate fully in the operations of markets and to share equitably in their benefits. Markets should serve people – instead of people serving markets. After all, markets are only the means – people the end. (UNDP 1993, p 4)

Discussions in this book demonstrate the limitations of current economic policies. The contributors have tackled a wide range of issues including globalisation, women's poverty, theoretical and conceptual considerations in poverty research, and direct effects of policy on vulnerable groups such as Indigenous people, families and the unemployed, and people with disabilities. Other authors shed light on the relationship between crime and poverty, on the possibilities and shortcomings of existing anti-poverty strategies, and on alternative definitions of what poverty means and how community-based approaches may be employed to alleviate the problem.

The contributions in this book have argued that neo-liberal conceptions of economy and society have great limitations. As the evidence presented suggests, the implementation of related policies contributes to the existence of extreme wealth and poverty rather than to building better futures. But as Frank Stilwell (Chapter 2) argues, this does not have to be an inevitable process and can be challenged. *Thinking about Poverty* hopes to make this prospect more likely, by questioning the assumptions of the current orthodoxy about poverty, by trying to raise awareness of the shortcomings and problems associated with present arrangements, and by contributing to future solutions of poverty alleviation.

Thus the way forward requires a re-conceptualisation of what poverty means, and a move away from narrow economic indicators towards more qualitative aspects of human needs.

In Australia, thinking about poverty lags behind European approaches, which integrate concepts such as social exclusion, which are richer and more complex than the limited definitions underpinning the Australian approach.

As Klaus Serr (Chapter 5) argues, non-monetary values and indicators have to be seriously considered when defining poverty. It is also essential that the voices and experiences of the poor themselves are integrated into poverty research. While not a focus of this book, Chapter 15 poses some alternative views on community, society and economy. It is argued that from past and current alternative theories and approaches, there are some lessons to be learned about the importance of community values and how to develop small-scale related projects to deal with poverty more effectively.

Failure to deal with poverty issues has increasingly devastating consequences, as da Silva points out:

> Hunger is actually the worst of all weapons of mass destruction, claiming millions of victims every year. Fighting hunger and poverty and promoting development are the truly sustainable way to achieve world peace ... There

CONCLUSION

will be no peace without development, and there will be neither peace nor development without social justice. (Brazilian President Luiz Inácio Lula da Silva, quoted in UNDP 2005, p 75)

The fight against poverty is therefore one of the most important challenges faced by the world, including Australia. Poverty relates to all aspects of human activity, social justice, morality, and the ever more important issue of peace and security.

References

Abbott, T, 2001a, 'Against the prodigal son', *Policy*, vol 17, no 3, pp 37-39.

Abbott, T, 2001b, *Four Corners*, Australian Broadcasting Commission, 10 July, 2001.

ABS (Australian Bureau of Statistics), 1996, 'Special article – poverty and deprivation in Australia', in *Year Book Australia 1996*, ABS, Canberra.

ABS, 1999, *Disability, ageing and carers: 1998*, Cat No 4430.8.040.001, *Summary tables*, ABS, Canberra.

ABS, 2001a, The health and welfare of Australia's Aboriginal and Torres Strait Islander Peoples, ABS, Canberra.

ABS, 2001b, *The health of older people, Australia*, ABS, Canberra.

ABS, 2004a, 'Health, health care delivery and financing', in *Year Book of Australia*, ABS, Canberra.

ABS, 2004b, *Measures of Australia's progress: multiple disadvantage*, ABS, Canberra.

ABS, 2005a, *Job Search experience, Australia*, Cat No 62222.0, ABS, Canberra.

ABS, 2005b, *Labour force, Australia*, Catalogue no 6202.0, ABS, Canberra.

ABS, 2005c, *Prisoners in Australia 2005*, ABS, Canberra, <www.abs.gov.au> (accessed 23 December 2005).

ACOSS (Australian Council of Social Services), 1998, *Budget 98 – time for 20/20 vision*, ACOSS, Sydney ACOSS, 2001a, *Breaching the safety net: the harsh impact of social security penalties*, ACOSS, Sydney.

ACOSS, 2001b, *Ending the hardship: submission to the Independent Review of breaches and penalties in the social security system*, ACOSS, Sydney.

ACOSS, 2003a, *Fairness and flexibility: reform of workforce age social security payments in Australia*, Paper 129, ACOSS, Sydney.

ACOSS ,2003b, *Living on the edge*, ACOSS, Sydney.

ACOSS, 2003c, *Emergency relief handbook: a guide for emergency relief workers*, 3rd edn, ACOSS, Sydney.

ACOSS, 2003d, *Living on the edge*, AOSS, Sydney.

ACOSS, 2004, *Community services report*, ACOSS, Sydney.

ACOSS, 2005a, *Issues arising from welfare to work package, ACOSS Fact Sheet*, ACOSS, <www.acoss.org.au/Publications.aspx?displayID=2> (accessed 3 October 2005).

ACOSS, 2005b, 'ACOSS and its members respond to welfare to work legislation', *ACOSS News*, 10 November 2005.

Alcock, P, 1993, *Understanding poverty*, Macmillan, London.

Anderson, J, 2000 'Gender, "race", poverty, health and discourses of health reform in the context of globalisation: a postcolonial feminist perspective in policy research', *Nursing Inquiry*, Vol 7, pp 220-229.

Anderson, T, 2006, 'The Howard Government, Australian aid and consequences', *Australian Review of Public Affairs*, February 2006, <www.australianreview.net/digest/2006/02/anderson.html>, (accessed 5 February 2006).

Andrews, G, Hall, W, Teeson, M & Henderson, S, 1999, *The mental health of Australians*, Commonwealth of Australia, Canberra.

REFERENCES

Andrews, K 2005, *Welcome from the Hon Kevin Andrews MP*, <www.mediacentre.dewr.gov.au/mediacentre/MinisterAndrews>, (accessed 5 December 2005).

Aspalter, C (ed), 2003, 'Welfare capitalism in Australia: from gender-discrimination to gender-sensitive social policies?', in *Neo-liberalism and the Australian welfare state*, Casa Verde Publishing, Taipei.

AusAID 2005, *Equal partners, gender awareness and Australian development cooperation*, Overseas Aid, AusAID, (accessed 27 October 2005), <www.ausaid.gov.au/publications/html/gender_development.cfm>.

Australian Catholic Social Justice Council (ACSJC), 2004, *The human costs behind the official unemployment rate*, A pastoral letter for the Feast of St Joseph the Worker, ACSJC, 1 May.

Australian Catholic Social Welfare Commission, 1997, 'Social obligation and public policy: the role of the market, the state and civil society in enhancing social welfare', in *Common Wealth: Applying Catholic Social Principles to Public Policy*, vol 6, no 1, pp 1-16.

Australian Government, 2006, Government response to Senate Community Affairs References Committee Report on Poverty and Financial Hardship, <www.aph.gov.au/senate/committee/clac_ctte/completed_inquiries/2002-04/poverty/gov_response.pdf> (accessed 21 April 2006).

Australian Government Attorney-General's Department, nd, Crime Prevention, <www.ag.gov.au/agd/WWW/ncphome.nsf/Page/Overview> (accessed 22 December 2005).

Australian Government Productivity Commission, 2004, Review of the *Disability Discrimination Act 1992*, Report No 30, Australian Government Publishing, Canberra.

Australian Health Ministers Advisory Committee, 1992, *National mental health policy*, Australian Government Publishing, Canberra.

Australian Institute of Health and Welfare, 1995, *Australia's welfare service and assistance*, Australian Government Printing Service, Canberra.

Australian Institute of Health and Welfare 2003, *Australia's welfare 2003*, <www.aihw.gov.au/publications/aus/aw03/aw03-c10.pdf> (accessed 21 November 2005).

Australian Institute of Health and Welfare, 2005, *Australia's welfare 2005*, <www.aihw.gov.au/publications/index.cfm/title/10186>, (accessed 30 November 2005).

Australian National Training Authority (ANTA), 2000, *Bridging pathways*, <http://antapubs.dest.gov.au/publications/images/publications/bridgingPathwaysNationalStrategy.pdf>, (accessed November 2005).

Bahar, S, 2000, 'Human rights are women's right', in B Smith (ed), *Global feminisms since 1945*, Routledge, Abington, pp 265-289.

Baldrey, E, McDonnell, D, Maplestone, P & Peeters, M 2003, *Ex-prisoners and accommodation: what bearing do different forms of social housing have on social reintegration?* Australian Housing and Urban Research Institute, Melbourne, <www.ahuri.edu.au>, (accessed 20 October 2005).

Baldry, E & Green, S, 2003, 'Indigenous welfare in Australia', in C Aspalter (ed), *Neoliberalism and the Australian welfare state*, Casa Verde Publishing, Taipei.

Baldwin, SM, 1985, *The costs of caring: families with disabled children*, Routledge and Keagan Paul, London.

Barns, G, 2003, *What's wrong with the Liberal Party?*, Cambridge University Press, Melbourne.

Barraket, J, 2004, *Community and social enterprise: what role for government*, report prepared for The Department of Victorian Communities, <www.dvc.vic.gov.au/enterprise.htm>, (accessed 10 May 2005).

Barratt Brown, M, 1984, *Models in political economy*, Penguin Books, London.

Beall, J, 1998, 'The gender and poverty nexus in the DFID White Paper: opportunity or constraint?', *Journal of International Development*, Vol 10, pp 235-46.

Beder, S & Cahill, D, 2005, 'Regulating the power shift: the state, capital and electricity', *Journal of Australian Political Economy*, no 55, December.

Beilharz, P, 1992, *Labour's utopias: bolshevism, fabianism, social democracy*, Routledge, London.

Beilharz, P, Considine, M & Watts, R, 1992, *Arguing about the welfare state. The Australian experience*, Allen and Unwin, Sydney.

Bello, W, 2002, *Deglobalisation: ideas for a new world economy*, Zed Books, London.

Berreen, R, 1994, 'And thereby to discountenance mendicity, practices of charity in early nineteenth century Australia', in M Wearing & R Berreen (eds), *Welfare and social policy in Australia: the distribution of advantage*, Harcourt Brace & Cos, Sydney.

Beveridge, W, 1943, *The pillars of security*, George Allen & Unwin, London.

Birchall, J, 2003, *Rediscovering the cooperative advantage poverty reduction through self-help*, International Labour Office, Cooperative Branch, Geneva.

Birrell, B & Rapson, V, 1997, 'Poor families, poor children: who cares for the next generation?', *People and Place*, vol 5, no 3, pp 44-53.

Bishop, B, 1999, *The national strategy for an ageing Australia: independence and self provision*, Discussion Paper, Commonwealth of Australia, Canberra.

Bishop, B, 2000, *The national strategy for an ageing Australia: world class care*, Discussion Paper, Commonwealth of Australia, Canberra.

Blagescu, M & Young, J, 2006, Working Paper 260, *Capacity development for policy advocacy: current thinking and approaches among agencies supporting civil society organisations*, Overseas Development Institute, London.

Bloy, M, 2002, *The 1601 Elizabethan Poor Law*, University of Singapore, <www.victorianweb.org/history/poorlaw/elizpl.html>, (accessed 15 May 2005).

Booth, C, 1969, *Life and labour of the people in London*, AM Kelley, New York.

Borland, J & Tseng, Y, 2005, 'Does "Work for the Dole" work?', Australian Conference of Economists, Sept 2005.

Borzycki, M, 2005, *Interventions for prisoners returning to the community*, Australian Institute of Criminology, Canberra.

Boschee, J & McClurg, J, 2003, *Toward a better understanding of social entrepreneurship: some important distinctions*, Social Enterprise London, <www.sel.org.uk/knowledge.aspx>, (accessed 29 July 2005).

Bottoms, A & Wiles, P, 2002, 'Environmental criminology', in M Maguire, R Morgan & R Reiner (eds), *The Oxford handbook of criminology*, 3rd edn, Oxford University Press, Oxford.

Bourdieu, P, 1983, 'Forms of capital' in JC Richards (ed), *Handbook of theory and research for the sociology of education*, Greenwood Press, New York.

REFERENCES

Bowman, M & Healy, J, 1988, 'Human services in South Australia and Victoria', in B Galligan (ed), *Comparative state politics*, Longman Cheshire, Melbourne.

Box, S, 1987, *Recession, crime and punishment*, Macmillan Education Ltd, Sydney.

Bradbury, B, Norris, K & Abello, D, 2001, *Socio-economic disadvantage and the prevalence of disability*, SPRC Report 1/01, Social Policy Research Centre, University of New South Wales, <www.sprc.unsw.edu.au/reports/Report1-01.pdf>, (accessed 3 November 2005).

Brandt Commission, 1983, The Independent Bureau on international development issues, *Common crisis. North-South co-operation for world recovery*, The MIT Press, Cambridge, MA.

Brandt, W, 1980, (Commission Chairperson), *North-South: a programme for survival*, Pan, London.

Bray, J, 2001, *Hardship in Australia: an analysis of financial stress indicators in the 1998-99*, Occasional paper no 4, Department of Family and Community Services, Canberra.

Brennan, S, 2006, *Without Cathy Freeman, Aborigines aren't in the race*, <www.universalrights.net/people/stories.php?category=indig>, (accessed 1 April 2006).

Broad, C, 2005, Media Release, Victorian Minister for Housing, Department of Human Services, 14 October, Melbourne.

Bryan, D & Rafferty, M, 1998, *The global economy in Australia*, Allen and Unwin, Sydney.

Bryson, L, 1992, *Welfare and the state*, MacMillan, Melbourne.

Bryson, V, 2002, 'Recent feminisms: beyond dichotomies: review article', *Contemporary Politics*, vol 8, no 3, pp 233-38.

BSL (Brotherhood of St Laurence), 2003a, *Napier Street Child and Family Resource Centre*, <www.bsl.org.au/main.asp?PageId=466>, (accessed 20 December 2005).

BSL, 2003b, *Submission to Senate Community Affairs References Committee Inquiry into Poverty and Financial Hardship in Australia*, BSL.

BSL, 2005, *Poverty line update*, Information Sheet no 3 May, BSL Melbourne.

Buber, M, 1958, *Paths to utopia*, Beacon Press, Boston.

Buckman, G, 2004, *Globalisation: tame it or scrap it?* Zed Books, London.

Bunch, C, 1995, 'Transforming human rights from a feminist perspective', in J Peters & A Wolper (eds), *Women's rights, human rights: international feminist perspectives*, Routledge, Abington, pp 11-17.

Burbach, R & Robinson, WI, 1999, 'The fin de siecle debate: globalisation as epochal shift', *Science and Society*, vol 63, no 1, p 10.

Burdekin, B, 1989, *Our homeless children*, Human Rights and Equal Opportunity Commission, AGPS, Canberra.

Bureau of Justice Statistics 2005, *Prisoners in 2004*, US Department of Justice, <www.ojp.usdoj.gov/bjs/abstract/p04.htm>, (accessed 23 December 2005).

Burke, P (ed), 1999, 'Just a few things to tide us over ...', in *Revealing the hidden city*, Inner City Administrators Group, Adelaide City Council, Adelaide.

Burkey, S, 1993, *People first*, Zed Books LTD, London.

Business Review Weekly, 2006, 'Rich 2000', vol 28, no 19, John Fairfax Publications Pty Ltd, Sydney.

Butterworth, P & Berry, H, 2004, 'Addressing mental health problems as a strategy to promote employment: an overview of interventions and approaches', *Australian Social Policy* 2004, Commonwealth Department of Families, Community Services and Indigenous Affairs, pp 19-49.

Butterworth, P, 2003, *Estimating the prevalence of mental disorder among income support recipients: approach, validity and finding,*. Policy Research Paper No 21. Commonwealth Department of Family and Community Services, Canberra.

Butterworth, P, Crosier, T & Rogers, B, 2004, 'Mental health problems, disability and income support receipt: a replication and extension using the HILDA survey', *Australian Journal of Labour Economics,* vol 7, no 2, pp 151-74.

Cadigal Wangal, 2005, *First encounters, Mambo,* <www.cadigalwangal.com.au/index2.php?option=com_content&do_pdf=1&id=23>, (accessed 4 July 2005).

Cagatay, N, 1998, *Gender and poverty,* Working Paper Series, WP 5, Social Development and Poverty Elimination Division, United Nations Development Programme.

Cage, R, 1992, *Poverty abounding, charity aplenty: the charity network in colonial Victoria,* Hale & Iremonger, Sydney.

Cameron, P & Flanagan, J, 2004, *Thin ice: living with serious mental illness and poverty in Tasmania,* Anglicare Tasmania, Hobart.

Cameron, S & Duncan, B, 2001, *Surviving, not living: disadvantage in Melbourne,* Catholic Social Services Victoria, East Melbourne.

Campfens, H (ed), 1997, *Community development around the world,* University of Toronto Press, Toronto.

Carney, T & Hanks, P, 1994, *Social security in Australia,* Oxford University Press, Melbourne.

Castles, FG, 1985, *Working class and welfare: reflections on the political development of the welfare state in Australia and New Zealand,* 1890-1980, Allen & Unwin, Wellington.

Castles, FG, 2001, 'A farewell to the Australian welfare state', *Eureka Street,* vol 11, pp 29-31.

Castles, FG, 2004, 'The future of families', *Eureka Street,* April, pp 1-4.

Centrelink, 2005a, *A guide to Australian Government payments,* 1 July–19 September, Canberra.

Centrelink 2005b, *A guide to Centrelink concessions,* Canberra.

Chambon, AS, 1999, 'Foucault's approach: Making the familiar visible' in AS Chambon, A Irving and L Epstein (eds), *Reading Foucault for social work,* Columbia University Press, New York.

Chapman, B, Weatherburn, D, Kapuscinski, C, Chilvers, M & Roussel, S, 2002, 'Unemployment duration, schooling and property crime', *Crime and Justice Bulletin,* no 74, NSW Bureau of Crime Statistics and Research, Sydney.

Chiricos, T, 1987, 'Rates of crime and unemployment: an analysis of aggregate research evidence', *Social Problems,* vol 34, pp 187-211.

Choo, C, 1990, *Aboriginal child poverty: child poverty policy review 2,* Brotherhood of St Laurence, Melbourne.

Chussodovsky, M, 1997, *The globalisation of poverty,* Third World Network, Penang.

City of Darebin, 2001, *Darebin Poverty Inquiry: final report, Community, Planning and Advocacy Branch,* City of Darebin, Preston.

REFERENCES

Clark, M (ed), 1957, *Sources of Australian history*, Oxford University Press, Melbourne.

Coburn, D, 2000, 'Income inequality, social cohesion and the health status of populations: the role of neo-liberalism.' *Social Science and Medicine*, vol 51, pp 135-46.

Cocks, E, 2001, 'Normalisation and social role valorisation: guidance for human service development', *Hong Kong Journal of Psychiatry*, vol 11, no 1, pp 12-16.

Coleman, JC, 1988, 'Social capital in the creation of human capital', *American Journal of Sociology*, vol 94, pp 95-120.

Commins, P, 1993, *Combating exclusion in Ireland 1990-1994: a Midway report*, European Commission, Brussels.

Commonwealth of Australia, 2002a, *Building a simpler system to help jobless families and individuals*, Canberra.

Commonwealth of Australia, 2002b, *National Aboriginal and Torres Strait Islander social survey 2002*, Commonwealth of Australia, Canberra.

Commonwealth of Australia, 2005a, *Employment and workplace relations legislation amendment (welfare to work and other measures) Bill 2005*, 28 November 2005.

Commonwealth of Australia, 2005b, *Family and community services legislation amendment (welfare to work) Bill 2005*, 28 November 2005.

Connell, RW & Irving, TH, 1980, *Class structure in Australian history*, Longman Cheshire, Sydney.

Consumer Credit Legal Centre, 2004, *Annual report for 2003/2004*, CCLC, Surrey Hills, Melbourne.

Cook, B, Dodds, C, Mitchell, W, 2003, 'Social entrepreneurship – false premises and dangerous forebodings' *Australian Journal of Social Issues*, vol 38, no 1, pp 57-72.

Coopers, Lybrand, & Scott WD, 1985, *Study into homelessness and inadequate housing*, vol 1 & 2, Department of Housing and Construction, AGPS, Canberra.

Corbridge, S, 1986, *Capitalist world development: a critique of radical development geography*, Macmillan Education Ltd, Houndmills.

Cox, E, 1995, *A truly civil society*. ABC Books for the Australian Broadcasting Corporation, Sydney.

Cox, J, 2001, 'The erosion of self-reliance: welfare dependency and family', *Policy [CIS]*, vol 17, no 3, pp 33-36.

Creed, P, 1998, 'Improving the mental and physical health of unemployed people: why and how?' *Medical Journal of Australia*, vol 168, pp 177-78.

Crime Prevention Victoria, 2002, *Safer streets and homes – a crime and violence prevention strategy for Victoria, 2002-2005*, Crime Prevention Victoria, Melbourne.

Curran, L, 2000, *Growing the community together? Why and how: occasional paper number 9*, Catholic Commission for Justice and Peace, Melbourne.

D'Souza, N, 1993, 'Aboriginal child welfare: framework for a national policy', in *Family Matters*, no 35, August 1993, pp 40-45.

Dag Hammarskjold Foundation, 1977, *Another development: approaches and strategies*, in P Ekins (ed) 1986, *The living economy: a new economics in the making*, Routledge & Keagan Paul, London.

Dalton, T & Ong, R, 2005, 'Precarious employment in the urban context: the case of public housing', *Just Policy: A Journal of Australian Social Policy*, vol 37, pp 42-50.

Danaher, G, Schirato, T, & Webb, J, 2000, *Understanding Foucault*, Allen and Unwin, Sydney.

Davidson, K, 1987, "JK Galbraith and the new economics", *Sydney Morning Herald*, 24 February.

Davidson, P, 2003, *Poverty, policy and the cost of raising teenagers*, paper presented to Australian Social Policy Conference, University of New South Wales, Sydney.

Davis, A & George, J, 1993, *States of health: health and illness in Australia*, 2nd edn, Harper Collins, Sydney.

Davis, JB, 2004, 'Transnational corporations: dynamic structures, strategies and processes', in PA O'Hara (ed), *Global political economy and the wealth of nations*, Routledge, Abington.

Day, D, 2005, 'A land seen for the first time: claiming and naming Australia 1788-1829', in *Claiming a continent: a new history of Australia*, Harper Perennial, Sydney.

de Lepervanche, M, 1975, 'Australian immigrants, 1788-1940: desired and unwanted', in EL Wheelwright & K Buckley (eds), *Essays in the political economy of Australian capitalism*, Australia and New Zealand Book Company, Sydney.

Dean, M, 1991, *The constitution of poverty: toward a genealogy of liberal governance*, Routledge, London.

Dennett, J, James, E, Room, G, & Watson, P, 1982, *Europe against poverty. The European poverty programme 1975-80*, Bedford Square Press, London.

Department for Victorian Communities (DVC), 2005, 'Community building', DVC, <www.dvc.vic.gov.au/building.htm>, (accessed 4 August 2005).

Department of Education, Training and Science (DETS), 2003, *An investigation into international best practice in facilitating the transition of tertiary education students with disabilities into their post-graduate careers*, DETS, <www.dest.gov.au/.../other_publications/ transition_of.tertiary_students_with_disabilities.htm>, (accessed 3 November 2005).

Department of Family and Community Services (FaS), 2003, *Discussion paper: emergency relief program*, March, National Office of FaS, Canberra.

Department of Human Services, 2000, *The aspirations of people with a disability within an inclusive Victorian community: summary report*, Victorian Government, Melbourne.

Department of Infrastructure, 2006, Action plan for accessibility, <www.doi.vic.gov.au/Doi/Internet/transport.nsf/AllDocs/208D198596C41F114A256B5800 2225E8?OpenDocument#summary>, (accessed 2 May 2005).

Department of Justice, 2003, *Victorian prisoner health study*, Department of Justice, Melbourne, Victoria.

Department of Justice, 2005, *Statistical overview of the Victorian prison system 1999/2000 to 2003/2004*, Department of Justice, Melbourne, Victoria.

Department of Social Services and Australian Council of Social Services, 1978, *Emergency relief: a study of agencies and clients*, Australian Government Publishing Services, Canberra.

REFERENCES

Department of Trade and Industry (DTI), 2002, *Social enterprise: a strategy for success*, Social Enterprise Unit, DTI, UK, <www.sbs.gov.uk/sbsgov/action/>, (accessed 27 July 2005).

Desai, M, 2004, *Marx's revenge: the resurgence of capitalism and the death of statist socialism*, Verso, London.

Dewan, R, 1999, 'Gender implications of the "new" economic policy: a conceptual overview', *Women's Studies International Forum*, vol 22, no 4, pp 425-29.

Dickey, B, 1980, *No charity there: a short history of social welfare in Australia*, Nelson Books, Melbourne.

Disability Services Act 1986, Commonwealth of Australia, Canberra.

Dodson, M, 2004, *Plenary presentation: The second international conference on New Directions in the Humanities*, Monash University Centre in Prato, Italy, <http://law.edu.au/anuiia/speeches/Parto%20speech.pdf accessed 03/03/06>, (accessed 22 July 2004).

Dohrenwend, B & Dohrenwend, B, 1969, *Social status and psychological disorders: a causal inquiry*, J Wiley, New York.

Douglas, J, 2005, 'The experience of food insecurity in a disadvantaged urban area', unpublished Honours thesis, University of South Australia, Adelaide.

Drakeford, M & Vanstone, M, 2000, 'Social exclusion and the politics of criminal justice: a tale of two administrations', *The Howard Journal of Criminal Justice*, vol 39, no 4, pp 369-81.

DTI, 2003, *Social enterprise: a progress report on social enterprise – a strategy for success*, Social Enterprise Unit, DTI, UK, <www.sbs.gov.uk/sbsgov/action/>, (accessed 27 July 2005).

Duclos, J & Gregoire, P, 2003, *Absolute and relative deprivation and the measurement of poverty: Working Paper 03-02*, Centre Interuniversitaire sur le risqué, les politiques economiques et l'emploi, Paris.

Dufty, G, 2000, *Winners and losers: changes in the purchasing power for Victorians 1990-1999*, Policy and Research Paper, VOSS, Melbourne.

Dunn, R, 1988, 'Cheque row bounces back to Greiner', *Sydney Morning Herald*, 13 September, p 4.

Dutton, P, 2005, *Disability and work: inclusion or coercion*, Paper presented to the Australian Social Policy Conference, University of New South Wales, 21 July 2005.

Eade, D, 1997, *Capacity building: an approach to people-centred development*, Oxfam, Oxford.

Eardley, T, 1998, *Working but poor? Low pay and poverty in Australia*, Discussion Paper No 91, Social Policy Research Centre, University of New South Wales, Sydney, pp 1-41.

Eardley, T, Brown, J, Rawsthorne, M, Norris, K & Emrys, L, 2005, *The impact of breaching on income support customers*, Final Report 5/05, Social Policy Research Centre Report, University of New South Wales, Sydney.

Economic Planning Advisory Council, 1989, *Economic and social implications of consumer debt*, Australian Government Publishing Service, Canberra.

Egan, J, 1999, *Buried alive, Sydney 1788-1792: eyewitness accounts of the making of a nation*, Allen & Unwin, Sydney, Sydney.

Ekins, P & Max-Neef, M (eds), 1992, *Real life economics: understanding wealth creation*, Routledge, London.

Ekins, P (ed), 1986, *The living economy: a new economics in the making*, Routledge & Keagan Paul, London.

Ekins, P, 1992, *A new world order: grassroots movements for global change*, Routledge, London.

Ekins, P, 1992, *A new world order: grassroots movements for global change*, Routledge, London.

Elwin, A, 1999, *Poverty and disability: a survey of the literature*, Social Protection Discussion Paper Series no 9932, World Bank, Washington, <www1.oecd.org/publications/e-book/8103021E.pdf>, (accessed 20 November 2005).

Emery, P, 1983, 'Commonwealth-state issues in welfare finance', in R Mendelsohn (ed), *Australian social welfare finance*, George Allen & Unwin, Sydney.

Engels, B, 2005, *The provision of emergency relief and contemporary pressures for change in metropolitan Melbourne*, School of Social Science and Planning, RMIT University, unpublished report for the Emergency Relief Victoria Forum, Melbourne.

Engels, B, 2005, *The provision of emergency relief and contemporary pressures for change in metropolitan Melbourne*, School of Social Science and Planning, RMIT University, unpublished report for the Emergency Relief Victoria Forum, Melbourne.

Enterprising Communities, 2005, 'About the Project', Enterprising Communities Cumbria Website, UK, <www.enterprisingcommunities.org.uk/>, (accessed 28 July 2005).

Estivill, J, 2003, *Concepts and strategies for combating social exclusion: an overview*, Social Security Policy and Development Branch International Labour Office, Geneva.

Ethiopian Catholic Church, 2004, *Social rehabilitation strategy: focusing on children*, Ethiopian Catholic Secretariat, Addis Ababa.

Etzioni, A, 1991, 'Socio-economics a budding challenge', in A Etzioni & PR Lawrence (eds), *Socio-economics: toward a new synthesis*, ME Sharpe, Inc, New York.

European Association of Co-operative Banks (EACB), 2004, *Cooperative banks in Europe: values and practices to promote development*, EACB, Brussels, <www.eurocoopbanks.coop/GetDocument.aspx?id=513>, (accessed 8 April 2006).

European Communities, 2002, *Joint report on social inclusion*, European Commission Directorate-General for Employment and Social Affairs, Unit EMPL/E.2, Office for Official Publications of the European Communities, Luxembourg.

Ezeilo, JN 2005, 'Feminism and human rights at crossroads in Africa: reconciling universalism and cultural relativism', in M Waller & S Marcos, (eds) *Dialogue and difference: feminism's challenge to globalisation*, Palgrave MacMillan, Melbourne.

Falshaw, L, Friendship, C, Travers, R & Nugent, F, 2003, *Searching for 'What Works': an evaluation of cognitive skills programmes*, Home Office Findings 206, Home Office, UK, <www.homeoffice.gov.uk>, (accessed 20 December 2005).

Families and Communities Strategy, *Stronger Families and Communities Strategy (SFCS) 2004-09*, Department of Families, Community Services and Indigenous Affairs, Australian Government, Canberra, <www.facs.gov.au/internet/facsinternet.nsf/aboutfacs/programs/sfsc-sfcs.htm>, (accessed 12 April 2006).

Farrall, S & Maruna, S, 2006, 'Desistance-focussed criminal justice policy research: introduction to a special issue on desistance from crime and public policy', *The Howard Journal of Criminal Justice*, vol 43, no 4, pp 358-367.

REFERENCES

Farrall, S & Sparks, R, 2006, 'Introduction', *Criminology and Criminal Justice*, vol 6, no 1, pp 7-17.

Farrington, D, 2002, 'Developmental criminology and risk-focussed prevention', in M Maguire, R Morgan & R Reiner (eds), *The Oxford handbook of criminology*, 3rd edn, Oxford University Press, Oxford.

FaS, 2005, Emergency relief program, (accessed 17 November 2005), <www.facs.gov.au/internet/facsinternet.nsf/family/ erprogram.htm>.

Feminist Majority Foundation, 2005, *About the Feminist Majority Foundation*, FMF Web site, <www.feminist.org/welcome>.

Fenna, A, 2004, *Australian public policy*, 2nd edn, Pearson Education Australia, Sydney.

Fergusson, D, Swain-Campbell, N & Horwood, J 2004, 'How does childhood economic disadvantage lead to crime?' *Journal of Child Psychology and Psychiatry*, vol 45, no 5, pp 956-66.

Fifer, D, 1998, 'Tackling the causes of poverty', *The Age*, Melbourne, 19 March.

Fincher, R & Nieuwenhuysen, J (eds), 1998, *Australian poverty then and now*, Melbourne University Press, Melbourne.

Fine, B, 2000, *Social capital versus social theory: political economy and social science at the turn of the millennium*, Routledge, London.

FitzGerald, V, 2004, *Governments working together: a better future for all Australians*, Victorian Government, Melbourne.

Flew, F, Bagilhole, B, Carabine, J, Fenton, N, Kitzinger, C, Lister, R & Wilkinson, S, 1999, 'Introducing local feminisms, global futures', *Women's Studies International Forum*, vol 22, no 2, pp 393-403.

Fook, J 1993, *Radical casework*, Allen & Unwin, Sydney, Sydney.

Forbes Magazine 2000, 'World's richest people 2000', <www.forbes.com/worlds richest>, (accessed 5 August 2000).

Forbes Magazine, 2004, 'World's richest people the rich get richer,' <www.forbes.com/maserati/billionaires2004/cz_lk_0226mainintrobill04.html>, (accessed 11 September 2000).

Forbes Magazine, 2006, 'Billionaire bacchanelia', <www.forbes.com/free_forbes/2006/0327/111.html>, (accessed 25 May 2006).

Forster, M & Mira d'Ercole, M, 2005, *OECD social, employment and migration working papers: no 22. Income distribution and poverty in OECD countries in the second half of the 1990s*, OECD, Paris.

Foucault, M, 1983, 'The subject and power', in HL Dreyfus & P Rabinow (eds), *Beyond structuralism and hermeneutics*, 2nd edn, University of Chicago Press, Chicago.

Foucault, M, 1991, 'Governmentality', in G Burchill, C Gordon, & P Miller (eds), *The Foucault effect: studies in governmentality*, Harvester Wheatsheaf, London.

France, A & Utting, D, 2005 'The paradigm of 'Risk and Protection- Focussed Prevention' and its impact on services for children and families', *Children and Society*, vol 19, pp 77-90.

Frank, R, 1999, *Luxury fever: money and happiness in an era of excess*, Princeton University Press, Princeton, NJ.

Frankel, B, 2001, *When the boat comes in: transforming Australia in the age of globalisation*, Pluto Press, Sydney.

Friedman, E, 1995, 'Women's human rights: the emergence of a movement', in J Peters & A Wolper (eds), *Women's rights, human rights: international feminist perspectives*, Routledge, Abington.

Friedman, M, 1962, *Capitalism and freedom*, University of Chicago Press, Chicago.

Galbraith, JK, 1995, *The world economy since the wars*, Mandarin, London.

Galtung, J, 1986, 'Towards a new economics: on the theory and practice of self-reliance' in P Ekins (eds), *The living economy: a new economics in the making*, Routledge & Keagan Paul, London.

Gamble, A, 2001, 'Neo-liberalism', *Capital and Class*, vol 75, pp 127-34.

Garton, S, 1990, *Out of luck: poor Australians and social welfare*, Allen & Unwin, Sydney.

Garton, S, 1994, 'Rights and duties: arguing charity and welfare, 1880-1920', in M Wearing & R Berreen (eds), *Welfare and social policy in Australia: the distribution of advantage*, Harcourt Brace & Co., Sydney.

George, S, 1992, *The debt boomerang: how third world debt harms us all*, Pluto Press, London.

George, V & Wilding, P, 2002, *Globalisation and human welfare*, Palgrave, Melbourne.

Geremek, B, 1997, *Poverty: a history*, Blackwell, Oxford.

Gibson, D & Abello, R, 2005, *Australia's welfare; the seventh biennial welfare report of the*, Australian Institute of Health and Welfare, Canberra.

Gibson, D & Means, R, 2000, 'Policy convergence: restructuring long-term care in Australia and the UK', *Policy and Politics*, vol 29, no 1, pp 43-58.

Gilley, T & Taylor, J, 1995, *Unequal lives? Low income and the life chances of three-year-olds*, Brotherhood of St Laurence, Melbourne.

Gilley, T, 2003, *Early days, much promise: an evaluation of the Home Instruction Program for preschool youngsters (HIPPY) in Australia*, Project Report, Brotherhood of St Laurence, Melbourne.

Girling, AD, 1983, *New age encyclopaedia*, Bay Books, Sydney.

Gittins, R, 2005, 'Budget's hidden "reform": a two-class welfare system', *Sydney Morning Herald*, 30 May.

Gleeson, B 1998, 'Disability and poverty', in R Fincher & J Nieuwenhuysen (eds), *Australian poverty: then and now*, Melbourne University Press, Melbourne.

Glendinning, C & Millar, J (eds), 1987, *Women and poverty in Britain*, Wheatsheaf Books Ltd, London.

Goldfinch, S, 2000, *Remaking New Zealand and Australian economic policy*, Victoria University Press, Wellington.

Goldsmith, E & Mander, J (eds), 2001, *The case against the global economy and for a turn towards the local*, Earthscan, London.

Gomm, R, 1996, 'Mental health and inequality', in T Heller, J Reynold, R Gomm, R Muston, & S Pattison (eds), *Mental health matters*, Macmillan Press and The Open University, London.

Goodman, J & Ranald, P, 1999, *Stopping the juggernaut*, Pluto Press, Sydney.

Goodman, J, 2002, 'Introduction', in J Goodman (ed), *Protest and globalisation: prospects for transnational solidarity*, Pluto Press, Sydney.

Gordon, D, Adelman, L, Ashworth, K, Bradshaw, J, Levitas R, Middleton, S, Pantazis, Patsios, D, Payne, S, Townsend, P, & Williams, L, 2000, *Poverty and social exclusion in Britain*, Joseph Rowntree Foundation, York.

REFERENCES

Grant, F & Grabosky, P, 2000, *The promise of crime prevention*, 2nd edn, Australian Institute of Criminology Research and Public Policy Series no 31, Canberra.

Gray, M, Healy & K, Crofts, P, 2003, 'Social Enterprise: is it the business of social work? *Australian Social Work*, vol 56, no 2, pp 141-54.

Graycar, A & Jamrozik, A, 1989, *How Australians live*, MacMillan Press, Melbourne.

Graycar, A & Jamrozik, Am 1993, *How Australians live*, 2nd edn, MacMillan Press, Melbourne.

Gregory, B & Sheehan, P, 1998, 'Poverty and the collapse of full employment', in R Fincher & J Nieuwenhuysen (eds), *Australian poverty: then and now*, Melbourne University Press, Melbourne.

Gregory, RG, 2002, 'It's full time jobs that matter', *Australian Journal of Labour Economics*, vol 5, no 2, June.

Gruen, D, & O'Brien, T, 2002, 'Introduction', in D Gruen, T O'Brien, & J Lawson (eds), *Globalisation, living standards and inequality: recent progress and continuing challenges*, Reserve Bank of Australia 2002 Conference, 27-28 May.

Gupta, G, 2005, *Statement at the informal interactive hearings of the United Nations General Assembly*, International Centre for Research on Women, <http://catalog.icrw.org/dbtw-wpd/exec/dbtwpub.dll>, (accessed 23 September 2005).

Haebich, A, 2000, *Broken circles: fragmenting indigenous families 1800-2000*, Fremantle Arts Press, Perth.

Hale, C, 2005, 'Economic marginalisation, social exclusion and crime', in C Hale, K Hayward, A Wahidin & E Wincup (eds), *Criminology*, Oxford University Press, Oxford.

Hamilton, C & Dennis, R, 2005, *Affluenza: when too much is never enough*, Allen & Unwin, Sydney.

Hamilton, C, 2003a, *Growth fetish*, Allen and Unwin, Sydney.

Hamilton, C, 2003b, 'Real and imagined hardship in Australia', *Journal of Australian Political Economy*, no 52, December.

Handa, M, 1985, 'Gandhi and Marx: an outline of two paradigms', in R Diwan & M Lutz (eds), *Essays in Gandhian economics*, Gandhi Peace Foundation, New Delhi.

Haralambos, M & Holborn, M, 1991, Sociology themes and perspectives, (3rd edn), Harper Collins Publishers, London.

Harding, A, Lloyd, R & Greenwell, H, 2001, *Financial disadvantage in Australia: the persistence of poverty in a decade of growth*, (NATSEM) The Smith Family, Melbourne.

Harrington, M, 1962, *The other America: poverty in the United States*, Macmillan, New York.

Harrington, M, 1984, *The new American poverty*, Penguin, New York.

Harris, E, Webster, IW, Harris, MF & Lee, PJ, 1998, 'Unemployment and health: the healthcare system's role', *Medical Journal of Australia*, vol 168, pp 291-96.

Hatfield, A & Lefley, H 1993, *Surviving mental illness*, Guildford Press, New York

Held, D, McGrew, A, Goldblatt, D, & Perraton, J, 1999, *Global transformations*, Polity Press, Cambridge.

Henderson, R, 1975, *Poverty in Australia: first main report, Commission of Inquiry into Poverty*, Volume 1, Australian Government Publishing Service, Canberra.

Henderson, RF, Harcourt, A & Harper, RJA, 1970, *People in poverty: a Melbourne survey*, The Institute of Applied Economics and Social Research, The University of Melbourne, Melbourne.

Hettne, B, 1995, *Development theory and the three worlds*, (Second edition), Longman Group Limited, London.

Hickey, S & Mohan G (eds), 2004, *Participation: from tyranny to transformation?– Exploring new approaches to participation in development*, Zed Books, London.

Hill, J & Scannell, H, 1983, *Due south: socialists and world development*, Pluto Press, London.

Hill, T, 2004, *Gender, income poverty and intra-household distribution*, School of Economics and Social Policy Research Centre, University of New South Wales, Sydney, <www.docs.fce.unsw.edu.au/economics/news/postgrad seminar/HillSeminarPaper2.pdf>, (accessed 5 August 2004).

Hills, S, 2004, *Response by Brotherhood of St Laurence to Senate community affairs reference committee inquiry into aged care*, Brotherhood of St Laurence, Melbourne.

Hirst, C, 1989, *Forced exit*, Crossroads Youth Network, Melbourne.

Hiscock, G, 2006, 'Poverty still the indigenous norm: despite gains, Aboriginal Australians lag behind other groups', in *CNN World*, <http://edition.cnn.com/2006/WORLD/asiapc/02/22/australia.aboriginal/index.html>, (accessed 3 March 2006).

Hoagland, J, 1999, 'Is the global economy widening the income gap?', *International Herald Tribune*, 27 April, p 8.

Hollin, C, 2002, 'Criminological psychology', in M Maguire, R Morgan & R Reiner (eds), *The Oxford handbook of criminology*, 3rd edn, Oxford University Press, Oxford.

Hollingworth, P, 1972, *The powerless poor*, Stockland Press, Melbourne.

Hollinsworth, D, 1998, *Race and racism in Australia*, 2nd edn, Social Science Press, Sydney.

Home Office, 2005, *Offender management caseload statistics 2004*, Home Office Statistical Bulletin December 2005, Home Office UK, <www.homeoffice.gov.uk>, (accessed 22 December 2005).

Homel, P, 2004, 'The whole of government approach to crime prevention', *Trends and Issues in Crime and Criminal Justice*, no 287, Australian Institute of Criminology, Canberra.

Howe, A, 2000, *HACC status report for Victorian local government: full report*, Municipal Association of Victoria, Melbourne.

Hudson, P, 1998, 'Tax reform to include overhaul of welfare', *The Age*, Melbourne, 4 May.

Hume City Council, 2003, *Hume tackling poverty together: an inquiry into poverty in Hume City*, Social Planning Unit, Hume City Council, Melbourne.

Huxley, P & Vick, N, 2005, *Promoting social inclusion through national mental health policy*, Paper presented at THMHS Conference, Adelaide

Huxley, P, Webber, M & Evans, S, 2005, *Measuring social inclusion*, Paper presented at THMHS Conference, Adelaide

IEA, 1996, 'Charles Murray and the underclass: the developing debate', *Choice in Welfare*, no 33, The IEA Health and Welfare Unit, London.

Ife, JW, 1995, *Community development: creating community alternatives – vision, analysis and practice*, Addison Wesley Longman Australia Pty Ltd, Melbourne.

REFERENCES

Ife, JW, 2002, *Community development: community-based alternatives in an age of globalisation*, Pearson Education, Sydney.

International Labour Office (ILO), 1976, *Declaration of principles and programme of action for a basic needs strategy of development*, ILO, Geneva.

International Labour Office (ILO), 2004, *Global employment trends 2004*, ILO, Geneva.

Inclusion International website, <www.inclusioninternational.org/en/ii_priority_areas/pr/index.html>, (accessed 14 November 2005).

Inglis, KS, 1974, *The Australian colonists: an exploration of social history 1788-1870*, Melbourne University Press, Melbourne.

International Co-operative Alliance (ICA), 1995, *Cooperatives and the poor: report of an experts' consultation*, ICA, London.

International Co-operative Alliance (ICA), 2006, Statistical information on the co-operative movement, <www.ica.coop/coop/statistics.html>, (accessed 4 May 2006).

International Institute for Labour Studies, 1996, *Social exclusion and anti-poverty strategy*, International Labour Organization, Geneva.

International Institute for Sustainable Development (IISD), 2000a, 'Communities and livelihoods' <http://iisd.ca/communities.htm>, (accessed 12 May 2000).

International Institute for Sustainable Development (IISD), 2000b, 'We the Peoples: 50 communities awards', <http://iisd1.iisd.ca/50comm/50_desc.htm>, (accessed 12 May 2000).

International Women's Development Agency, 2005, *Annual report, 2004-2005: empowerment through partnerships*, <www.iwda.org.au/about.htm>, (accessed 20 May 2005).

Irwin, DA, 2002, *Free trade under fire*, Princeton University Press, Princeton, New Jersey.

Jablensky, A, McGrath, J, Herrman, H, Castle, D, Gureje, O, Morgan, V & Korten, A, on behalf of the Low Prevalence Disorders Study Group, 1999, *National survey of mental health and wellbeing. Report 4: People living with psychotic illness: an Australian study 1997-98*. Commonwealth of Australia, Canberra.

Jaggs, D, 1986, *Neglected and criminal: foundations of child welfare legislation in Victoria*, Phillip Institute of Technology, Melbourne.

Jamrozik, A & Nocella, L, 1998, *The sociology of social problems*, Cambridge University Press, Cambridge.

Jamrozik, A, 2001, *Social policy in the post-welfare state*, Longman, Melbourne.

Jamrozik, A, 2005, *Social policy in the post-welfare state*, 2nd edn, Longman, Melbourne.

Jefferson, T & Preston, A, 2005, 'Australia's "other" gender wage gap: baby boomers and compulsory superannuation accounts', *Feminist Economics*, vol 11, no 2, pp 79-101.

John, M, 2002, 'Feminism, poverty and globalization: an Indian view', *Inter-Asia Cultural Studies*, vol 3, no 3, pp 351-67.

Johnson, J & Taylor, J, 2000, 'The invisible Australians: conception of poverty in Australia', paper presented to AIFS Conference Family Futures, Sydney, 24-26 July.

Johnson, J, 2000, *The invisible Australians: community understandings of poverty*, Brotherhood of St Laurence, Melbourne.

Johnson, J, 2002, *Poverty in Australia: developing community dialogue. Report of a qualitative research study*, Brotherhood of St Laurence, Melbourne.

Johnston, E, 1991 *Royal Commission into Aboriginal deaths in custody*, AGPS, Canberra.

Jones, M, 1993, *Transforming local government in Australia: making it work*, Allen and Unwin, Sydney.

Jones, MA, 1972, *Housing and poverty in Australia*, Melbourne University Press, Melbourne.

Jones, MA, 1996, *The Australian welfare state*, 4th edn, Allen and Unwin, Sydney.

Kaplan, G, 1992, *Contemporary Western European feminism*, Allen and Unwin, Sydney.

Keck, M & Sikkink, K, 1998, *Activists beyond borders*, Cornell University Press, Ithaca, New York.

Kelly, S, 2001, 'Trends in Australian wealth – new estimates for the 1990s', The National Centre for Social and Economic Modelling, University of Canberra, <www.natsem.canberra.edu.au>, (accessed 1 November 2001).

Kendall, K, 2002, 'Time to think again about cognitive behavioural programmes', in P Carlen (ed), *Women and punishment: the struggle for justice*, Willan Publishing, Cullompton, UK.

Kendig, H & Duckett, S, 2001, *Australian directions in aged care: the generation of policies for generations of older people, Sydney*, The Australian Health Policy Institute, Sydney.

Kennedy, R 1985, *Charity warfare: the charity organisation society in colonial Melbourne*, Hyland House, Melbourne.

Kenwood, AG, 1995, *Australian economic institutions since federation*, Oxford University Press, Melbourne.

Kewley, T, 1973, *Social security in Australia 1900-72*, 2nd edn, Sydney University Press, Sydney.

King, J & Stilwell, F, 2005, 'The industrial relations 'reforms': an introduction', *Journal of Australian Political Economy*, no 56, December.

Kinnear, P, 2003, 'The idea of "mutual obligation" in Australian social security policy', in C Aspalter (ed), *Neoliberalism and the Australian welfare state*, Casa Verde Publishing, Taipei.

Kitching, G, 2001, *Seeking social justice through globalization: escaping a nationalist perspective*, The Pennsylvania State University Press, University Park, PA.

Korten, DC, 1995, *When corporations rule the world*, Earthscan Publications Ltd, London.

Korten, DC, 2000, *The post-corporate world: life after capitalism*, Berret-Koehler Publishers, Inc, in conjunction with Pluto Press, Sydney.

Kryger, T, 1998, *Do official figures understate 'true' unemployment?* Australian Parliamentary Library, Research Note 33 1997-98, <www.aph.gov.au/library/pubs/rn/1997-98/98rn33.htm>, (accessed 7 November 2005).

Land, K, Cantor, D & Russell, S, 1995, 'Unemployment and crime rate fluctuations in the post-World War II United States', in J Hagan & R Peterson (eds), *Crime and inequality*, Stanford University Press, Palo Alto, CA.

Layard, R, 2003, 'Happiness: has social science a clue?' *Lionel Robbins Memorial Lecture*, London School of Economics, March.

REFERENCES

Leahy, M, 2001, *Big Brother is watching us: justice and privacy implications of Centrelink's Enhanced Investigation Initiative*, Welfare Rights Centre South Australia, <www.wrcsa.org.au/publications/issueone.html>, (accessed 28 February 2006).

Leech, M, 2001, *Families on the margins: a snapshot*, Mission Australia, <www.mission.com.au/uploaded files/families/>, (accessed 12 May 2002).

Leonard, M 2003, 'Women and development: examining gender issues', in G McCann & S McCloskey (eds), *From the local to the global: key issues in development studies*, Pluto Press, London.

Lewis, D & Johnson, D, 2005, 'Costs of family care for individuals with developmental disabilities', in R Stancliffe & K Lakin (eds), *Costs and outcomes of community services for people with intellectual disabilities*, Brookes, Baltimore.

Lister, R, 2003, *Citizenship, feminist perspectives*, 2nd edn, Palgrave, Melbourne.

Lloyd, R, Harding, A & Payne, A, 2004, *Australians in poverty in the 21st century*, paper presented to 33rd Conference of Economists, NATSEM National Centre for Social and Economic Modelling, University of Canberra, 27-30 September 2004.

Lopes, C & Theisohn T, 2003, *Ownership, leadership and transformation: can we do better for capacity development?* Earthscan Publications Ltd, London.

Lopez-Claros, A & Zahidi, S, 2005, 'Women's empowerment: measuring the global gender gap: special report', *Harvard Business Review*, World Economic Forum, Boston.

Lutz, MA, 1999, *Economics for the common good*, Routledge, London.

Lynch, M, Buckman, J & Krenske, L, 2003, 'Youth justice: criminal trajectories', *Trends and Issues*, paper no 265, Australian Institute of Criminology, Canberra.

Lyons, M, 2001, *Cooperatives in Australia – a background paper*, The Australian Centre for Co-operative Research and Development, University of Technology, Sydney.

Mabbett, D & Bolderson, H, 2000, *Non-discrimination, free movement and social citizenship in Europe: Contrasting provisions for EU nationals and asylum-seekers*, Paper presented at International Research Conference on Social Security 'Social security in the global village' Helsinki, 25-27 September 2000.

Mack, J & Lansley, S, 1985, *Poor Britain*, George Allen & Unwin (Publishers) Ltd, London.

Mack-Canty, C, 2004, 'Third-wave feminism and the need to reweave the nature/culture duality', *NWSA Journal*, vol 16, no 3, pp 154-79.

Madden, D, 2000, 'Relative or absolute poverty lines: a new approach', *Review of Income and Wealth*, Series 46, no 2, June 2000.

Maddox, M, 2005, *God under Howard: The rise of the religious right in Australian politics*, Allen & Unwin, Sydney.

Maguire, M & Raynor, P, 2006, 'How the resettlement of prisoners promotes desistance from crime: or does it?', *Criminology and Criminal Justice*, vol 6, no 1, pp 19-38.

Marmot, M, 2004, *Status syndrome: how your social standing directly affects your health and life expectancy*, Bloomsbury, London.

Marrone, J & Golowka, E, 1999, 'If work makes people with mental illness sick, what do unemployment, poverty and social isolation cause?', *Psychiatric Rehabilitation Journal*, vol 23, no 2, pp 187-193.

Marshall, TH, 1950, *Citizenship and social class and other essays*, Cambridge University Press, Cambridge.

Marston, G & Watts, R, 2004, 'The problem with neo-conservative social policy: rethinking the ethics of citizenship and the welfare state', *A Just Policy*, vol 33, October 2004, pp 34-45.

Martinson, R, 1974, 'What works? Question and answers about prison reform', *The Public Interest*, vol 35, pp 22-54.

Marx, K 1954, *Capital 1*, Progress Publishers, Moscow.

Mathers, C & Schofield, D, 1998, 'The health consequences of unemployment: the evidence', *Medical Journal of Australia*, vol 168, pp 178-82.

Mathews, R, 1987, *Employee ownership: Mondragon's lessons for Australia*, Australian Fabian Society, Melbourne.

Maunders, D, 1984, *Keeping them off the streets: a history of voluntary youth organisations in Australia 1850-1980*, Philip Institute of Technology, Melbourne.

McArdle, J, 1999, *Community development in the market economy*, Vista Publications, Melbourne.

McBride, S, 2005, 'Living precariously: A Canadian perspective on economic security', *Just Policy: A Journal of Australian Social Policy*, vol 37, pp 9-17.

McCausland, R, 2005a, 'Petrol bowsers for washing kids' faces: a new conversation', in *Indigenous Policy*, Australian Social Policy Conference 2005, University of New South Wales, Sydney.

McCausland, R, 2005b, 'Shared Responsibility Agreements: practical reconciliation or paternalistic rhetoric?', *Indigenous Law Bulletin*, July 2005, vol 6, issue 12, Sydney.

McChesney, R, 1999, 'Introduction', in *Profit over people: neo-liberalism and global order*, N Chomsky (ed), Seven Stories Press, New York, pp 7-16.

McGuire, J, 1995, 'Reviewing 'What Works': past, present and future', in J McGuire (ed), *What works: reducing reoffending*, John Wiley and Sons Ltd, Chichester.

McGuire, J 2004, 'Commentary: promising answers, and the next generation of questions', *Psychology, Crime & Law*, vol 10, no 3, pp 335-345.

McKnight, D, 2005, *Beyond right and left: new politics and the culture wars*, Allen & Unwin, Sydney.

McNaughton, S & Hanson, T, 2005, *Emergency Relief funding allocation for Victoria 2005-2006: a summary of methodology and guideline changes*, Paper presented to Victorian FaS Emergency Relief Advisory Committee, Melbourne.

Meadows, G & Singh, B (eds), 2002, *Mental health in Australia*, Oxford University Press, Melbourne.

Mechanic, D, 1971, 'Social class and schizophrenia: some requirements for a plausible theory of social influence', *Social Forces*, vol 50, pp 304-08.

Melbourne Criminology Research and Evaluation Unit, 2003, *Bridging the gap: a release transition support program for Victorian prisoners. Final evaluation report*, Department of Criminology, University of Melbourne, Melbourne.

Melbourne Institute, 2003, *Household income and labour dynamics in Australia (HILDA) survey: Annual Report 2003*, Melbourne Institute of Applied Economic and Social Research, University of Melbourne, Melbourne.

Mendelsohn, R, 1979, *The condition of the people: social welfare in Australia 1900-1975*, George Allen & Unwin, Sydney.

REFERENCES

Mendelsohn, R, 1983, 'Social welfare finance: the past', in *Australian social welfare finance*, R Mendelsohn (ed), George Allen & Unwin, Sydney.

Mendes, P, 2003, *Australia's welfare wars: the players, the politics and the ideologies*, UNSW Press, Sydney.

Metcalf, B, 1995, *From utopian dreaming to communal reality*, University of New South Wales Press, Sydney.

Metcalf, B, 1996, *Shared visions shared lives: communal living around the globe*, Findhorn Press, Findhorn.

Mies, M, 1998, *Patriarchy and accumulation on a world scale: women and the international division of labour*, Zed Books, London.

Milne, G, 2005, 'Uncharitable clampdown', *The Australian*, Sydney, 18 April.

Minister for Community Services, Dept of Human Services, press release, 29 April 2005.

Minister for Health, Housing and Community Services, 1991, *Social justice for people with disabilities*, Australian Government Printing Service, Canberra.

Mishel, L, Bernstein, J, Boushey, H, 2003, *The state of working America 2002-03*, Cornell University Press, Ithaca.

Mission Australia, 2002, *'There's something different about this place', local, national and global directions in community capacity building* Mission Australia Report, <www.mission.com.au/cm/p.aspx?n=SKXRK-OGYPC-GHYAH-OOCGA-WLKIT>, (accessed 16 May 2005).

Mitchell, W and Carlson, E (eds), 2001, *Unemployment: the tip of the iceberg*, Centre for Applied Economic Research, University of NSW, Sydney.

Mitchell, W, Cowling, S & Watts, M, 2003, *A community development job guarantee. A new paradigm in employment policy*, Centre for Full Employment and Equity, University of Newcastle, Newcastle.

Mondragon Corporacion Cooperativa (MCC), 2005, Annual Report 2004, MCC, <http://mondragon.mcc.es/ing/magnitudes/memoria2004.pdf>, (accessed 15 May 2006).

Mukhopadhyay, M, 2003, 'Creating citizens and just governance: gender and development in the twenty-first century', *Gender and Development*, vol 11, no 3, pp 45-56.

Murali, V & Oyebode, F, 2004, 'Poverty, social inequality and mental health', *Advances in Psychiatric Treatment*, vol 10, pp 216-24.

Murray, C, 1984, *Losing ground*, Basic Books, New York.

Murray, C, 2001, 'Beyond the welfare state: Susan Windybank talks to Charles Murray', *Policy [CIS]*, vol 17, no 3, pp 25-28.

Narayan, D, Chambers, R, Shah, MK & Petesch, P, 1999, Global synthesis. *Prepared for the Global Synthesis Workshop: Consultations with the Poor*, World Bank, Washington, DC.

Narayan, D, with Patel, P, Schafft, K, Rademacher, A & Koch-Schulte, S, 2000, *Voices of the poor: can anyone hear us?*, published for the World Bank by Oxford University Press, New York.

Narayan, U, 1997, *Dislocating cultures, identities, tradition and Third World feminism*, Routledge, Abington.

National Crime Prevention, 1999, *Pathways to prevention: developmental and early intervention approaches to crime in Australia*, National Crime Prevention, Commonwealth Attorney-General's Department, Canberra.

Neil, C & Fopp, R, 1992, *Homelessness in Australia: causes and consequences*, CSIRO, Melbourne.

NESEP, 2005, 'About Us' North East Social Enterprise Partnership Website, UK, <www.ccda.org.uk/>, (accessed 28 July 2005).

Neville, A, 2002, *State of the family 2002*, Anglicare, Melbourne.

Neville, J, 1997, *Economic rationalism: social philosophy masquerading as economic science, background paper no 7*, The Australian Institute, May, ACT.

Newman, J, 1999, 'The challenge of welfare dependency in the 21st century', Discussion Paper, Federal Minister of Family and Community Services, Canberra.

Nicholas-Casebolt, A & Krysik, J, 1993, *The economic well-being of ever- and never-married single mother families: a cross-national comparison*, School of Social Work, Virginia Commonwealth University, Richmond, VA.

Nitsch, TO, 1990, 'Social economics: the first 200 years' in MA Lutz (ed), 1990, *Social Economics: retrospect and prospect*, Kluwer Academic Publishers, Massachusetts.

Nnaemeka, O, 2005, 'International conferences as sites for transitional feminist struggles: the case of the first international conference on women in Africa and the African diaspora', in M Waller & S Marcos (eds), *Dialogue and difference: feminism's challenge to globalisation*, Palgrave MacMillan, Melbourne.

Noble, T & Wroe, D, 2005, 'Asylum seekers need Medicare', *The Age*, 23 November, p 11.

Novak, T, 1988, *Poverty and the state*, Open University Press, Milton Keynes.

Nussbaum, M, 2000 *Women and Human Development, The Capabilities Approach*, Cambridge University Press, Cambridge.

O'Boyle, EJ, 2004, 'World poverty, hunger and disease', in PA O'Hara (ed), *Global political economy and the wealth of nations*, Routledge, Abington.

O'Brien, J & Dempsey, I, 2004, 'Comparative analysis of employment services for people with disabilities in Australia, Finland, and Sweden', *Journal of Policy and Practice in Intellectual Disabilities*, vol 1, p 126.

O'Brien, M & Penna, S, 1998, *Theorising welfare: enlightenment and modern society*, Sage, London.

O'Connor, I, Wilson, J, & Setterlund, D, 2003, *Social work and welfare practice*, 4th edn, Pearson Education Australia, Sydney.

Office of Indigenous Policy Co-ordination (OIPC), 2006a, *Five principles: a whole-of-government commitment and changed engagement*, <www.oipc.gov.au/About_OIPC/Indigenous_Affairs_Arrangements/2FivePrincipals>, (accessed 10 January 2006).

Office of Indigenous Policy Co-ordination (OIPC), 2006b, *Shared responsibility agreements: flexibility and responsiveness at the local level*, <www.oipc.gov.au/About_OIPC/Indigenous_Affairs_Arrangements/6SharedRes>, (accessed 1 January 2006).

Office of Indigenous Policy Co-ordination (OIPC), 2006c, *Shared responsibility agreements: sport and recreation activities for young people*, <www.indigenous.gov.au/sra/nsw/fact_sheets/nswnov0506.html>, (accessed 10 January 2006).

Organisation for Economic Co-operation and Development (OECD), 1999, *Social enterprises*, OECD Publications, Paris, <www.oecd.org/publications/>, (accessed 16 June 2005).

REFERENCES

Organisation for Economic Co-operation and Development (OECD), 2003, *Transforming disability into ability: policies to promote work and income security for disabled people*, OECD, Paris, <www1.oecd.org/publications/e-book/8103021E.pdf>, (accessed 2 May 2006).

Otis, N & Howe, A, 1991, 'Trends in reporting disability in the Australian aged population: interpretation of preliminary ABS survey findings', *Australian Health Review*, vol 14, no 4, pp 380-93.

Owen, R, 1966, *A new view of society*, Everyman's Library, Dent.

Ozdowski, S, 2004, Back to basics, Speech to ACROD National Convention, <www.humanrights.gov.au/disability_rights/speeches/2004/acrod.htm>, (accessed 20 November 2005).

Painter, M, 1996, 'Economic policy, market liberalism and the "end of Australian politics"', *Australian Journal of Political science*, vol 31, no 3, pp 287-99.

Palmer, M, 1988, 'What is happening to emergency relief?', *OSS News*, vol July, 1988, p 3.

Pearson, A, 2004, *Recovery: challenging the paradigm*, VICSERV Conference, Melbourne 2004.

Pearson, N, 2001a, *On the human right to misery, mass incarceration and early death*, Dr Charles Perkins Memorial Oration 2001.

Pearson, N, 2001b, 'Rebuilding indigenous communities', in P Botsman & M Latham (eds), *The enabling state: people before bureaucracy*, Pluto Press, Sydney.

Peel, M, 2003, *The lowest rung: voices of Australian poverty*, Cambridge University Press, Melbourne.

Peet, R, 2003, *Unholy trinity: the IMF, World Bank and WTO*, Zed Books, London.

Penter, C, 2005, *Report of the Emergency Relief Sector Mapping Project*, Matrix Consulting Group, Perth.

Perkins, D & Angley, P, 2003, *Values, unemployment and public policy: the need for a new direction*, Working for an Australia free of poverty, Brotherhood of St Laurence, Melbourne.

Phillips, K, 1990, *The politics of rich and poor*, Random House, New York.

Piper, A, 2004 'Admission to charitable institutions in colonial Tasmania: from individual failing to social problem, *Tasmanian Historical Studies*, vol 9, p 43.

Power, J, Wettenhall, R & Halligan, J (eds), 1981, *Local government systems of Australia, Advisory Council For Inter-Governmental Relations Information Paper no 7*, Australian Government Publishing Service, Canberra.

Pownall, E, 1983, *Australian pioneer women*, Curry O'Neill Ross Pty Ltd, Melbourne.

Pressman, S, 2003, 'Feminist explanations of the feminisation of poverty', *Journal of Economic Issues*, vol 37, no 2, pp 353-61.

Pusey, M, 1991, *Economic rationalism in Canberra: a nation-building state changes its mind*, Cambridge University Press, Cambridge.

Pusey, M, 1993, 'Reclaiming the middle ground ... from new right to "ER"', in S King & P Lloyd (eds), *Economic rationalism*, Allen and Unwin, Sydney.

Pusey, M, 2003, *Experience of middle Australia: the dark side of economic reform*, Cambridge University Press, Melbourne.

Putnam, RD, 1993, *Making democracy work. Civic traditions in modern Italy*, Princeton University Press, Princeton.

Putnam, RD, 1995, 'Bowling alone: America's declining social capital', *Journal of Democracy*, vol 6, no 1, Jan, pp 65-78.

Putnam, RD, 2000, *Bowling alone: the collapse and revival of American community*, Simon and Schuster, New York.

Putnam, RD, 2005, *'Community engagement in a changing America'*, Keynote Address, International Conference on Engaging Communities, Brisbane, 14-17 August.

Rabinow, P (ed), 1991, *The Foucault reader: an introduction to Foucault's thought*, Penguin Books, London.

Rawsthorne, M, 1994, *No poverty of spirit: families in Fairfield*, Ettinger House, Canley Vale, Sydney.

Raynor, P, 2002, 'Community penalties: Probation, punishment and "what works"', in M Maguire, R Morgan & R Reiner (eds), *The Oxford handbook of criminology*, 3rd edn, Oxford University Press, Oxford.

Reddy, S & Pogge, T, 2003, *How not to count the poor*, Columbia University, New York, <www.socialanalysis.org>,(accessed 14 May 2004).

Reece, RHW, 1974, *Aborigines and colonists: Aborigines and colonial society in New South Wales in the 1830s and 1840s*, Sydney University Press, Sydney.

Re-entry Policy Council, 2004, *Report of the Re-entry Policy Council: charting the safe and successful return of prisoners to the community*, Re-entry Policy Council, USA, <www.reentrypolicy.org>, (accessed 21 December 2005).

Renner, M & Starke, L, 2003, *Vital signs 2003: the trends that are shaping our future*, Worldwatch Institute, New York.

Reynolds, H, 2001, *The question of genocide in Australian history: an indelible stain?*, Allen & Unwin, Sydney.

Reynolds, H, 2005, *Nowhere people*, Viking Penguin Group, Melbourne.

Rieger, E & Leibfried, S, 2003, *Limits to globalisation*, Polity Press, Cambridge.

Roe, J, 1975, 'Social policy and the permanent poor', in EL Wheelwright & K Buckley (eds), *Essays in the political economy of Australian capitalism*, Australia and New Zealand Book Company, Sydney.

Rose, D & Serr, K, 2006, *The coffee shop development feasibility study: an income generating project for the disadvantaged*, Catholic Social Services (Vic), Melbourne.

Rowntree, S, 1901, *Poverty: a study of town life*, Howard, Fertig.

Rutter, M, Giller, H & Hagell, A, 1998, *Antisocial behaviour by young people*, Cambridge University Press, Cambridge.

Ryan, J, 2005, 'Vulnerable at risk: workplace changes far from fair', *Justice Trends*, vol 119, pp 1-4.

Ryan, V, 1988, 'Canberra told – put money in poor box', *The Advertiser*, Canberra, 21 September, p.3.

Sachs, W (ed), 1992, *The development dictionary*, Zen Books Ltd, London.

Salhi, ZS, 2004, 'Algerian women, citizenship and the family code', in C Sweetman (ed), *Gender development and citizenship*, Oxfam GB, Oxford.

Sampson, R, 1995 'The community', in J Wilson & J Petersilia (eds), *Crime*, Institute for Contemporary Studies Press, San Francisco.

Saraceno, B & Barbui, C, 1997, 'Poverty and mental illness', *Canadian Journal of Psychiatry*, vol 42, no 3, pp 1-7.

REFERENCES

Saunders, P & Tsumori, K, 2002, *Poverty in Australia: beyond the rhetoric*, Policy Monograph no 57, Centre for Independent Studies, Sydney.

Saunders, P, 2004a, 'Lies, damned lies and the Senate poverty inquiry report', *Issues Analysis*, no 46, pp 1-16.

Saunders, P, 2004b, 'The welfare reform agenda', in P Boreham, G Stokes & R Hall (eds), *The politics of Australian society: political issues for the new century*, 2nd edn, Pearson Education, Sydney.

Saunders, P, 2004c, *Australia's welfare habit and how to kick it*, Duffy & Snellgrove, Sydney.

Saunders, P, 2005a, 'A headlong dash into the chasm of hyperbole', Centre for Independent Studies (CIS), *Issue Analysis*, no 59, June 2005.

Saunders, P, 2005b, 'The $85 billion tax/welfare churn', *Issue Analysis (CIS)*, no 57, 7 April.

Saunders, P, 2005c, 'Six arguments in favour of self-funding', *Issue Analysis (CIS)*, no 61, 14 July.

Saunders, Peter, 1994, *Welfare and Inequality*, Cambridge University Press, Cambridge.

Saunders, Peter, 1996, *Poverty, income distribution and health: an Australian study*, Reports and Proceedings no 128, Social Policy Research Centre, University of New South Wales, Sydney.

Saunders, Peter, 1998, *The direct and indirect effects of unemployment on poverty and inequality*, Discussion Paper no 118, December, Social Policy Research Centre, University of New South Wales, Sydney.

Saunders, Peter, 2002a, 'Introduction: the reality and costs of unemployment', in Peter Saunders & R Taylor (eds), *The price of prosperity: the economic and social costs of unemployment*, University of New South Wales Press, Sydney.

Saunders, Peter, 2002b, *The ends and means of welfare*, Cambridge University Press, Cambridge.

Saunders, Peter, 2003, The meaning and measurement of poverty: towards an agenda for action, Submission to the Senate Community Affairs References Committee Inquiry into Poverty and Financial Hardship, Social Policy Research Centre, University of New South Wales.

Saunders, Peter, 2005a, 'Disability, poverty and living standards: reviewing evidence and policies', SPRC Discussion Paper no 145, Social Policy Research Centre, Sydney.

Saunders, Peter, 2005b, *The poverty wars: reconnecting research with reality*, UNSW Press, Sydney.

Saunders, Peter, 2005c, *Disability, poverty and living standards: reviewing Australian evidence and policies*, unpublished paper.

Saunders, Peter, 2005d, 'Welfare to work in practice: introduction and overview', in P Saunders (ed), *Welfare to work in practice: social security and participation in economic and social life*, Aldershot, London.

Saunders, Peter, 2006, 'Lost horizons?: social justice and the re-distributional imperative', *A Just Policy*, vol 39 March 2006, pp 5-12.

Savage, A, 2004, *Food and emergency relief: policy and research paper*, VOSS, Melbourne.

Sawer, G, 1963, *Australian federal politics and law 1929-1949*, Melbourne University Press, Melbourne.

Schiller, BR, 1989, *The economics of poverty and discrimination*, (5th edn), Prentice-Hall Inc, New Jersey.

Schubert, M, 2005, 'Work for dole "not working"', *The Age*, 27 September.

Schubert, M, 2006, 'More coalition women join child-care revamp call', *The Age*, January 17, p 4.

Schumacher, EF, 1973, *Small is beautiful: a study of economics as if people mattered*, Blond & Briggs Ltd, London.

Scrivener, G, 2000, Parental imposition or police coercion? The role of parents and police in committals to the industrial school in New South Wales, 1867-1905, *Journal of the Royal Australian Historical Society*, vol 86, part 1, p 23.

Seelig, T, Jones, A, Bland, R & Thompson, A, 2004 *A Evaluation of Local Partnership Agreements between Department of Housing Area Offices and Local Mental Health Services, Final report*, Queensland Department of Housing, Brisbane.

Seelos, C & Mair, J, 2005, 'Social entrepreneurship: creating new business models to serve the poor' *Business Horizons*, vol 48, pp 241-46.

Sen, AK, 1992, *Inequality re-examined*, Oxford University Press, Oxford.

Sen, AK, 1999, *Development of freedom*, Anchor Books, New York.

Senate Community Affairs Reference Committee, 2004, *A hand up not a hand out: report on poverty and financial hardship*, Commonwealth of Australia, Canberra.

Senate Standing Committee on Social Welfare, 1982, *Homeless youth: report*, AGPS, Canberra.

SenScot, 2005, 'About SenScot' SenScot Website Scotland, <http://senscot.spl21.net/>, (accessed 8 August 2005).

Serr, K, 1996, 'Pubs as low cost housing?', *Parity*, Council to Homeless Persons, vol 9 issue 9, November 1996, pp 4-7.

Serr, K, 1998, 'Working with the unemployed: a participatory approach' *Victorian Social Work*, vol 2 May 1998, pp 7-9.

Serr, K, 2000, *Community based anti-poverty strategies*, unpublished PhD Thesis, La Trobe University, Bundoora.

Serr, K, 2001, 'Towards a theory and practice of alternative economics', *A Just Policy*, vol 21 March 2001, pp 28-36.

Serr, K, 2003, 'Senate Inquiry: inquiry into poverty in Australia', *AASW National Bulletin*, vol 13, issue 2, April 2003, pp 20-22.

Serr, K (ed), 2004a, *Thinking about poverty*, 2nd edn, Professional Practice Publications Series, Social Work Services Pty Ltd, Melbourne.

Serr, K, 2004b, 'Poverty solutions: listening to the poor', in K Serr (ed), *Thinking about poverty* (2nd edn), Professional Practice Publications Series, Social Work Services Pty Ltd, Melbourne.

Serr, K, 2004c, 'Voices from the bottom', *Australian Social Work*, vol 57, no 2, June 2004, pp 137-149.

Serr, K, 2004d, 'Poverty and wealth in a global context', *Victorian Social Work*, vol 12, no 4, July 2004, pp 3-4.

Serr, K, 2006, *Shattered dreams*, Catholic Social Services (Vic.), Melbourne.

Shakespeare, T & Corker, M (eds), 2002, *Disability/postmodernity: embodying disability theory*, Continuum, London.

Shaver, S, 1998,'Poverty, gender and sole parenthood', in R Fincher & J Nieuwenhuysen (eds), *Australian poverty: then and now*, Melbourne University Press, Melbourne.

REFERENCES

Shaver, S, 2001, 'Australian welfare reform: from citizenship to social engineering', *Australian Journal of Social Issues*, vol 36, no 4, pp 227-93.

Shields, J, 2005, 'Setting the double standard: chief executive pay the BCA way', *Journal of Australian Political Economy*, no 56, December.

Shipman, A, 2002, *The globalization myth*, Allen and Unwin, Sydney.

Simmons, R, 2000, *Social Enterprises: An opportunity to harness capacities* The Smith Family Research and Advocacy Briefing Paper no 7, December 2000, <www.smithfamily.org.au>, (accessed 7 August 2005).

Sinha, K, 2004, 'Citizenship degraded: Indian women in a modern state and pre-modern society', in C Sweetman (ed), *Gender development and citizenship*, Oxfam GB, Oxford.

Skinner, S, 1997, *Building community strengths. A resource book on capacity building*, Community Development Foundation, London.

Smallwood, H, Webster, M & Ayres-Wearne, V, 2002, *User pays. Who pays? A report into the impact of government fees and charges on people living with low incomes*, Good Shepherd Youth and Family Service, Collingwood, Melbourne.

Smeeding, T, 2005 'Poor people in rich nations: the United States in comparative perspective', Luxembourg Income Study Working Paper Series, Working Paper no 419, <www.lisproject.org>, (accessed 21 March 2006).

Smith, G, O'Keefe, J, Carpenter, L, Doty, P, & Kennedy, G, 2000, *Understanding Medicaid home and community services: a primer*, US Dept of Health and Human Services, Office of the Assistant Secretary for Planning and Evaluation, Washington DC.

Smyth, C, Rawsthorne, M & Siminski, P, 2005, *Women's life work*, Report prepared for the Commonwealth, State, Territories and New Zealand Minister's Conference on the Status of Women (MINCO), Social Policy Research Centre, University of New South Wales, Sydney.

Social Enterprise Coalition, 2005, 'About SEC' SEC Website, UK, <www.socialenterprise.org.uk/>, (accessed 27 July 2005).

Social Enterprise London, nd, *Starting point guide: guide for established social enterprises, social enterprise start-ups and social entrepreneurs*, SEL, <www.sel.org.uk/knowledge.aspx>, (accessed 29 July 2005).

Social Enterprise Unit, 2005, 'Social enterprise', SEU Department of Trade and Industry, UK, <www.sbs.gov.uk/sbsgov/action/>, (accessed 27 July 2005).

Social Exclusion Unit, 2002, *Reducing re-offending by ex-prisoners*, Social Exclusion Unit, Office of the Deputy Prime Minister, London, <www.socialexclusionunit.gov.uk>, (accessed 20 December 2005).

Social Exclusion Unit, 2004 *Tackling social exclusion: taking stock and looking to the future*, Social Exclusion Unit, Office of the Deputy Prime Minister, London, <www.socialexclusionunit.gov.uk>, (accessed 20 December 2005).

Social Exclusion Unit, 2004 *Taking stock and looking to the future*, Office of the Deputy Prime Minister, London.

Social Watch, 2005 *Social Watch Report 2005: fear and want obstacles to human security*, Monocromo, Montevideo.

Spenceley, G, 1980, 'Charity relief in Melbourne: the early years of the 1930s Depression', *Monash Papers in Economic History*, no 8, Monash University, Melbourne.

Spenceley, G, 1986, 'Social control, the Charity Organisation Society and the evolution of unemployment relief policy in Melbourne during the Depression of the 1930s', *Historical Studies*, vol 22, no 87, pp 232- 251.

Spencer, H, 1969, *The man versus the state*, D MacRae (ed), Penguin, Harmondsworth, UK.

Spicker, P, 1993, *Poverty and social security*, Routledge, London.

Spooner, C, Hall, W & Lynskey, M, 2001, *Structural determinants of youth drug use*, Australian National Council on Drugs, Canberra.

Squires, P, 1990, *Anti-social policy*, Harvester Wheatsheaf, New York.

Stark, A, 2005, 'Warm hands in cold age – on the need of a new world order of care', *Feminist Economics*, vol 11, no 2, pp 7-36.

Steering Committee for the Review of Government Service Provision, 2005, *Report on government services: health, community services and housing*, vol 2, Australian Government Publishing Services, Canberra.

Stiglitz, J, 2003, 'The insider: what I learned at the world economic crisis', *The New Republic*, 17 April.

Stiglitz, JE, 2003, *Globalization and its discontents*, WW Norton, New York.

Stilwell, F, 2000, *Changing track: a new political economic direction for Australia*, Pluto Press, Sydney.

Stilwell, F, 2002, *Political economy: the contest of economic ideas*, Oxford University Press, Melbourne.

Stilwell, F, 2003, 'Economic inequality', in G Argyrous & F Stilwell (eds), *Economics as a social science*, 2nd edn, Pluto Press, Sydney.

Stilwell, F & Jordan, K, 2005, 'Land tax in Australia: principles, problems and policies', in J Laurent (ed) *Henry George's legacy in economic thought*, Edward Elgar, Cheltenham, UK & Northhampton, MA.

Stretesky, P, Schuck, A & Hogan, M, 2004 'Space matters: an analysis of poverty, poverty clustering, and violent crime', *Justice Quarterly*, vol 21, no 4, pp 817-41.

Stutz, F & Warf, B, 2005, *The world economy: resources, location, trade, and development*, 4th edn, Pearson Prentice Hall, Upper Saddle River, NJ.

Swan, W, 2005, *Postcode: the splintering of a nation*, Pluto Press, Canberra.

Sweetman, C (ed), 2004, *Gender development and citizenship*, Oxfam GB, Oxford.

Tabb, WK, 2004, *Economic governance in the age of globalisation*, Columbia University Press, New York.

Talbot, C (ed), 1999, 'The state we're in', in *Revealing the Hidden City*, Inner City Administrators Group, Adelaide City Council, Adelaide.

Talbot, C, Tregilgas, P, & Harrison, K, 2002, *Social enterprise in Australia: an introductory handbook*, Adelaide Central Mission, Adelaide, <www.ucwesley adelaide.org.au/publications/resources.htm>, (accessed 10 May).

Tasmanian Council of Social Service, 2001 (TCSS), *Dead man's shoes: unemployment in Tasmania and the stories of jobseekers looking for work*, TCSS, Hobart.

Taylor, BK, 1992, *Imagine no possessions: towards a sociology of poverty*, Harvester Wheatsheaf, Hemel Hempstead.

Taylor, J, 2002, 'Unemployment and family life', in P Saunders & R Taylor (eds), *The price of prosperity: the economic and social costs of unemployment*, University of New South Wales Press, Sydney.

REFERENCES

Taylor, J & Fraser, A, 2003, *Eleven plus: life chances and family income*, Brotherhood of St Laurence, Melbourne.

Taylor, R & Morrell, S, 2002, 'The health effects of unemployment', in P Saunders & R Taylor (eds), *The price of prosperity: the economic and social costs of unemployment*, University of New South Wales Press, Sydney.

The Gungil Jindibah Centre, 1994, *Learning from the past: Aboriginal perspectives on the effects and implications of welfare policies and practices on Aboriginal families in New South Wales*, South Cross University, Lismore.

Thompson, D, 2001, *Radical feminism today*, SAGE Publications, Warwick, WA.

Thompson, G, 2004, 'Global inequality, economic globalization and technological change', in W Brown, S Bromley, & S Athreye (eds), *Ordering the international: history, change and transformation*, Pluto Press in association with The Open University, Sydney.

Tönnies, F, 1963, *Community & society*, Harper and Row, New York.

Topsfield, J, 2006, 'Poverty report naïve and faulty', *The Age*, 16 March, p 11.

Townsend, K, 1996, 'Official welcome', in G Moon (ed), *Making her rights a reality: women's human rights and development*, Community Aid Abroad, Melbourne.

Townsend, P (ed), 1970, *The concept of poverty*, Heinemann, London.

Townsend, P, 1979, *Poverty in the United Kingdom: a survey of household resources and standards of living*, University of California Press, Berkeley.

Townsend, P, 1984, 'The development of an anti-poverty strategy', in JC Brown (ed), *Anti-poverty policy in the European community: papers prepared for a working party*, Policy Studies Institute, London.

Townsend, P, 1993, *The international analysis of poverty*, Harvester Wheatsheaf, New York.

Trainer, T, 1996, *Towards a sustainable economy*, Envirobook, Sydney.

Travers, P & Richardson, S, 1993, *Living decently: material well-being in Australia*, Oxford University Press, Melbourne.

Treasury, 2005, *Budget Paper no 1, 2004-2005 Budget Papers*, <www.budget.gov.au/2004-2005/bp1/html/bst4.htm>, (accessed 7 November 2005).

Trewin, D & Madden, R, 2005, *The health and welfare of Australia's Aboriginal and Torres Strait Islander Peoples*, Australian Bureau of Statistics and Australian Institute of Health and Welfare, Commonwealth Government, Canberra.

Turner, R, Wheaton, B & Lloyd, D, 1995, 'The epidemiology of social stress', *American Sociological Review*, vol 60, pp 104-25.

Twomey, C, 1999, 'Courting men: mothers, magistrates and welfare in the Australian colonies', *Women's History Review*, vol 8, no 2, p 231.

United Nations (UN), 2004, *World population prospects: the 2004 revision: highlights*, UN Department of Economic and Social Affairs Population Division, <http://esa.un.org/unpp/> (accessed 1 May 2004).

United Nations (UN), 2005, *UN millennium development goals*, Department of Public Information, UN, <www.un.org/millenniumgoals>, (accessed 5 February 2006).

United Nations Development Program (UNDP), 1993, *Human Development Report 1993*, Oxford University Press, Oxford.

United Nations Development Program (UNDP), 1996, *Human Development Report 1996*, Oxford University Press, Oxford.

United Nations Development Program (UNDP), 1997, *Human development report, 1997*, Oxford University Press, Oxford.

United Nations Development Program (UNDP), 1998, *Human Development Report 1998*, Oxford University Press, Oxford.

United Nations Development Program (UNDP) 1990, *Human Development Report 1990*, Oxford University Press, Oxford.

United Nations Development Program (UNDP), 1999, *Human development report 1999*, Oxford University Press, Oxford.

United Nations Development Program (UNDP), 2000, *Human Development Report 2000*, Oxford University Press, Oxford.

United Nations Development Program (UNDP), 2002, *Human Development Report 2002*, Oxford University Press, Oxford.

United Nations Development Program (UNDP), 2003, *Human Development Report 2003*, Oxford University Press, Oxford.

United Nations Development Program (UNDP), 2004, *Development partnership in Ethiopia*, UNDP, Addis Ababa.

United Nations Development Program (UNDP), 2005, *Human development report 2005*, Oxford University Press, Oxford.

United Nations International Children's Fund (UNICEF), 2002, *The state of the world's children*, Oxford University Press, Oxford.

United Nations International Children's Fund (UNICEF), 2005, *Child poverty in rich countries 2005*, Innocenti Research Centre Report Card no 6. UNICEF, Florence, <www.unicef-icdc.org/publications/pdf/repcard6e.pdf>, (accessed 12 May 2006).

United States Bureau of Statistics, 1997, *Poverty statistics on population groups*, Current Population Survey, March 1996.

UnitingCare Australia, 2000, *UnitingCare Australia's response to independence and self-provision*, Discussion Paper, UnitingCare, Melbourne.

van Krieken, R, 1992, *Children and the state: social control and the formation of Australian child welfare*, Allen and Unwin, Sydney.

Victorian Concessions Unit, 2005, *State concessions 2003-2004: annual report, Community are Division*, Victorian Government Department of Human Services, Melbourne.

Victorian Council of Social Services (VCOSS), 2005, *Generating a community legacy: VCOSS State budget submission 2005-2006*, VCOSS, Melbourne.

Victorian Council of Social Services (VCOSS), 2005, *Noticeboard*, vol 18, no 5.

Victorian Council of Social Services (VCOSS), 2005, *Sustaining a fairer Victoria: VCOSS State budget submission 2006-07*, Melbourne.

Victorian Office of Housing (VOH), 2004, *Waiting and transfer list: June 2004*, Melbourne.

Victorian Office of Housing (VOH), 2005, *Annual report: 2004-05*, Melbourne.

Victorian Relief Committee, 2005, *Annual report: 2004-05*, Melbourne.

Victorian State Government (VSG), 2005, *2005-06 Service delivery: budget paper no 3*, VSG Publisher, Melbourne.

Vimpani, G, 2001, 'Health inequalities: the seeds are sown in childhood, what about the remedies?', in R Eckersley, J Dixon & B Douglas (eds), *The social origins of health and well-being*, Cambridge University Press, Cambridge.

REFERENCES

Vinson, T, 2004, *Community adversity and resilience: the distribution of social disadvantage in Victoria and New South Wales and the mediating role of social cohesion*, Jesuit Social Services, Melbourne.

Wade, R, 2002, 'Globalisation, poverty and income distribution: does the liberal argument hold?', in *Globalisation, living standards and inequality: recent progress and continuing challenges*, Reserve Bank of Australia, <www.rba.gov.au/publicationsandresearch/conferences/2002/index.htm>, (accessed 24 November 2002).

Waghorn, G & Lloyd, C, 2005, 'The employment of people with mental illness', *Australian e-Journal for the Advancement of Mental Health (AeJAMH)*, vol 4, no 2 (Supplement), <www.auseinet.com/journal/vol4iss2suppl/waghornlloyd.pdf>, (accessed 1 December 2005).

Ward, A, 2004, *Educational maintenance allowance and emergency relief: research report*, Emergency Relief Victoria Forum, VOSS, Melbourne.

Ward, L, 2001, *Transition from custody to community: transitional support for people leaving prison*, Department of Justice, Melbourne, Victoria.

Wearing, M & Berreen, R (eds), 1994, *Welfare and social policy in Australia: the distribution of advantage*, Harcourt Brace & Co, Sydney.

Weatherburn, D & Lind, B, 1998, 'Poverty, parenting, peers and crime-prone neighbourhoods', *Trends and Issues in Crime and Criminal Justice*, vol 85, pp 1-6.

Weatherburn, D, 2002, 'The impact of unemployment on crime', in P Saunders and R Taylor (eds), *The price of prosperity: the economic and social costs of unemployment*, University of New South Wales Press, Sydney.

Weatherburn, D, 2004, *Law and order in Australia: rhetoric and reality*, The Federation Press, Sydney.

Webb, S & Webb, B, 1963, *English Poor Law history. Part 1: The old Poor Law*, Frank Cass & Co, London.

Webber, R & Bessant, J, 2001, 'Techniques for negotiating workplace "reform" in Australia', *Youth and Policy: The Journal of Critical Analysis*, vol 72, pp 35-49.

Weeks, W & Quinn, M, 2000, 'Change and the impact of restructure on Australian families', in W Weeks & M Quinn (eds), *Issues facing Australian families: Human Services respond*, 3rd edn, Longman, Sydney.

Weston, J, 2002, *Choosing, getting and keeping a job: a study of supported employment for people with complex needs: final report*, Scottish Human Services Trust, Edinburgh.

Wheelwright, EL & Buckley, K (eds), 1975, *Essays in the political economy of Australian capitalism*, Australia and New Zealand Book Company, Sydney.

White, A, 1998, 'Tax office accused of Packer blunder', *The Australian*, Sydney, 15 October.

White, R & Habibis, D, 2005, *Crime and society*, Oxford University Press, South Melbourne.

Whyte, WF & Whyte KK, 1988, *Making Mondragon: the growth and dynamics of the worker cooperative complex*, ILR Press, Ithaca.

Wicks, J, 2005, *The reality of income inequality in Australia*, St Vincent de Paul Society Social Policy Issues Paper No 1, May 2005, Sydney.

Wilkinson, RG, 2001, *Unhealthy societies: the afflictions of inequality*, Routledge, London.

Wilson, R, 1997, *Bringing them home: Report of the National Inquiry into the separation of Aboriginal and Torres Strait Islander children from their families*, HREOC, Sydney.

Wilson, S, 2000, 'Welfare to work policies in Australia and the welfare reform process', paper presented at *The Year 2000 International Research Conference on Social Security: Social Security in the Global Village*, Helsinki.

Wilson, S, Meagher, G, Gibson, R, Danemark, D & Western, M (eds), 2005, *Australian social attitudes: the first report*, UNSW Press, Sydney.

Wilson, WJ, 1987, *The truly disadvantaged: the inner city, the underclass and public policy*, University of Chicago Press, Chicago.

Wilton, R, 2003, 'Poverty and mental health: a qualitative study of residential care facility tenants', *Community Mental Health Journal*, vol 39, no 2, pp 139-56.

Wiseman, J, 1992, 'The development and outcomes of the Victorian social justice policy', in M Considine & B Costar (eds), *Trials in power: Cain, Kirner and Victoria, 1982-1992*, Melbourne University Press, Melbourne.

Wiseman, J, 1998, *Global nation: Australia and politics of globalisation*, Cambridge University Press, Cambridge.

Wolf, M, 2002, 'Doing more harm than good', *Financial Times*, 8 May, p 13.

Women's Edge Coalition, 2005, *Women's economic equality*, Women's Edge Coalition Web Site, Washington, <www.womensedge.org/pages/reference materials/referencematerial.jsp?id=273>, (accessed 27 February 2005).

World Bank, 1999, 'What is social capital?', *Poverty.Net*, <www.worldbank.org/poverty/scapital/whatsc.htm>, (accessed 13 June 2000).

World Bank, 2000a, *'Poverty in an age of globalisation'*, Briefing Paper, The World Bank, <www1.worldbank.org/economicpolicy/globalization/>, (accessed 13 December 2000).

World Bank 2000b, *World Development Report 2000*, Oxford University Press, New York.

World Bank 2005, *'05 World Bank indicators: 1 reducing poverty and hunger'*, <www.worldbank.org/data/wdi2005/wditext/Section2.htm>, (accessed 3 October 2005).

World Commission on Environment and Development, 1987, *Our common future*, Oxford University Press, Oxford.

World Commission on the Social Dimension of Globalisation, 2004, *A fair globalisation: creating opportunities for all*, International Labour Office, Geneva.

World Health Organisation (WHO) 2000, International Classification of Functioning, Disability and Health, Prefinal draft full version, WHO, Geneva.

Wroe, D, 2005, 'Benefits at risk if parents refuse 25-hour job', *The Age*, 22 November, p 8.

Wynhausen, E, 2005, *Dirt cheap: life at the wrong end of the job market*, Pan Macmillan Australia, Sydney.

Yarwood, AT, 1977, *Samuel Marsden: the great survivor*, Melbourne University Press, Melbourne.

Yates, J, Wulff, M & Reynolds, M, 2004, *Changes in the supply of and need for low rent dwellings in the private rental market*, AHURI Sydney Research Centre, Sydney.

Yeatman, A, 1996, *Getting real: the interim report of the Review of the Commonwealth/State Disability Agreement*, Australian Government Printing Service, Canberra.

Yuval-Davis, N, 1997, *Gender and nation*, Sage Publications, London.

Index

Aborigines
  assimilation, effect of past
    policy, 122-3
  dispossession, process of, 119, 129
  entrenched disadvantages of
    Aboriginal communities, 11
  exclusion, process of, 119, 129
  experience, Aboriginal, in
    Australia, 118-30
  First Fleet, impact of arrival, 72
  'handouts' for Aborigines,
    critique of, 38
  imprisonment,
    rates of Aboriginal, 110
  integration, effect of past policy,
    123-4
  invasion, dispossession and, effect
    of past policy, 120-1
  levels of poverty, 9, 118
  mutual obligation, impact of Shared
    Responsibility Agreements, 127-8
  poverty, Aboriginal
    levels of, 9, 118
  past policies and, 120-6
  protection,
    effect of past policy, 121-2
  rights, awareness of, 124-5
  self-determination, 129
    effect of past policy, 125
  self-management, policy of, 125
  structural inequalities, vulnerability
    of Indigenous Australians to, 39
  unemployment, rates of for
    Indigenous Australians, 95
Affective disorders, 134
Africa
  imperialism, problems of, 15
  living standards, deterioration in, 9
  sub-Saharan, deterioration of
    economic conditions, 14
Aged
  colonial society, position of
    dependency in, 76
  crackdown,
    on pensioners, 45

  government policy,
    impact on older people, 79-91
  health costs, increased of ageing
    population, 86
  homelessness, 88
  income support, proportion of
    people receiving, 45
  pensions, 44
    Commonwealth government
    income support, as, 156-61
    introduction of schemes, 76
    poverty, vulnerability to, 82
Anglicare
  economic rationalism, account of
    negative impact of policies, 81
Anti-poverty strategies
  alternative, 183-96
  Australia, in, 155-69
  capacity building, 194-6
  Commonwealth
    government, 156-61
  community based, 184-5
  concessions
    Commonwealth government
    strategies, 156-61
    States' strategies, 161-4
  fiscal federalism, 156-61
  government sector, and, 155-6
  income support, as Commonwealth
    government, 156-61
  local government, 164-6
  participation 187-8
  self-reliance, 185-7
  social capital, 193-4
  social enterprise, 190-2
    criticism of approach, 1923
  States, of, 161-4
  Territories, of, 161-4
  welfare services
    State, 161-4
    Territory, 161-4
Anxiety disorders, 133-4
Australia
  child poverty, 3
  colonial contexts, 71-2

Australia (cont)
  disability, extent in, 145
  foreign aid contributions,
    current commitment, 11
  inequalities in society, 3
  penal colony,
    establishment as, 68, 71
  poverty
    analysis of, 35
    colonial society, in context of, 73
    incidence, 11
    rates, 3, 35
    responses to, before social security legislation, 66
  wealth and income inequalities, 4
Australian Council of Social Services (ACOSS)
  emergency relief, survey of persons seeking, 170
  structural inequalities, identification of groups vulnerable to, 39
Austudy
  Commonwealth government income support, as, 156-61
Bancor
  world bank, proposal for, 2
Bank
  world, proposal for, 2
Booth, Charles
  subsistence approach to poverty, 52
Brandt Commissions, 5, 54
Bretton Woods
  American model at, 2
  system, effect, 4
Brotherhood of St Lawrence
  concerns raised by, 3
  economic rationalism, account of negative impact of policies, 81
  Home Instruction Program conducted by, 41
Capability, 58
  deprivation, 58
Capital
  globalisation of, positive claims concerning effect, 12
  social capital, 193-4
Capitalism
  distributional inequality, 21
  historical context, 183-4
  inequality as feature of system, 24
  insecure employment and, 52
  poverty as feature of system, 24
  processes of economic growth in capitalist economies, 9
Carer payment
  Commonwealth government income support, as, 156-61
Case management
  failure to utilise approach, effect, 84
Catholic Social Services Victoria
  economic rationalism, account of negative impact of policies, 81
Centre for Independent Studies (CIS)
  poverty status quo, defence of, 46
  'right-wing' approach to poverty debate, 35-6
  St Vincent de Paul Society report, reaction to, 51
  welfare, view of, 37, 51
Charity
  church-based from 500s to 1500s, 69
  colonies, charitable assistance in, 74-7
  punishment and, convergence, 69
Children
  abuse, 83
  child-care
    redesign of system, need for, 89
    social protection afforded by accessible, 34
    user-pays systems, disadvantage of women by, 40
  colonial society, position of dependency in, 74-5
  crime, juvenile
    involvement in, 83, 108
  impact of poverty on, 83
  male, preference for, 29
  marginal living, impact on, 83-4
  rates of child poverty
    Australia, 3, 82
    unemployment-related poverty, in families affected by, 103
    US, 2
China
  economic progress in, 12
  living standards,
    changes in, 9

INDEX

Churches
  charity, church-based from 500s to 1500s, 69
Citizenship, 27
  definition, 27
  economic, 30
  employment security as determinant of, 29
  global, 27
  income as determinant of, 29
  poverty, relationship with, 29
  social, and welfare state, 29
  status, improvement of women's, 25
  women's, need to improve, 28-30
Commonwealth Commission of Inquiry into Poverty, 3
Community
  anti-poverty strategies, community based, 184-5
  importance of, 184-5
  services, impact of economic rationalism, 84-5
Competitiveness
  international, effect on workers' incomes, 10
  promotion of, by neo-liberal philosophy, 85
Constitution
  financial assistance to States, 157
  income support, power of Commonwealth government to provide, 156-61
Consumer behaviour
  poverty traps and, 42
Cooperatives
  locally organised, to combat neo-liberal globalism, 19, 188-90
Costs
  unemployment, of, 99-100
Credit
  purchases using, 42
Crime
  criminal justice system, 110-2
  imprisonment, characteristics of, 110-1
  juvenile involvement in, 83, 108
  patterns of, and link to poverty, 108-10
  poverty and, 107-17
  policy responses, 112-4
  program responses, 112-4
  prevention, 112-4
  prisoners
    characteristics of, 110-1
    poverty and, 111-2
    rehabilitation, 114-6
    release, 114-6
  what causes, perspectives on, 107-8
Currency
  US dollar, domination of global economy by, 2
  world, proposal for, 2
Debt
  private, current explosion in, 42
Deglobalisation
  progressive internationalism and, 18
Deprivation
  capability, 58
  extreme, in developing nations, 5
  poor, as experts on, 62
  relative, 57
Deregulation
  neo-liberal view of, 80
Developing nations
  deprivation, extreme, in, 5
Development
  idea of, 54
  model, 54
Disabled persons
  Australia, extent of disability in, 145
  colonial society, position of dependency in, 74-5
  defining disability, 143-5
  disability support pension
    Commonwealth government income support, as, 156-61
    number of people receiving, 140
    targeting of eligibility arrangements, 131
  employment exclusion, 146-7
  exploitation, 146-7
  income deprivation, 150-3
  medical model of disability, 143
  pensioners, crackdown on, 45
  poverty, and people with a disability, 142-54

Disabled persons (cont)
　social model of disability, 144
　social service inadequacy, 147-50
　structural inequalities, vulnerability to, 40
Domestic violence, 33
　sexual, 33
　social policy issue, as global, 28
Ecological sustainability
　challenge of, 12
Economics
　capitalist economies, processes of economic growth in, 9
　citizenship, economic, 30
　economic thinking, concepts of, 49-51
　growth, justification for emphasis on, 20, 50
　orthodox, 9
　rationalism, economic
　community services, impact on, 84-5
　social services, impact on, 84-5
Education
　Commonwealth-funded programs, 160
　disabled persons, access to, 146
　free school, social protection afforded by, 33
　low level, as indicator of unemployment, 94
　moving between homes, impact on, 88
　policies, 88
　user pays policies, effect, 88
　women, inequality in, 33
Egalitarian society
　outcomes, towards more egalitarian, 19-23
　promotion of principles, 12
Elite social groups
　poverty, benefits from, 46
Emergency relief
　funding, 170-82
　　Commonwealth, 171-3
　　States, 173
　provision of, 170-82
　　local level, at, 177-80
　urgent reform, need for, 181

Employment
　disabled persons, exclusion, 146-7
　government commitment to full, 43
　policies, 89-90
　public, provision to deal with poverty, 22
　security, as determinant of citizenship, 29
Engels, Friedrich
　structural explanation of poverty, 38
Equality
　freedom without, 39
　opportunity, of, 21
Fair Pay Commission
　minimum wage, charged in respect of, 44
Families
　impact of poverty on, 83
　inclusion, family relationships as dimension of, 139
　income support, by family tax benefits, 156-61
　low income, with teenage children, 83
　unemployment, effect on family well-being, 102-4
　workless, 95
Feminism
　post-colonial, 26
　post-modern, 26
　third-world, 26
　women's poverty, and, 25-7
　　application in overcoming, 24-34
　　broad perspective of, 25
Foreign aid
　commitment, current, 11
　Gender and Development approach to, 33
Free trade policies
　large-scale implementation of, 2
Galbraith, JK
　neo-liberal legitimation of inequality, view on, 16
Gender inequality
　life expectancy, gender gap in, 30
　poverty, as direct cause of, 25, 31, 32-4

INDEX

state infrastructure, importance in addressing, 30
superannuation, gender gap in compulsory accumulations, 91
Global economy
negotiations at Bretton Woods, 2
Globalisation
capital of, positive claims concerning effect, 12
definition of poverty, internationalisation of, 54-5
economic inequality, forces generating, 10
income distribution, and, 12-5
processes of, 8-23
protests against, 18
women, benefits from, 25
Governmentality, 67, 74
Governments
economic inequalities, role in ameliorating, 10
neo-liberal ideology, policies promoting, 16
Great Depression
key factors in, 1
Green politics, 19
neo-liberalism, challenge to, 23
Happiness
enhancement, by eradication of poverty, 20
increased levels of consumption and, 57
Health
Commonwealth-funded programs, 160
housing, effect of inadequate, 87
insurance, 85, 86
mental, 133
policies, 85-7
poor, health problems of, 40
reproductive, 33
socio-economic status, link between, 83
structural inequalities, vulnerability of chronically ill persons to, 40
unemployment, impact on individual well-being, 104-5

universal health care, social protection afforded by, 34
user pays system, via access to private hospitals, 85
Henderson
Commonwealth Commission of Inquiry into Poverty, 3
Poverty Line, 3, 56
relative poverty conceived by, 55
Hillsong Church
private supplier of welfare, as, 47
Homelessness, 88
Housing
built environment, accessibility for persons with disability, 153
Commonwealth-funded programs, 160
inclusion, as dimension of, 139
policies, 87-8
public, provision to deal with poverty, 22
Howard Government
Aboriginal issues, policy of self-management, 125
mutual obligation, impact of Shared Responsibility Agreements, 127-8
emergency relief funding formula, 171
neo-liberal ideology, policies promoting, 16
obligations, shift of focus from rights to, 37
welfare, change instigated since 1996, 35
HR Nicholls Society (HRNS)
'right-wing' approach to poverty debate, 35-6
Human Development Index, 14, 55
Human Poverty Indexes, 55
Human Rights and Equal Opportunity Commission
report findings, 1989, 3
Human rights movement
violence against women, as advocacy cause, 28
Imprisonment
characteristics of, 110-1
rates of, 110

Incentivation
  economic inequality, neo-liberal legitimation of, 16
Inclusion
  social, 139, 154
Income
  citizenship, as determinant of, 29
  disabled persons, income deprivation, 150-3
  fair distribution of, 1
  globalisation, and income distribution, 12-5
  inclusion, finances as dimension of, 139
  mental illness, and income security, 137-8
  middle, determination of poverty line, 56
  mobility data, 38
  policy instruments that redistribute, 21
  security policies, social protection afforded by, 33
  social exclusion, income poverty as indicator of, 59
  support, as Commonwealth government strategy, 156-61
  payment differentials, 167
  wealth and, inequalities, 1
  Australia, 4
India
  citizenship in, 29
  economic progress in, 12
  living standards, changes in, 9
Industrial relations reforms, 44
Industrial Revolution, 50
  poverty, historical context, 183-4
Inequality
  capitalist system, as feature of, 24
  culture of, brought by British to colonies, 74
  distributional, 21
  economic inequality
    forces generating, 10
    global, 14
    neo-liberal view of, 20
    poverty, and in different countries, 12
    socially damaging effects, 20
  gender see Gender inequality
  market, neo-liberal view of, 80
  Marxist view of, 39
  policy instruments to reduce, 21
  structural, 39-43
  women's, 24-34
Institute for Public Affairs (IPA)
  'right-wing' approach to poverty debate, 35-6
International Monetary Fund (IMF)
  globalisation, role in, 10
  neo-liberal policy manifest through practices of, 17
  structural adjustment programs of, 15
  US, domination by, 2
Internationalism
  progressive, 11, 17-9
Isolation
  mental illness, impact on social relationships, 138
Keynes
  Bretton Woods meeting, contribution at, 1
Labour
  unequal division of, 33
Life expectancy
  gender gap in, 30
Local government
  anti-poverty strategies, 164-6
Localism
  alternative, 17-9
Malthus, Thomas
  neo-classical economics, 80
Marx, Karl
  historical context, 183-4
  poverty, view of, 50, 52
  structural explanation of poverty, 38
Medicare, 85, 160-1
Melbourne Institute of Applied Economic and Social Research
  'left-wing' approach to poverty debate, 35-6
  research from, 38
Men
  unemployment, impact on individual well-being, 104-5

INDEX

Mental illness
- affective disorders, 134
- anxiety disorders, 133-4
- income security and, 137-8
- poverty and, 131-41
  - cause, or consequence, 132
  - dimensions of poverty, 136
  - policy development, 139-41
- psychotic disorders, 134-5
- social inclusion, 139
- social relationships and, 138
- substance use disorders, 134
- understanding, 132-3
- work, access to, 137

Migrants
- recent, from non-English speaking countries, levels of poverty, 8

Millennium Declaration, 5

Mission Australia
- economic rationalism, account of negative impact of policies, 81

Multi-lateral Agreement on Investment
- attempt to introduce, 18

Mutual obligation
- conservative policies, 37, 45

National Centre for Social and Economic Modelling (NATSEM)
- 21st century, study of Australians in poverty in, 82

Nationalism
- defensive, 11, 17-9

Nations
- competition between, for investment by multinational corporations, 10
- developing see Developing nations
- disparities between, 4

Needs
- basic, and subsistence definition of poverty, 54
- neglect, and increased risk of juvenile offending, 109

Neo-classicism
- poverty, historical context, 183-4

Neo-liberalism
- assumptions, basic, of, 80
- influence of, 15-7
- market, emphasis on, 47, 53
- moralising tendencies, 36
- practical operation of, 16
- practice, 80-1
- rise of, effect, 23
- theory, 80-1
- unemployment, approaches to, 92
- welfare, criticism of, 46

Newstart allowance
- Commonwealth government income support, as, 156-61

Nutrition
- ill health, as aspect of, 86

Obligations
- Aboriginal communities, impact of Shared Responsibility Agreements, 127-8
- breaching, penalties for, 98
- conservative mutual obligation policies, 37, 90

Organization for Economic Cooperation and Development (OECD) countries
- Half Median Poverty Line, 82
- income mobility in, 38

Parenting payment
- Commonwealth government income support, as, 156-61

Participation
- anti-poverty strategy, as, 187-8

Pawnbrokers, 43

Politics
- poverty, of, 46-7
- women, lack of political representation, 33

Poor see Poverty

Poor Laws
- avoidance of state obligations by, 72
- Elizabethan, 70
- history, tracing, 68

Poverty
- absolute, 24, 52-3, 119
  - increase in, 25
- analysis of, in Australia, 35
- capability, 58-60
- capitalist system, as feature of, 24
- citizenship, relationship with, 29
- concepts of, 49-65

Poverty (cont)
  policy responses, 112-4
  program responses, 112-4
  definition
    combined, case for, 63-4
    homeless men, developed by, 60
    internationalisation of, 54-5
    self-definitions of the poor, 61-3
  demonising the poor, 81-2
  deprivation
    non-monetary aspects, 49
    relative, 57-8
  disability, and people with, 142-54
  employment, provision of public to deal with, 22
  gender inequality as cause of, 25, 31, 32-4
  historical context, 183-4
  individual explanations of, 36-8, 47
  internationalisation of
    definition, 54-5
  line, 56
    conceptualisation of, 52
  locating the poor, 82
  margins, impact on people living on, 83-4
  mental illness and, 131-41
    cause, or consequence, 132
    dimensions of poverty, 136
    policy development, 139-41
  multifaceted dimensions, 61
  policy instruments to reduce, 21
  politics of, 46-7
  qualitative experiences of, 50, 136
  quantitative concepts, 50
  rates of, 9
  relative, 24, 42, 55-7, 119
  self-definitions of the poor, 61-3
  social exclusion, 58-60
  structural explanations of, 38-9
  subsistence model, 50
  traps, 22
  understanding, 35-48
  unemployment, correlation with, 22, 89, 95-6
  income support, 96-9
  wealth and *see* Wealth
  welfare, and, 43-6
  what constitutes, 49-65
  women and, 24-34

Prisoners
  characteristics of, 110-1
  poverty and, 111-2
  rehabilitation, 114-6
  release, 114-6
Privatisation
  neo-liberal view of, 80
Psychotic disorders, 134-5
Rationalism
  economic, 80
    community services, impact on, 84-5
    social services, impact on, 84-5
Relative deprivation, 57
  index, 57
Ricardo, David
  neo-classical economics, 80
  poverty, view of, 50
Rights
  obligations, and, 37
Rowntree, Seebohm
  poverty, view of, 52, 53
Safety
  inclusion, as dimension of, 139
Salvation Army
  concerns raised by, 3
  unemployment, increased demand for assistance because of, 102
Self-reliance
  anti-poverty strategy, as, 185-7
Senate Community Affairs Reference Committee
  inquiry into poverty, 2004, 3
Senate Report on Poverty
  2004, 82, 170
Senate Standing Committee on social Welfare
  findings, 1982, 3
Sickness allowance
  Commonwealth government income support, as, 156-61
Single parent families
  female-headed households, need for social protection, 31
  levels of poverty, 8, 82
  structural inequalities, vulnerability to, 40
  unemployment, rates for, 95

INDEX

Welfare-to-Work legislation, effect, 90
women's poverty, research on, 30
Smith, Adam
  neo-classical economics, 80
  poverty, view of, 50
Social enterprise, 190-2
  criticism of approach, 1923
Social exclusion (SE), 59
  income poverty as indicator of, 59
  poverty-related problems, strategy to reduce, 59
Social justice
  fight against poverty and, 198-9
Social Policy Research Centre
  'left-wing' approach to poverty debate, 35-6
Social security
  policies, 90-1
  unemployment, and income support, 96-9
Social services
  Commonwealth-funded programs, 160
  disabled persons, inadequacy for, 147-50
  economic rationalism, impact on, 84-5
Spencer, Herbert
  19th century British attitudes expressed by, 36
St Vincent de Paul Society
  CIS, reaction to report by, 51
  unemployment, increased demand for assistance because of, 102
State
  dividing practices of, 73-4
  modern, emergence of, 67
Structural adjustment programs
  IMF, of, 15
Substance use disorders, 134
Superannuation
  gender gap, in compulsory accumulations, 91
Taxation
  goods and services tax, impact on poor, 41

income tax, equitable redistribution of wealth by, 41
inequality, as policy instrument to reduce, 21
minimisation, 41
poverty, as policy instrument to reduce, 21
structural problems in tax system, 41
Third World nations
  feminism, third-world, 26
  financial crisis, of 1980s, 4
  living conditions, attack on, 24
Trade liberalisation
  poverty reduction, link with, 12
  push for, by WTO, 18
Trade unions
  economic inequalities, role in ameliorating, 10
  neo-liberal view of, 80
Transport
  disability standards, 153
UN Millennium Summit, 5, 55
Unemployment, 92-106
  Australia, in, 93-106
  benefits, 44
  community well-being and, 100-2
  costs of, 99-100
  crime/poverty interface, and, 108
  extent of problem, 93-4
  family well-being and, 102-4
  individual well-being and, 104-5
  insecure, and capitalism, 52
  long-term unemployed, levels of poverty, 8
  mutual obligation policies and, 37
  neo-liberal policies, 92
  poverty, correlation with, 22, 89, 95-6
  income support, 96-9
  rates of, 92
  structural inequalities, vulnerability of single unemployed to, 39
  who is affected by, 94-5
  work for dole programs, negative results, 45
  workforce, policies to force unemployed into, 35

United States
  children, plight in, 3
  dollar, domination of global economy by currency, 2
  foreign aid contributions, current commitment, 11
  poverty rate, 2
UnitingCare Australia
  economic rationalism, account of negative impact of policies, 81
Utopian socialists, 184
Violence
  domestic, 33
  sexual, 33
  women, against, as global social policy issue, 28
Wage
  justice, calibrated to need, 43
  minimum, government guarantee of, 43
  productivity, setting by, 43
  welfare state, wage-earner's, 76
Wealth
  income, and, inequalities in Australia, 4
  poverty, and
    drivers of, 8-12
    generation of, 8-23
  unequal distribution, in US, 3
Weaponry
  annual expenditure on, 4
Webb, Beatrice
  subsistence approach to poverty, 52
Welfare
  benefits, hierarchy of, 44
  'cheats', crackdown on, 35
  'dependency', 43, 97, 98
  eligibility tests, 44
  inequities in character and delivery of benefits, 44
  'middle-class', subsidisation of choice by, 45
  neo-liberals, criticism of, 46
  policies, 85-7
  poverty and, 43-6
  privatised, 47
  safety-net, changes in, 44
  state
    social citizenship, and, 30
    wage-earner's, 76
  Welfare-to-Work legislation
    disability support pension, 131
    effect, 90
Widow allowance, 158
Women
  globalisation, benefits from, 25
  life expectancy, 30
  poverty, and, 24-34
    research on, 30-32
  structural inequalities, vulnerability to, 40
  user-pays systems, disadvantage by, 40
  violence against, as global social policy issue, 28
Work
  mental illness, and access to, 137
Workplace legislation, 89
World Bank
  globalisation, role in, 10
  neo-liberal policy manifest through practices of, 17
  US, domination by, 2
World Commission on Environment and Development, 5, 54
World Commission on Social Dimension of Globalisation, 5
World Social Forum
  progressive internationalism, airing of concerns of, 18
World Summit for Social Development, 55
World Trade Organisation (WTO)
  globalisation, role in, 10
  neo-liberal policy manifest through practices of, 17
  US, domination by, 2
Youth allowance
  Commonwealth government income support, as, 156-61